Curious Cases

Curious Cases

A Series of Short Pastoral Case Studies

By
Mark J. Renner

Foreword by Benjamin D. Haupt

RESOURCE *Publications* · Eugene, Oregon

CURIOUS CASES
A Series of Short Pastoral Case Studies

Copyright © 2024 Mark J. Renner. All rights reserved. Except for brief quotations in critical publications or reviews, no part of this book may be reproduced in any manner without prior written permission from the publisher. Write: Permissions, Wipf and Stock Publishers, 199 W. 8th Ave., Suite 3, Eugene, OR 97401.

Resource Publications
An Imprint of Wipf and Stock Publishers
199 W. 8th Ave., Suite 3
Eugene, OR 97401

www.wipfandstock.com

PAPERBACK ISBN: 979-8-3852-0455-7
HARDCOVER ISBN: 979-8-3852-0456-4
EBOOK ISBN: 979-8-3852-0457-1

VERSION NUMBER 020524

Scripture quotations are taken from the Holy Bible, New International Version®, NIV®. Copyright © 1973, 1978, 1984, 2011 by Biblica, Inc.™ Used by permission of Zondervan. All rights reserved worldwide. www.zondervan.com The "NIV" and "New International Version" are trademarks registered in the United States Patent and Trademark Office by Biblica, Inc.™

For Dana Marie
I love you

Contents

Foreword by Benjamin D. Haupt | ix
Preface | xi
Chapter 1—Caring for the Poor | 1
Chapter 2—Conflict Resolution | 19
Chapter 3—Dealing with Racism | 36
Chapter 4—Death and Dying | 51
Chapter 5—Engagement and Marriage | 63
Chapter 6—Missions | 76
Chapter 7—Pastoral Counseling | 96
Chapter 8—Prison Ministry | 110
Chapter 9—Raising Children | 123
Chapter 10—Rural and Small-Town Ministry | 137
Chapter 11—Separation and Divorce | 152
Chapter 12—Sexual Misconduct | 168
Chapter 13—Shut-Ins and Homebound Ministry | 183
Chapter 14—Urban and Inner-City Ministry | 198
Chapter 15—Youth and Young Adult Ministry | 212

Bibliography | 229

Foreword

I met the author of this book, Pastor Mark Renner, at Concordia Seminary, where he was enrolled in one of my classes. A few years prior, I had been to a leadership workshop at Harvard University where I learned their famous case study discussion methodology as a way to grow in leadership. Having been a student of leadership for decades, I had experienced many other ways to learn and grow leaders, but nothing rivalled what I experienced at that workshop. I was immediately hooked on case studies and implemented them in my classroom teaching of pastoral leadership. Mark quickly got the hang of writing and discussing case studies, and before he graduated, he told me that he would like to write a whole book of them. I told him that there are way too few case studies for Christian congregations and that he should give it a go. The case studies could be used by pastors and lay leaders to grow in their understanding of each other. For example, they might serve as a few minutes of training and discussion time at an elders' meeting. Gatherings of pastors could use the case studies as conversation starters for their time of casuistry. Professors of pastoral leadership would certainly make use of the wide variety of case studies to teach seminarians or experienced pastors how to sharpen their leadership skills. "Mark, go for it!" I told him. Just a few years later, Mark sent me the draft of the book you hold in your hands. Mark is incredibly creative! Some of these case studies come from his own experiences, others are situations he heard about from friends, and still others are born from Mark's pastoral heart and imaginative mind as he contemplated the many situations a pastor and/or lay leaders might find themselves in as they lead their local congregation. But this case study methodology isn't just some novel or brand-new way of learning and discussing congregational leadership.

For centuries and perhaps millennia, pastors and lay leaders have gathered together to discuss how to be the body of Christ in their locale. Whether it was how to deal with a particular person, a particular situation, or a particular teaching, Christians have long benefited from talking together about the ministry given to them by the Lord Jesus. Paul wrote, "Let the word of Christ dwell in you richly, teaching and admonishing one another in all wisdom, singing psalms and hymns and spiritual songs, with thankfulness in your hearts to God" (Col 3:16 ESV) Martin Luther called this the "mutual conversation and consolation" and said that when Christians do this it is nearly sacramental, that is, a holy moment where Christ himself brings his grace and the forgiveness of sins to his people.

This book is packed with case studies. They will challenge your thinking and may not always lead you to simple answers or to full agreement in just a matter of minutes. They might actually problematize or complicate the way you have been leading God's people. However, my prayer is that these case studies would lead to the mutual conversation and consolation by which the Holy Spirit might work through the word as you work with other Christians to improve your congregational leadership.

Rev. Dr. Benjamin D. Haupt
Reformation Day, 2023
Concordia Seminary, St. Louis

Preface

THE WRITING OF THIS book all began at seminary in St. Louis years ago. I had just submitted a case study for a pastoral leadership course, and one of my professors, Reverend Dr. Ben Haupt, emailed me back and said, "Mark, I just read your case study. That was one of the funniest things that I've ever read in my entire life! I was laughing so hard that faculty and staff were coming into my office to check on me to make sure that I was alright. If that's real then wow! If it's made it up then wow too! You should definitely try to get this published."

A few days later, I told Dr. Haupt that I was planning on writing a book of short pastoral case studies. He was intrigued and then mentioned that the seminary was in need of more case studies under the new curriculum. Over the next two and a half years, I worked tirelessly writing this book. It was a lot of fun, but a ton of work! Many of these case studies are based on my own unique experiences in service to the church over the course of my adult life, while others are based on the diverse experiences of trusted friends and colleagues, and others on what I imagine a leader of the church doing in a particularly challenging situation.

While writing these case studies in my living room or kitchen, I drew on my various experiences in ministry since the age of nineteen when I first served the church as a missionary and English teacher. Time flew by, as it was so much fun writing these and knowing that I would have the chance to share my experiences with readers who are faithfully serving the Lord all over the world! The mere thought that I would be blessed to assist leaders of the church in thinking through a wide variety of challenges and opportunities while serving the Lord in their own unique and diverse contexts, gave me more than enough energy to write *Curious Cases*. I hope and pray that this book is a help to everyone who reads it and that it encourages readers to be curious about the many curious situations that they will encounter in ministry.

Young leaders in the church were at the forefront of my mind when I wrote this book of short pastoral case studies; the young leader who grew up at a healthy church with a full-time staff of two pastors, the missionary couple who felt led by the Holy Spirit to move their family thousands of miles away, the director of Christian education, and the worship director fresh out of college. This book is for the congregation looking to develop leaders, for the young pastor who had a fantastic experience in seminary and then accepted an immensely challenging first call upon graduation. I wrote this book to ignite conversation, bring real scenarios our leaders face day to day to be discussed, and challenge the leaders of our churches to reflect on how and why they respond to these real-life issues presented in this book. My hope is these writings bless all those who chose to serve the church in a leadership role. May these case studies bless you and your ministry tremendously as God leads you to make informed and responsible decisions in the name of Jesus Christ.

Chapter 1

Caring for the Poor

Janet's Prayer Request

JANET IS A SINGLE mother of two living in a five-hundred-square-foot studio apartment in between the downtown of the city and an old industrial park. She has recently lost her job as a hostess due to a lack of in person dining at the restaurant she worked at. Even more devastatingly for Janet, her rent is scheduled to be raised significantly on the first of next year, which is only five months away.

These difficulties in life have caused Janet to pray a great deal. She has found herself asking God for help every morning when she wakes up and every evening when she goes to bed. Janet has tried to reach out to her network of girlfriends and acquaintances for guidance and tips on new job opportunities, but unfortunately, many of her friends are facing similar hardships due to the recent economic downturn in their city.

Three weeks to the day after Janet lost her job as a hostess, she is playing with her two sons at a local elementary school playground when she notices a sign for a new church. The sign reads "Come worship Jesus Christ with us at Full of Hope Church. Sunday Worship is at 9:00 a.m. followed by 10:15 a.m. Bible study and free breakfast. We are meeting in the school gymnasium. All are welcome!!"

The next day Janet attends Full of Hope Church with her two sons and really enjoys the sermon and praise music. She even found the little explanation on communion for next week's worship service interesting. The people at this church actually believe that they are eating Jesus' body and drinking his blood in communion. That's a new thing for Janet.

For Bible study she goes to Pastor Jason's group. It is a small group of seven people including Pastor Jason. The Bible study is focused on the time that Jesus fed the huge crowd in Luke 9: 12–and also the fourth petition of the Lord's Prayer, "*Give us this day our daily bread.*"

Janet is impressed by how Pastor Jason stresses that the fourth petition of the Lord's Prayer puts a high emphasis on how God leads us to remember that all of our daily needs are cared for by him, even the needs of all evil people, and regardless if someone remembers to pray or not. And that we pray in this petition that God would help us to remember this, and that he would remind us to receive our daily bread with joy and thanksgiving.

At the end of the Bible study, each person is asked if they have any prayer requests. Nearly every person in the group gives Pastor Jason a prayer request concerning work or housing needs. Pastor Jason's prayer request is that his home church will be able to find the resources to pay for his health insurance. Janet is the last person in the group to offer a prayer request. Looking down at the floor for a moment silently for a few seconds, she speaks up and says, "I don't know how I should say this exactly. I've been out of work for just over three weeks. I've been praying for help and asking friends if they know of any good job opportunities and nothing has come up. A guy I knew in high school heard that I was desperate for work and emailed me the other day . . . and he said that he manages this club near where I live. In fact, I could walk to work and not spend money on gas. It's a strip club. And he said I could probably get a job stripping. All he has to do is interview me. It would pay over five times what I was making before as a hostess. To be honest, I really need this job to pay the rent and provide food and clothes for my two sons. Please pray that I get this job at the strip club. I'm really desperate."

Please thoughtfully answer the following questions:

1. If you were Pastor Jason, how would you respond to Janet's prayer request?

2. What biblical or extrabiblical passages might be good to read in this situation?

3. What are some practical things Pastor Jason and the congregation of Full of Hope Church could do to help Janet and her sons?

A Conversation over Breakfast

Father Dev is a priest in an impoverished shanty town located about forty meters outside of the nation's largest city. He views everyone in this town as one of his sheep regardless of their religion, philosophy, age, or political affiliation. Each morning, he and Sister Hannah turn their small church sanctuary into a kitchen and dining room, where they serve a breakfast of rava upma, masala dosa, and often a rice pudding called kheer. When the majority of the people have been served, Father Dev and Sister Hannah sit down and eat breakfast with the flock. This is always a great opportunity for friendships to be strengthened and new bonds to be formed.

On one memorable Thursday, Father Dev sat down next to a young man by the name of Ashley who had recently graduated from university. He was an admirer of the ministry that Father Dev and Sister Hannah had to the poor. Ashley soon began to tell Father Dev of a service that he was providing to the poor in that same community.

Ashley proudly and confidently said, "You know, I recently graduated from university top of my class with a bachelors in animal biology. I had a lot of great opportunities as far as graduate school was concerned. However, I felt that the Lord wanted my skills to be put to use in caring for people. So, I built a little house down the road from here; that's where I live and run my dentistry office. I care for about two dozen patients a day, six days a week and I'm learning something new all of the time. It's really amazing how one can think that they will be doing a certain career and yet God has other plans for them."

Father Dev is disturbed to learn that a person who has never been to dental school or to a medical school for the care of human persons is practicing dental medicine in the shanty town. Nevertheless, Father Dev says little to Ashley about his practice at breakfast, and instead exchanges contact information with the young man and sets up a lunch appointment with him for the following day.

After breakfast, Father Dev sits down with Sister Hannah and explains to her the situation. They both agree that the circumstances are far from ideal. However, they know that this is the closest thing to an actual professional dentist that is available for the majority of the residents of the shanty town. They both conclude that it is highly likely that Ashley has the ability to carry out basic dental tasks thanks to his training in animal biology, needed tasks that would likely include cleaning teeth, being able to spot an infected tooth, and administering small amounts of anesthetic to patients.

Father Dev and Sister Hannah conclude that they have two options in front of them. They can either meet with Ashley and ask him to stop his practice of dental medical care to the people of the shanty town. Or they can try and gift him with materials and resources to better learn this profession. Sister Hannah has a first cousin that is a dentist that would likely be willing to spend two or three weeks with Ashley training him in dental medicine.

Please thoughtfully answer the following questions:

1. Do you believe it would be wise for Father Dev or Sister Hannah to ask Ashley to stop practicing dental medicine?
2. Do you believe it's wise to consider trying to gift Ashley with greater materials and resources so he can begin learning this medical profession?
3. Are there any verses from the Bible you would recommend that Father Dev and Sister Hannah meditate upon before speaking with Ashley?

A Cold Spring Night

Pastor Tim serves a large historic congregation in the inner suburbs of a massive metropolitan area. Grand brick and stone homes make up the neighborhood where his congregation is located. A few streets to the east there are several neighborhoods that are in drastic decline and are experiencing poverty.

Occasionally, Pastor Tim will mention some of the hardships that the neighboring communities are facing during Bible studies and sermons. Most parishioners say little to nothing in response to the concerns that Pastor Tim expresses. This is tremendously disappointing to him, and he has expressed his disappointment at a recent elders meeting, saying, "There are people just a few streets over that are in a desperate situation. Our congregation is financially blessed with the resources to help these people. Yet every time that I draw up a plan to try in some way address the needs of these people, I get little to no support. Instead, the conversation is moved to strengthening the general endowment or the educational endowment. This is incredibly disappointing to me! Do we love our neighbors or don't we?"

Two days after the elders' meeting Pastor Tim is finishing up writing his sermon in his office when he hears the sound of a baby crying. At first, he believes that his secretary is watching a show on one of her devices, but he soon realizes that there is a child in the facility somewhere. He first checks the north sanctuary and doesn't see anyone, but upon checking the south sanctuary he immediately hears a cry again.

Caring for the Poor

Pastor Tim slowly walks up to the balcony of the south sanctuary and finds six people camped out in sleeping bags next to the organ: an adult man, an adult woman, three girls all under the age of ten, and a baby boy no older than one year old. Pastor Tim smiles and says hello to them. The man responds, "Hey Father. My name's Will and we're really sorry to intrude like this, but the house of refuge is completely filled today, and we are supposed to get freezing rain tonight. I had to get my wife and kids into a warm place to rest. The door was unlocked this morning so we just walked right in. We promise to leave first thing in the morning. I swear. You have my word, man to man."

Pastor Tim says, "Well, first things first. The school nurse's office has a shower in the bathroom. Let's take you down there so everyone can clean up and we will get you some fresh clothes. And I bet you're hungry, so I'll find something for you to eat in the cafeteria. How does that sound?" The entire family is overjoyed at Pastor Tim's hospitality.

After everyone has showered, they sit down to eat together and Will begins to tell Pastor Tim his story. "You know, I made cars in the factory down the road for sixteen years. I had a good life. I'm not lazy, I just haven't been able to find work for the last year. I just want to provide for my family. That's it. Would the church have any work for me here, Father?" Just at that moment Alexandria, the church secretary, approaches Father Tim and hands him a note saying, "Elder Green—Hi Pastor, I received your voicemail, and I'm afraid there is no way under any circumstances our church can allow homeless people to spend the night in the south sanctuary. Sorry, insurance won't allow it."

Pastor Tim looks up at Will, his wife, and his four children and says, "Hey guys, I would like you to come and spend a couple of nights at my home with my wife and kids. How does that sound?" Will responds by saying, "We really appreciate this, Father! Thank you!"

Please thoughtfully answer the following questions:

1. What biblical character does Will remind you of?
2. Do you believe Pastor Tim's behavior in this situation was Christlike?
3. Do you believe Elder Green responded to Pastor Tim's voicemail in an appropriate way?
4. If you were in Pastor Tim's position, would have you volunteered to bring Will, his wife, and four young children to stay at your home for a few nights with your wife and kids?

Finding a Home for Ashland

Ashland is a fifty-five-year-old veteran who is currently homeless. He lives in a tent in an alleyway in between two of the most luxurious apartment complexes in the city. By coincidence, he has noticed that the organist of his church lives in an apartment within view of his tent. As Ashland eats his fast-food dinner, he struggles to remember the organist's name . . . when suddenly it comes back to him. "Freddy! Yeah, that's right!"

As it pours down rain, Ashland ponders whether Freddy has any idea that he is his neighbor or that his neighbor is a homeless man. He then begins fantasizing about Freddy inviting him to be his roommate. There would be plenty of room for them both inside of the spacious apartment. He meditates about this as he drifts off to sleep on his rain-soaked pillows.

Over the next several weeks, Ashland's funds begin to dry up until both his checking and savings accounts are overdrawn. He is now feeling the pain of hunger on a daily basis. One evening he watches Freddy through the window feed his family of Scottish Fold cats. There appear to be seven or eight well groomed, highly pampered cats in all. At the end of the feeding, several cans of half-eaten gourmet cat food are thrown away into the trash bin. About two hours later, Freddy's housekeeper, Apple, brings out the trash bags and tosses them into the dumpster in the alleyway. Once Apple goes back inside, Ashland is overcome by hunger and flips open the dumpster lid searching for Freddy's trash bags. He pulls the large bags out and rips through them until he spots the half-eaten gourmet cat food cans. Ashland scoops the cat food into his mouth and then licks every crumb of the remains from the cans. In the process, he accidentally cuts his tongue on one of the lids. It doesn't matter to him though, because he's had something to eat. His hunger has been satisfied for the day.

The following Sunday Freddy arrives at church just after six in the morning and is greeted by Pastor Williams. They make small talk and share stories about how the last week went. Freddy then casually shares, "I didn't get much sleep last night. I spotted this man going through my trash on my security camera. Apparently, he has been living in an alleyway outside of my apartment for about a month. I called the police and when they arrived this guy said that he went to church with me. I think maybe I've seen him here before a few times. His name is Ashland. He's a rough looking guy. Anyway, the police made him move on, and I think they took him to a homeless shelter for veterans not far from here. Pastor, have you met this Ashland person before?"

Pastor Williams is noticeably concerned by the news that Freddy has shared with him and says, "Yes, yes, I know him a little bit. He's been attending here sporadically for the last six months. We had lunch about three months ago. He's a veteran and has been through a lot. I wasn't aware that he was homeless. Thanks for letting me know about this. After the service today, I'll phone the local precinct and see if they can tell me which homeless shelter Ashland was taken to. Maybe the church can help him find safe permanent housing, and resources."

Please thoughtfully answer the following questions:

1. Do you believe Freddy was right in calling the police on Ashland?
2. What biblical and extrabiblical passages might be helpful for Pastor Williams, the congregation, and Ashland in searching for solutions to Ashland's housing crisis?
3. In your view, what could Pastor Williams and his congregation do to help Ashland obtain safe, permanent housing and resources?

A City with a Little Light

Sammy lives in one of the most densely populated places on earth. The apartment complex that he and his family dwell in is fourteen stories high and is next to a busy airport. Each night neon signs glow through his barred window as massive airplanes continually fly only feet above the roof of the complex.

Sammy's two-hundred-and-fifty-square-foot apartment acts not only as a dwelling for his wife, Cindy, mother, Amy, and his three sons, Andy, Jacky, and Tony, but it also serves as his bicycle repair shop. Each evening around eleven following dinner, Sammy and his whole family get down on their knees and thank God the Father for sending Jesus to die for them on the cross. They thank God the Father that they are together as a family, and they always pray for a better life filled with abundant opportunities and a larger living space.

One night around three in the morning, Sammy hears a knock on his door. He looks through his peephole and sees his first cousin Leon with his wife ,Joey, and their infant daughter Grace. Sammy turns on the light and lets them into the apartment. Cousin Leon tells a captivating story of fleeing his home country to escape religious persecution, of being smuggled with his wife and four-month-old daughter across a border at night in the back of a truck and, once across the border, locating Sammy's apartment based on his memory of visiting him fifteen years earlier.

Before Cousin Leon even has a chance to ask, Sammy insists that Leon, Joey, and baby Grace stay with them until they can find work and a place of their own to live. Cindy and Amy prepare dinner, beds, and a warm bath for the family. All nine family members then end the night by praising God the Father that they are safely together, that work opportunities would arise for Leon in the morning, and finally that Leon, Joey, and Grace would eventually be able to obtain citizenship.

The following morning at about 11 a.m. Sammy introduces Leon to Lidia, the owner of a restaurant inside of the apartment complex. She offers him a job as a dishwasher and janitor at her restaurant. Leon happily accepts and begins working immediately. The next six months are filled with joy and some sleepless nights for the family of nine as baby Grace has trouble sleeping due to sleep regression and teething. There is a sense of excitement in the air as Leon, Joey, and Grace prepare to move into their own one-hundred-and-twenty-square-foot apartment just down the hall from Sammy's apartment!

In the early morning before the move to the new apartment, there is a ferocious pounding on Sammy's apartment door. He hears men identifying as police officers yelling, "Open the door! We know you are hiding illegal aliens in your apartment! Open up or we will break down the door!" Sammy says, "Yes, just a minute!" Cindy and Amy quickly open a hidden door built into the closet floor and Leon, Joey, and baby Grace cram down into the hole. As Cindy closes the secret door, police in swat gear and semi-automatic weapons begin tearing the apartment apart, searching for any trace of the young family. After nearly four hours of questioning each family member individually, the police conclude that the family was either never there or left a long time before. They decide to leave with the stern warning of returning at a later date.

A few minutes after the police leave, Cindy opens the secret door and helps Leon, Joey, and baby Grace out of the hole. They look visibly shaken and exhausted after nearly four hours of being crammed in a hole hiding from the police. The entire family says a prayer of thanksgiving to Jesus Christ for his hand of protection upon them during the police search, and they ask that God will continue to bless Leon, Joey, and baby Grace as they move into their new apartment.

Please thoughtfully answer the following questions:

1. If you had been in Sammy and his wife Cindy's position, would have you housed Leon, Joey, and baby Grace at your apartment?

2. If you had been in Sammy, Cindy, Amy, Andy, Jacky, and Tony's shoes, would have you hidden Leon, Joey, and baby Grace from the police and lied about their whereabouts?

3. If you were the pastor to this family of nine, how would you specifically pray for them?

4. If you were the pastor to this family of nine, what advice would you give this close-knit group of Christians?

5. In your opinion, should their pastor give drastically different advice to Leon, Joey, and baby Grace than to Sammy, Cindy, Amy, Andy, Jacky, and Tony?

A Good Big Sister

G.G. is a twenty-seven-year-old woman who loves painting, free museum Mondays and singing in her church choir. She is currently an underemployed singer who performs backup vocals on two or three moderately successful albums per year. G.G.'s best friend at church is an accomplished, family-oriented small business owner and pastor named Tiffany. They jokingly tell church visitors that they are "sisters from another mother!"

During a Wednesday evening women's Bible study, G.G. reveals that she has moved back in with her ex-boyfriend, Clyde Mitchell. The typically calm and professional Pastor Tiffany shouts at G.G. in front of the other twenty ladies. "G.G. girl! What are you thinking moving back in with that man after he beat you and treated you like he did? Have you lost your mind?! If we weren't in the house of the Lord, I'd be saying a lot stronger words, girl!"

G.G. answers quickly, "I got evicted from my apartment! I haven't worked in almost half a year. I'm completely broke! It was either move back in with Clyde or sleep in the dumpster near my old apartment! What did you want me to do?" Pastor Tiffany says without hesitation, "Girl, you know that you can always depend on me. You're my little sister in the Lord and you're moving in with me, Berry, and the kids until you get back on your feet. I have room in the guest house for you ,and also, I'll do my best to help you find more paying singing gigs."

After the Bible study, Tiffany has four of her male employees who are military veterans accompany her and G.G. over to Clyde's apartment to gather up G.G.'s belongings. They knock on the door, and Pastor Tiffany instructs Clyde on what is going to happen and says, "Clyde, we are gathering up G.G.'s belongings. She's moving in with me. You two are never seeing each other again. We are getting her things and getting out. We had better not have any trouble from you." Clyde is agreeable and complies.

Please thoughtfully answer the following questions:

1. In your opinion, did Pastor Tiffany act like a good big sister in the Lord to G.G.?
2. If you were Pastor Tiffany's bishop, what words of pastoral support and comfort would you offer to her?
3. What biblical or extrabiblical passages might be helpful for G.G. to read as she adjusts to a new living situation in Pastor Tiffany's guest house?

Dwayne's Commute

Dwayne lives in a semi-impoverished rural county with a population of just over thirty thousand people. For seven and a half years he worked on an assembly line at the county's main employer. Unfortunately though, Dwayne's employer moved their operations to the other side of the state five months ago, and he is currently unemployed.

He has found it nearly impossible to cope with the stress of being unemployed even with the basic security of unemployment checks. Upon the advice of his sister, he has started attending free counseling sessions at a Lutheran social services office near his house. His counselor, Joy, provided a compassionate, non-judgmental ear to Dwayne as he has told her about his job loss and his divorce from his wife Nicki.

In fact, during his most recent counseling session, Dwayne said, "I don't know if I really have any friends. Sometimes, I'm not sure if anyone truly loves me," to which Joy responded, "I can tell you for a fact that you are loved. Jesus loves you unconditionally, Dwayne, and he will always be your friend."

After several months of counseling sessions, Dwayne's ability to cope with the loss of his job has moderately improved. However, he has recently received a notice from his bank that they will be foreclosing on his home due to lack of payment on his loan. Dwayne is devastated by the news and decides to drive twenty-five miles to the north to an affluent city named Foxly, which is located in the neighboring county. He begins filling out applications at every factory and restaurant that he comes across.

Two days later, he receives a phone call from the owner of a small factory; a gentleman by the name of Irving Franklin. He interviews Dwayne over the phone and by the end of the conversation has offered him a position as a tow motor driver and truck loader. Dwayne happily accepts the position. Five days a week he makes the twenty-five-mile drive from his new apartment located in his hometown to Foxly.

As Dwayne gets to know his new boss Irving Franklin, he is impressed by his hands-on, lead-by-example approach, as well as by his generous pay and benefits package that he offers all of his employees. Dwayne is making slightly more than he did at his previous job and is treated overall with more respect as well. During break time, several of his coworkers have pointed out to him that their boss Irving is a part-time Lutheran pastor at a small church that pays him very little, so he supports himself through his earnings at the factory.

This information about his new boss resonates with Dwayne, because his counselor is a Christian who works for a Lutheran organization. The next Sunday, Dwayne decides to visit Irving's church and is impressed by the welcoming atmosphere and is intrigued by the sermon on the saving power of holy baptism. This is the first time that Dwayne has heard salvation described as a totally free gift from God. One month later, Dwayne is baptized during Sunday morning service by his boss and pastor—Irving.

Two weeks later, as Dwayne is driving back to his apartment after work, he falls asleep at the wheel. Dwayne drives into a deep ditch and is tragically killed in a car wreck. Pastor Irving Franklin presides over his funeral and the congregation plants a sycamore fig tree in Dwayne's honor on account of the fact that Dwayne loved the story in the Gospel of Luke of Zacchaeus climbing the sycamore fig tree to see Jesus over the crowd.

Please thoughtfully answer the following questions:

1. What is your opinion of Joy the counselor's words of encouragement to Dwayne when she said, "I can tell you for a fact that you are loved. Jesus loves you unconditionally, Dwayne, and he will always be your friend"?
2. In your opinion, do you believe God played a part in Dwayne finding a job at the factory Irving Franklin owned?
3. Had you been in Dwayne's position, do you believe you would have desired to be baptized?
4. Even though Pastor Franklin was kind and generous to Dwayne, do you think he could have possibly done more for him as far as trying to help him find an apartment closer to work?

The Church Garden

Justin Stanford and his classmates are getting to know each other during their week-long seminary orientation. On the fourth day of orientation, everyone breaks into groups of five or six students and one professor. Each group works together on a community service project in the city.

It is an excruciatingly hot August day that is made more unbearable by the dense buildings, concrete, and blacktop attracting heat in an area, with very few trees to provide shade. As Justin's group cleans the littered street for about an hour and a half, they eventually take a break under a giant walnut tree.

As they sip their lemonade and wait for the pizzas they ordered for lunch, they hear a woman from the doorway of a nearby church say, "Hello, I'm the pastor here. Why don't you come inside to the fellowship hall and enjoy the air conditioning while you rest? The heat and humidity are horrible today!" The group happily accepts the invitation.

Once inside, their host introduces herself and says, "Hello I'm Pastor Susan. But you can just call me Susan. Welcome to St. Paul's in the City." Each member of the group also introduces themselves, including Justin's professor, who says, "Hi, it's a pleasure to meet you, I'm Chris Parkman. I'm one of their professors. I teach systematic theology and I'm also a parish pastor of a small congregation in the outer suburbs."

A few minutes later their pizzas arrive and Susan begins to share a little bit about her congregation and the services that they provide to the community. The group is impressed to hear St. Paul in the City has a food pantry, a social service agency, and a clothing room with new and gently used clothing items. A large portion of the people that benefit from these services are either homeless or barely make enough money to survive and are one missed paycheck away from being homeless.

Susan only asks the people that benefit from the services to volunteer at the church from time to time if they are able to, with unpacking clothing items, organizing the food pantry, or cleaning an area of the church to offset costs. Volunteering also helps each person feel invested in the church as partners as opposed to merely beneficiaries. However, very few people do volunteer, which Susan speculates is because they do not feel comfortable inside the church building itself, which led her and the congregation to start a street service at 8 a.m. each week. This service has about fifty people in attendance with a time of coffee and donuts afterwards.

The street service has actually surpassed in size the 10 a.m. in-building service, which only has about thirty-five to forty people each week and about twenty people enjoying coffee and donuts afterward in the fellowship hall.

The coffee and fellowship time at the street service frequently has ninety to a hundred people in attendance. Susan adds, "No matter if it's raining out or snowing or incredibly hot, people in our community love the street service. We have some regulars and a lot of new faces each week."

Susan then takes a deep sigh and says, "The reality of the matter is we are an aging congregation with very few volunteers. I'm sixty-seven-years old and have been close to retiring or at least moving to a part-time role twice now. Each time my bishop has implored me to stay, saying, 'Susan, I truly have no one to replace you at this time. There are so few people that are interested in this type of ministry. Yet it is so needed. Please can you just hold on for another year or two while I search for someone to take your role and you can have an emeritus role?'"

Susan pauses for a moment and then continues on, "There are a lot of joys in serving here. I have been at St. Paul for most of my career, but it's not easy. About eight years ago, I created a resting place for some of the people that we serve. Nearly once a month we get a call from someone in law enforcement or with the county coroner who tells us that a body was recovered on a sidewalk or in a doorway, and that person has either no identification or family contact information on them. And the only thing that the officer or coroner can find out about the deceased person is that they have a business card or a piece of clothing that has "St. Paul in the City" written on it. So, they call us and ask if we would like their ashes to display or scatter, and we take them. Would you like to see where we scatter their ashes?"

Everyone in the group is interested to see where Susan and her congregational leaders scatter the ashes. They follow her out the cathedral Gothic church to a little courtyard that has a garden. The area is unkept with weeds, old leaves, sticks, and clumps of ashes. Susan points to the garden and says, "Well, here is the garden where we scatter their ashes. I'm embarrassed by how this looks, but I am not physically able to keep up with raking and weeding anymore, and most of our members are not physically able to at this point. Right now, this is the best that we can do."

After a few seconds of pause, seminarian Justin asks, "What is the typical cause of death of the homeless people that have their ashes scattered here?" Susan responds, "From what we are told by the authorities, sometimes people freeze to death, or it's cancer, and in some cases, they die of an overdose . . . in one case a person was beaten to death for no apparent reason." Professor and pastor Chris Parkman is so moved by what he has seen and heard he gives Susan a hug and says, "Lord bless you, Susan."

Please thoughtfully answer the following questions:

1. What practical steps could be taken by the group of seminarians and their professor to assist Susan and the congregation of St. Paul in the City with their efforts to care for the homeless?
2. If you were a part of the group from the seminary, how would you specifically pray for Susan each day and the congregation of St. Paul in the City?

Blessing Robinson

Robinson is a private man who does not like to complain about hardships that he has faced. However, his older sister Diamond is well aware of the misfortunes he has suffered in his young life. At eighteen, his dream of going to college was lost when their father, Robert, died unexpectedly of a stroke, and Robinson had to go straight to work upon graduating high school in order to support his mother and younger siblings.

At twenty, his fiancée left him days before their wedding and moved to the neighboring state with their three-month-old daughter, Tiana, to live with another man. Robinson then had to fight through the courts for shared custody of his daughter and spent nearly every penny he saved working maintenance for the city.

At twenty-two, Robinson and Diamond's beloved mother, Sarah, died of cancer, and Robinson paid for the entire funeral and burial expenses. And finally last month Robinson's home burned down while he was at work after an electrical fire broke out. Thankfully no one was harmed, but all of Robinson's possessions, other than his car, were destroyed in the inferno.

This is a lot for any twenty-six-year-old to have to endure in their young life. Thankfully Diamond has contacted her church family at Jesus Is with Us Church for help. Pastor Jacob Theodore, along with the entire congregation, wants to bless Robinson mightily. This is a fantastic opportunity for God's people to be good stewards of what God has entrusted to them and help a member of the community who is in need.

Pastor Jacob Theodore invites Robinson out for dinner to the best steak house in town and, over cocktails, says to him, "Young man, your character and love for your family have been an inspiration not only to my entire congregation, but also to me personally as a pastor and leader. That's why my congregation of Jesus Is with Us Church and I have decided to use money from our mission and outreach budget, along with a personal contribution from myself, to build you a brand-new modern home with four bedrooms and three bathrooms. We will be paying for you to stay in a nice apartment until your home is completed. And also, we will be paying for you to go to college and obtain your bachelors degree and, if you so choose, your masters degree as well. We want you to reclaim your dream of going to college. We are thankful that Christ is blessing us with this opportunity to bless you, young man."

Robinson is overwhelmed with emotion by the news that Pastor Jacob Theodore has shared with him. He begins to cry tears of joy, shock, and confusion all at once. Robinson embraces the pastor and promises that he won't let him or the church down, and says over and over again how thankful he is.

Five weeks later a young man by the name of Jax makes an appointment to meet with Pastor Jacob Theodore and says, "Pastor, I'm happy for Diamond's younger brother Robinson. I truly am, but I've been a member at Jesus Is with Us Church most of my life and I've suffered just as much as Robinson, and I've hardly received any help from the church. I've had vehicles stolen from my driveway multiple times, my house was foreclosed on by the bank last summer, I never had an opportunity to attend college, and both of my daughters refuse to speak to me. Don't I need help too?"

Pastor Jacob Theodore takes a drink of his lemonade and then responds, "Yes Jax, you certainly do need help. At twenty-five you are still a young man, and you have an opportunity to turn your life around. If you have a trade that you would like to pursue, the church will financially assist you in attending a trade school. If you are determined to attend college to obtain an associate's degree, bachelor's degree, or possibly eventually a master's degree, the church will assist you in that pursuit so that you can begin a career with the degree you earned. Our church has money designated to assist young people such as yourself to pursue education."

Jax seems to be shocked, and responds with, "Okay, cool! Thank you, Pastor! Would you visit schools with me and help me pick one that is a good fit?" Pastor Jacob Theodore responds, "Of course, Jax, it would be my pleasure. Also, my administrative assistant, Tina, will assist you in filling out and sending in the proper paperwork for the application process."

Please thoughtfully answer the following questions:

1. How do you feel about the words of encouragement and generosity that Pastor Jacob Theodore shared with Robinson?
2. Does the story of Robinson's hardships and the generosity of Pastor Jacob Theodore, and his congregation of Jesus Is with Us Church, put you in mind of any stories from the Bible?

3. Do you think Pastor Jacob Theodore made a generous offer to Jax in offering him financial assistance from the church so he can obtain further education?

Opening the Doors to a Beautiful Family

Misty is a twenty-three-year-old single mother of a beautiful and happy eight-month-old baby boy named Clement. They live in a rent-controlled apartment on the thirty-ninth floor of a forty-story complex. Several times a week, Misty washes out one of Clement's disposable used diapers so that she can use it on him again. This practice is of course not very sanitary, but it's basically her only option as she cannot afford to buy new diapers on a regular basis. Sadly, Misty knows of another five mothers on her floor that are in a similar situation.

Four days a week, Misty's sixty-five-year-old, wheelchair-bound mother Sonya babysits Clement, while Misty works a twelve-hour shift as a custodian at a parochial elementary. And just last week Sonya, moved into Misty and Clement's apartment to help share the cost of rent and other expenses. Sonya treasures the time that she has to babysit her grandson Clement, but there are moments when caring for him is so physically demanding she is almost unable to handle it.

One unseasonably cold Friday afternoon, Sonya decides that she needs to talk with Misty about the possibility of her daughter working eight-hour shifts moving forward to make the job of babysitting Clement a little bit easier. However, before Sonya can make this suggestion, Misty says, "Mommy, I know you are probably going to be disappointed in me but, I have to tell you something. I'm pregnant. It happened on the date with that guy I met through the online dating service. We only had two dates. I don't know what I'm going to do! We are barely making ends meet now! You couldn't even afford your prescriptions yesterday! How can we afford another baby?"

Sonya responds to her daughter and says, "This is really scary right now, honey, but God is going to provide. We are in this together as a family." Misty answers, "I know, when I told the guy I went on dates with he started to insist that I get an abortion, and I told him that I'm a Christian and I can't do that because God creates life at conception, but I have to be honest Mommy, I'm afraid that we are going to end up on the streets. I'm not saying that I want to have an abortion, but I might have to put the baby up for adoption." Sonya answers, "Well, before we start talking about an adoption why don't we try and meet with Pastor Milton and see if he would have any ideas on getting connected with a group that can provide resources or possibly a work situation with better benefits?"

The following Wednesday, Sonya, Misty, and baby Clement meet with the kindly and outgoing Pastor Milton. The ladies explain their situation to him in depth over yogurt cake and espresso. With rapid response, Pastor Milton says, "Ladies, the best situation for you and your beautiful family is to live and work in a country that provides universal health care, and gives each new mother at least two months or possibly four months of paid maternity leave as an investment in the public good and well-being. Our Lord Jesus Christ said in Matthew's Gospel, 'The spirit is willing, but the flesh is weak.' You are a family that is strong in your faith, but your basic health care needs, paid vacation time, and paid maternity leave is almost nonexistent in the current system that you are in. In the country that I was born in, your needs will be a high priority, as are the needs of all of its citizens. If you would like, I can help you with the paperwork to apply for citizenship. Also, if you make this transition, I can put you in contact with my good friend Alain who is a priest in one of the main cities. His church actually has wonderful rent-controlled housing that is subsidized by the government. Honestly, it is nicer and more suitable for your needs than what you have now. Also, I will ask him to help you find an improved work situation, Misty. He owes me a favor."

After only one day of reflection, Sonya and Misty decide to accept Pastor Milton's offer to allow him to assist with their paperwork in applying to become citizens of the country he was born in. They also accept his offer of putting them in contact with his good friend Alain with the hope that he and his church can assist them in finding suitable housing and an improved work situation for Misty. Sonya is hopeful for the future as she helps raise her grandson Clement, and looks forward to meeting her second grandchild who has not been born yet.

Please thoughtfully answer the following questions:

1. In your opinion, did Misty give a biblically sound response to the guy who was trying to insist she get an abortion?
2. Do you believe Sonya acted as a wise and caring mother to Misty upon hearing the news of the pregnancy?
3. What is your opinion of Pastor Milton's advice and offers of help to this family?
4. If you had been in Sonya and Misty's place, would have you accepted Pastor Milton's offer to help in an immigration process?

5. Does the story of this family remind you of any specific stories from the Bible?

Chapter 2

Conflict Resolution

How to Respond to This Text Message?

PASTOR PATTI HAS NOTICED that a young woman named Alice, who attends weekly services while in college, has recently spent a great deal of time with a wealthy local businessman named Eric Carrington. They are often seen doing yard work and general repairs together on Eric's home on Saturday afternoons. Pastor Patti simply assumes that Alice and Eric have developed a friendly working relationship and nothing more due to the fact that Eric is married with children.

The following Friday afternoon, Pastor Patti's phone shows a text message from Alice that is also addressed to the head elder of the congregation. The text message reads as follows: "How dare you people judge me!! You sit back in your positions of power and wealth, and judge me while I try to attend one of the most expensive colleges in the world!! What would I do if I didn't have the option to live in Eric's guest house?! Are you going to let me live with you? Yeah, I bet!! Elder Frank, you think that you can accuse me of living with someone outside of marriage because I'm renting their guest house? Are you nuts?! And Pastor Patti, if you really do agree with Elder Frank, you're even crazier!! In fact, don't worry about it, I'll never be back at your church again!!! Elder Frank, how dare you insinuate that I'm some type of prostitute!!! Mr. Carrington has been a perfect gentleman to me since day one!!! He's a class act, and you have no class!!!!"

Please thoughtfully answer the following questions:

1. If you were Pastor Patti, how would you respond to Alice's unexpected text message?

2. If you were Pastor Patti, what type of questions would you ask Elder Frank over a phone call or an in-person meeting?

3. In your opinion, is there anything theologically or practically wrong with Alice renting Eric Carrington's guest house as a single woman while she is attending college?

4. What Scripture passages or extrabiblical resources might Pastor Patti use in working to resolve this conflict?

Providing Pastoral Care to Craig and the Entire Congregation

After supervising an all-night youth group lock-in, Pastor Alexis is finishing her fourth cup of coffee. As she greets the congregation at the start of the service, Pastor Alexis notices a person who strongly resembles Nancy Greystone—a member of her congregation. Yet this person's mannerisms seem to be a little different than Nancy's, and Pastor Alexis is not completely sure if it is her or not.

About forty-five minutes later, as congregation members line up and approach the front of the sanctuary to receive communion, Pastor Alexis notices the person who bears a striking resemblance to Nancy approaching to receive the Lord's Supper. Suddenly it dawns on her that this person is not Nancy. Instead, it is Nancy's son Craig, dressed in a black dress and neon pink high heels and wearing a great deal of makeup and a reddish orange wig. This is the first time that Pastor Alexis has seen Craig since the young man moved away to attend college on the other side of the country last year. Pastor Alexis smiles warmly at Craig as she hands him the wafer and says, "The body of Jesus Christ, given for you."

A few minutes after the service, Ms. Debbie Hancock walks confidently into the sacristy and proclaims, "Pastor, I must say that I was thrilled to begin the process of joining this congregation, but after what I saw this morning, I must reconsider! It is disturbing enough that a young man dressed as a woman would enter this church in the sight of God, women, children, and the elderly, and not so much as a word of instruction or rebuke would be given to him by an elder or the pastor. What is more frightening was your happy willingness to give him communion. I'm not sure where you went to seminary or who ordained you for ministry; but I must say that your behavior is an abomination in the sight of God! I will not be joining this church! This is the last time that you will see me near this property! Good day to you, madam!"

After Debbie walks out of the sacristy, Pastor Alexis sits down and begins her fifth cup of coffee for the day. She prays for wisdom from God on whether she should attempt to resolve things with Ms. Debbie Hancock, or if she should leave the situation be for a while. Pastor Alexis also begins thinking about possible questions and concerns that some of her congregation members may have about Craig's appearance. Pastor Alexis anticipates that some in her congregation may believe that Craig is committing a sin by dressing as a woman. A few members may even want Craig excommunicated.

Please thoughtfully answer the following questions:

1. If you were in Pastor Alexis's shoes, would you bring up Craig's new style of dress or Debbie's speech at your Monday night elders meeting?
2. What biblical or extrabiblical writings may be helpful to Pastor Alexis in reflecting on Craig's new style of dress and Debbie's speech?
3. How might these biblical and extrabiblical writings assist Pastor Alexis in speaking about these situations to elders and congregation members who are not in a leadership position?

The Situation with Winchester

Pastor Edward is less than three months away from retirement. He and his wife, Alice, are looking forward to moving to a warmer climate and relaxing with their children and grandchildren. To be frank, Pastor Edward nearly retired after thirty years of service, but was not in a stable enough place financially to do so. Therefore, he held on to reach thirty-five years. He can't help but count down the days until he is officially retired. In fact, tonight is his last elders' meeting before retirement.

It should be a pretty uneventful meeting. The only real order of business will be to welcome Winchester, a sixty-five-year-old retiree, on as a new elder. Pastor Edward does not know him especially well since Winchester only became a member last year. However, most of the other members know him well and several went to school with him years ago.

After the opening devotion and a short introduction of Winchester, each elder goes around the table and gives a quick report of needs that they feel should be met in the congregation and community at large. Elder Ken brings up the fact that long-time congregation member, Marjorie Hendy, is not happy with the lack of updates on the church social media accounts, and also, that it has been reported by several reliable sources that she has been making toasts at various community Christmas parties saying, "Here's to being one day closer to Pastor Edward's retirement! At least we won't have to listen to another one of his sad sermons in the new year!"

The room is taken over by an awkward silence until Winchester, the new elder, decides to speak up. "Marjorie Hendy is a crazy old hen! I've known her since I was five years old, and she has only become more putrid and distasteful since the first day that I met her! Her mom and both her aunts were the exact same way. I'm proud to say that every time Marjorie tried to seduce me, I shot her down cold. The same way I shot down her mom and aunts. They all had the hots for me, but I never took an interest. She's probably angry that I was asked to join the board of elders so she's now trying to stir up trouble and make nasty remarks toward pastor. Well, I won't hear of it! I'm going to give her a good piece of my mind over coffee tomorrow and set her straight!" Most of the other elders seem to agree with what Winchester had to say. And the meeting smoothly moves onto other orders of business.

Please thoughtfully answer the following questions:

1. Do you believe Winchester's comments about Marjorie were warranted given the circumstances?
2. Do you believe it is a good idea for Winchester to speak with Marjorie over coffee?
3. What responsibility does Pastor Edward have in this situation regarding Marjorie?
4. What responsibility does Pastor Edward have as far as mentoring his new elder, Winchester?

Entering Jamie's Room

Jamie B. is a thirty-eight-year-old bachelor who lives with his widowed sixty-year-old mother, Gretchen. He works five days a week, twelve to twelve at a local automotive plant. Jamie prides himself on being a hard worker at the factory and at home, performing household chores for his mother.

About four times a year he makes a point of attending a church service with his mother, because it means a lot to her, and he feels that if his dad were still alive, he would want Jamie to accompany Gretchen to church occasionally. In fact, Jamie has recently been looking forward to attending the upcoming Christmas Eve service as he's reflected on good memories from his childhood of putting up Christmas decoration in the sanctuary with his family and friends.

One evening about two weeks before Christmas, Gretchen invites over friends from church that have known her, Jamie, her daughter, Bridgette, and of course Jamie's late father, Rick, for decades. The friends include Head Elder and next-door neighbor, Derek Frymann, Elder and Chairman of the Congregation, Robert White, forty-year-old Elder Wes Thompson, who grew up playing sports with Jamie in school, and Pastor Greg's wife, Betty Jane.

These friends from the church are not stopping by the house to Christmas carol or to simply exchange pleasantries. Instead, Gretchen has invited them over for an emergency prayer meeting. She tells them about a massive book shelf in Jamie's room that takes up the entirety of his north wall. It is filled with pornographic movies and video games that he views on his giant projector screen. In fact, it almost seems as if Jamie is proud of his pornographic collection, as he makes no effort to conceal it and often leaves his bedroom door open where family members and guests accidentally notice his gigantic display of films and video games.

As Gretchen leads the group up the stairs into Jamie's bedroom, Betty Jane yells out, "Wow! This place looks like a dirty movie store! I can't believe my eyes!" It isn't long before Derek Frymann begins anointing the room with oil and praying aloud for Jamie with the other elders. Instead of praying with the group, Betty Jane picks up a large black garbage bag and begins filling it with Jamie's movies and video games. She insists that the other guests as well as Gretchen help in the removal of the pornography saying that the collection is "not from God, but from a place of evil." Hesitantly, everyone begins helping place the movies and video games into large black trash bags.

Suddenly footsteps can be heard coming up the stairs. To everyone's surprise, Jamie has arrived home early from work with drinks and smokes. He ducks through the bedroom doorway, which barely allows his six foot nine, three-hundred-and twenty-five-pound frame to enter. After taking a moment to assess the situation, Jamie speaks up. "What is this? Why are you putting my movies and video games into trash bags?!" Betty Jane responds, "This is for your own good! How dare you bring this filth into your mother's home!" Jamie replies, "The reason I'm bringing this into my bedroom is because I have needs. And I've earned this! And if you will all kindly remove yourselves and leave my movies and games here, I have a special film that I'm going to watch after another big day at work making cars!"

Derek Frymann lets out a deep sigh and says, "Jamie, your father is no longer here to watch out for you, but your family at the church is. I have been deeply concerned about you for the last ten years and your mother has been concerned about you for the last fifteen. Robert, Betty Jane, your mother, Wes, and I are doing this for your own good."

Jamie's face turns beet red and he replies, "First off, you two-faced sacks of crap, you have manipulated my mother. Worst of all, you brought this rat punk Wes, who is a slimy hypocrite, with you! Yeah, I said it. Wes slept with every lady he could in high school and brought porn magazines into the locker room before every practice! Now Wes Thompson and this merry group of hypocrites are trying to steal my possessions. And yes, I have a sex doll as well! And if I look into my closet and it's missing, there's going to be a problem. Now all of you leave my room, now! And oh, by the way, I'm not stepping foot back in the church until I get a big, giant apology from each of you! Good night!"

Derek, Robert, Wes, and Betty Jane all exit Jamie's room with Gretchen, leaving the bags of movies and video games behind. They then proceed to the living to pray for Jamie. After about two minutes of prayer, they hear his bedroom door slam and a pornographic movie playing full blast from his bedroom. With that, the entire group leaves the property and Betty Jane insists that Gretchen stay with her and Pastor Greg for several days until a solution to the conflict with Jamie can be worked out.

Please thoughtfully answer the following questions:

1. Was it appropriate for Gretchen to allow her friends from the church to enter Jamie's room and start the process of putting his movies and video games into trash bags?
2. Was Jamie right to be upset about his mother and church friends entering his room without his permission and attempting to trash his property?
3. What might be some first steps that can be taken by either Jamie or Gretchen and the rest of the group to reach some type of reconciliation?
4. What is the role and responsibility of Pastor Greg in this situation?

Meeting Antonio and BB

Kyle is in his first month serving as an associate pastor at a large congregation in the outer suburbs of the state capital. There is a lot of excitement around his arrival, partly due to the fact that he is a youthful, extroverted twenty-five-year-old. Almost immediately Kyle connected with parishioners in the congregation. In fact, many people have taken to just calling him Kyle, and not pastor. Nearly every night of his first month has been spent at

Conflict Resolution

a barbecue or restaurant with new friends and, recently, he has been invited to enjoy a private luxury box with one of his parishioners at a college football game. And, of course, some pre-game tailgating before kickoff.

As Kyle enjoys a glass of hard apple cider with his parishioner Dustin and many new friends, he is introduced to Dustin's old college fraternity brothers, Antonio and BB. They are friendly to Kyle and are excited that he is serving as a pastor at the church that Antonio grew up at. In fact, Antonio even attended the church's day school until the sixth grade. After a few minutes of chatting, the men express interest in coming to a service sometime to hear him preach. Antonio says, "Yeah, I haven't been to church there in almost five years. Ever since I started dating BB, I have felt weird about going back there. No one has really said anything, but I know that it's super traditional, so I've wanted to avoid awkwardness." Upon saying this, Antonio grabs BB's hand and gives him a kiss on the lips.

Suddenly a group of four college students walk by and yell, "Homos! Go to hell!" Dustin bursts up and gets in their faces and yells, "You got a problem with my cousin and his boyfriend kissing?! We can settle it right here! Let's go!" The students keep walking and have become noticeably shaken as they walk away, but Dustin has a few more things to say to them. "I actually think it's really beautiful to see them kiss! It's something your ignorant minds can't handle!"

Dustin walks back to Antonio, BB, and Kyle and says, "Sorry you guys have to listen to crap like that still. We've made so much progress, but there are still idiots like that running around. It's unbelievable." Pastor Kyle adds, "Yeah, Jesus loves you guys. In fact, he loves everyone, and harassing people with hateful language is not Christian at all." BB has a look of real surprise and says, "I'm surprised to hear you say that, Pastor Kyle. I thought that your church was super conservative and teaches that gay people go to hell?"

Pastor Kyle responds, "No, orthodox traditional Christianity does not teach that people go to hell for being gay. No way. It teaches that gay people should live a chaste and pure life. They should not act upon same-sex desires. Instead, gay people should either live lives of celibacy or marry someone of the opposite sex." BB responds, "Oh okay . . . so sort of like pray the gay away?" Pastor Kyle says, "No, it's not that. If someone is struggling with same-sex attraction, that might be something that they struggle with their entire lives. The fact of the matter is, Jesus loves people no matter what their sexual orientation is. He died for them on the cross and rose again for them, laying down his life for the whole world."

Please thoughtfully answer the following questions:

1. Do you believe Dustin was justified in being hurt and upset by the comments that the college students made toward Antonio and BB?
2. What is your opinion of how Pastor Kyle responded to the four college students harassing Antonio and BB with hateful speech?
3. Do you believe Pastor Kyle was pastoral in the way that he spoke to Antonio and BB?

A Fishy Situation

Pastor Hudson is finishing his first week as the new associate pastor at a large, growing congregation. He serves alongside three other pastors, two directors of Christian education, three secretaries, two music directors, a property manager, and two media/ IT coordinators, all of whom are employed on a full-time basis. The church also employs another ten to twelve part-time employees at any given time and has no shortage of volunteers in the congregation. He is thankful to be serving at such a stable church, both administratively and financially.

At lunch on Friday at the end of his first week, Allison and Christie invite Pastor Hudson to join them for lunch in the church café. Since all of the sofas, chairs, and tables are occupied, they eat their gourmet sushi picnic style on the carpet. Pastor Hudson has a fantastic time getting to know two of his new colleagues. Allison and Christie have gone out of their way to make him feel welcomed and loved!

The following Monday, right before morning staff meeting, the senior pastor, Greg, pulls Pastor Hudson aside and gives him a heads up that Ms. Stabler, one of the church music directors, is furious with Allison, Christie, and the new associate pastor. She is claiming that she clearly marked her gourmet sushi as being hers before placing it in the staff room refrigerator, and that it was stolen from her. She is demanding repayment and a public apology from all three perpetrators. Pastor Greg is not super concerned about this, but wanted Hudson to be aware that Ms. Stabler might be bringing this up during the staff meeting.

To Hudson's relief not a word of the missing sushi is mentioned during the staff meeting, and he has every intention of apologizing to Ms. Stabler for eating her gourmet sushi that he thought was purchased by Allison and Christie. However, she leaves as soon as the meeting concludes and disappears into the hallways of the massive complex. When Hudson goes to her office, he sees a note on her door informing visitors that she is taking the rest of the day as a personal day.

Conflict Resolution

The following Sunday morning, Pastor Hudson enters his office prior to the start of worship and is struck by a thick, putrid smell.... It's the smell of rotting fish. Short for time, he does not have an opportunity to search out where the smell is originating from. He hurries off to the west sanctuary for the start of the traditional service. Hudson preaches at each of the three services that day, and has the memory of being hit with the putrid smell stuck in his mind. The same two thoughts continue to run through his mind: "Why does my new office stink of rotting fish? Someone must have forgotten to empty the trash can, that's all it is."

After the service, Pastor Hudson walks back into his office and sees that his waste basket is empty. He then begins looking through the drawers of his desk and, upon opening the top left drawer, he finds three large containers of sushi; a California roll, a spicy tuna roll, and a dynamite roll, to be exact. All were rotting away and stinking up his office. He goes next door to Pastor Greg's office and brings him back to show him what he has discovered.

Pastor Greg then phones Ms. Stabler and asks her to meet him and Pastor Hudson in Hudson's office. Ten minutes later she arrives with a tickled look on her face. Pastor Greg begins the conversation by saying, "Hi, Ms. Stabler, Pastor Hudson found something in his desk, and I think we should talk about it. I'll let him start first."

Hudson sits up in his chair and says, "Listen Ms. Stabler, I always want to put the best construction on things, and I never want to jump to conclusions, but were you so upset with me for eating your gourmet sushi with Allison and Christie that you put three packages of sushi in my desk to make my office smell?" After a brief pause Ms. Stabler lets out a pretentious little laugh and responds with, "Oh that wasn't a prank! When I found out how much you and those girls love sushi, I bought each of you three packages of sushi to enjoy. Late Friday afternoon I bought each of you a California roll, a spicy tuna roll, and a dynamite roll. I hand delivered the girls their sushi and they loved it! When you weren't in your office, I just put it in the top left-hand drawer of your desk."

With a great sigh of relief Pastor Greg says, "Well this was just a little misunderstanding. Thank you so much for your thoughtful gifts to Pastor Hudson, Allison, and Christie. Why don't the three of us go out to lunch, my treat?" Pastor Hudson looks at Pastor Greg and Ms. Stabler and says with an ironic tone, "Are you in the mood for sushi?"

Please thoughtfully answer the following questions:

1. Do you believe Allison and Christie didn't know the gourmet sushi in the staff room refrigerator belonged to Ms. Stabler when they had it for lunch?

2. In your opinion, should Pastor Hudson have called Ms. Stabler up on the phone after the church staff meeting to apologize when he saw she was not in her office?

3. Is it more likely in your opinion that Ms. Stabler put the sushi in Pastor Hudson's desk as a gift because she knew how much he loved sushi, or as a prank to get back at him for eating her gourmet sushi with Allison and Christie?

Is Pastor Liberal or Conservative?

The congregation of Old Grey Brick Church is excited to have received a new graduate from the seminary. The call committee was united in the statement read to the voters' assembly by call committee chairman, K.C. Nichol, which read, "We are thankful to God that we are receiving a seminary graduate as our new pastor by the name of Donald Newhouse. We are pleased that he attended the most open-minded and progressive seminary in our Synod. We are confident that he and his wife and daughters will fit in well with the culture of our congregation and community as a whole. Please remember to keep Pastor Newhouse and his family in your prayers as they prepare to join our community."

For the first six months after Pastor Newhouse's ordination/installation service, parishioners at Old Grey Brick Church are satisfied with their new pastor's overall performance. He is a solid and personable preacher, teacher, and shepherd to the entire congregation. The congregation is especially delighted to hear Pastor Newhouse mention from time to time in Bible studies or day to day conversations the need for everyone to have health care regardless of their race, gender, age, economic status, religion, etc. They are especially pleased that he can support his positions in a concrete and systematic fashion using biblical passages such as Luke 6:31:

"Do to others as you would have them do to you."

Or Matt 22:37-40, when Jesus replied:

"Love the Lord your God with all your heart and with all your soul and with all your mind." This is the first and greatest commandment. And the second is like it: "Love your neighbor as yourself." All the Law and the Prophets hang on these two commandments.

He even goes as far as to say, "When a person is suffering and is being afflicted by illness, and we clearly have the opportunity to help a person in their hour of pain and decide not to help care for their needs and, in fact, turn a blind eye to their suffering, to some degree we are contributing to their pain. To some degree we are breaking the fifth commandment in that inaction, and committing a degree of murder against that person to some extent."

However, many in the congregation were absolutely aghast to hear Pastor Newhouse in Sunday morning Bible study share his concern for the unborn, using the same exact biblical teachings to support health care for all people. When asked to further expound on his support for the unborn, he answered, "All life has been created by God. It says in Psalm 51: 5–6,

> Surely, I was sinful at birth,
> sinful from the time my mother conceived me.
> Yet you desired faithfulness even in the womb;
> you taught me wisdom in that secret place.

Therefore, if a person is sinful from the moment of conception and is sinful from the moment of birth, then they need a savior. They need to hear the good news of Jesus Christ, and Jesus wants to use his church to share with them the gift of holy baptism. A person needs Jesus regardless of their race, gender, age, economic status, intellectual abilities, or whether they are in the womb or outside of the womb. In fact, it's a great idea to start talking to your child about how much Jesus loves them before they are even born."

Only a few days after Pastor Newhouse shared words of concern for the unborn in a Sunday morning Bible study, his two elders decide that it is appropriate to ask him out for lunch in order to better understand where he stands. Before their waiter even has the opportunity to take their orders, Head Elder Kelly Worchester says, "Pastor the reason that Jay and I invited you to lunch today is because we as elders need to know, in fact, the entire congregation needs to know where you stand. Are you a liberal or are you a conservative? We thought that, since you graduated from the seminary that you did . . . well, you would be a liberal. And we appreciate that you want everyone to have health care, but you really shocked us when you used the same type of reasoning to stand against abortion rights."

Pastor Newhouse answers slowly and calmly, "I don't really think of myself as being either liberal or conservative. I simply try to faithfully represent and teach the doctrines of the Christian church to you gentlemen and to the rest of the congregation. I am not here to tickle anyone's ears. I am here to be faithful to the ordination vows that I made before God. I know that someday I will have to stand before Jesus Christ and give an account for everything that I have said and done. And only by Jesus' blood and righteousness will I receive eternal life. That's true for all of us. Now why don't we order lunch?"

Please thoughtfully answer the following questions:

1. In your opinion, was Pastor Newhouse theologically consistent in the way he used the same biblical passages and reasoning to support everyone having access to health care and also showing concern for the unborn?

2. Do you think it was wise for Pastor Newhouse's two elders to ask him out for lunch in order to better understand his perspectives and beliefs?

A Cry from Tuggle

Tuggle is an eighty-five-year-old church organist at a small congregation. He is proud of the fact that he primarily led the campaign to purchase the new organ and was the majority financial contributor. Even though it is difficult and time consuming for Tuggle to climb the flight of stairs to the balcony each week, he joyfully does in order to play his favorite instrument to the glory of God.

One gorgeous, sunny September afternoon, custodian Mr. Frito decides to open the windows of the sanctuary and let in some fresh air while he cleans the church. As he makes his way up to the balcony, he begins to detect a musty odor emanating from the space around the organ. He approaches and opens up a cupboard near the organ bench and discovers ten mason jars filled with urine. Mr. Frito is puzzled as to why they would be there, and decides that it's best to pretend that he did not see the mason jars of urine in the first place. He speedily finishes cleaning the church and leaves for the day.

Almost three months later to the day, Pastor Buckle is preaching her Christmas Eve sermon when she hears a pained cry echoing from the balcony. Elder Louis and Mr. Frito decide to check on what is happening. As they reach the top of the stairs, they see Tuggle the organist urinating blood into a large mason jar that is overflowing. He has a tortured look on his face and is crying out in pain.

Elder Louis yells, "Tuggle! What the heck are you doing?" He only receives more cries from Tuggle, and he also hears Mr. Frito phoning for an ambulance and saying, "Yes, we have a medical emergency at Trinity Church. We need an ambulance right away. Our elderly organist is urinating out blood and seems to be in excruciating pain. He is in the balcony up a flight of stairs. Please hurry."

Tuggle is rushed to the hospital in an ambulance with his dear wife, Ethel, by his side. But as he is being loaded into the ambulance he looks toward Pastor Buckle, Elder Louis, and Mr. Frito and says, "Over the last six months it started getting too difficult for me to get down the stairs every time I needed to use the little boy's room. So, I started urinating in old mason jars every time I had to go during the service. I didn't mean any harm. Thanks for understanding. Lord bless you."

The three then discuss the events of the evening and are all in agreement that everyone at Trinity is really concerned about their long-time organist, and will be there for him and his family no matter what. Mr. Frito then says, "Yeah, I discovered ten mason jars full of urine last September in the cupboard and I had no idea how they got there so I thought that it was best to just ignore them. But looking back now I wish that I would have said something."

Elder Louis responds, "What?! You knew about his disgusting habit of urinating in those mason jars and didn't say anything to Pastor or any of the elders? You're sick! There is no way that you should continue to be paid to clean our church!" Elder Louis then storms away while Mr. Frito repeats, "Louis, Louis, Louis, I didn't know what to do. I wasn't even sure what was going on! I swear!" Pastor Buckle then does her best to assure Mr. Frito that he will not be fired as the church custodian as long as she has anything to say about it.

Please thoughtfully answer the following questions:

1. In your view, was Tuggle the organist acting in an inappropriate manner by urinating in mason jars during the worship service because of his inability to get down the stairs every time he needed to use the restroom?

2. In your opinion, was Mr. Frito acting unethically by not informing Pastor Buckle or the elders about the ten urine jars as soon as he discovered them?

3. Do you believe Pastor Buckle was right in assuring Mr. Frito his position for the church as the custodian would not be eliminated as long as she had anything to say about it?

Katherine's New Boss

Katherine has recently graduated from an accredited liberal arts university with a bachelor's degree in early childhood education. She has a strong faith in Christ and recently accepted a call to serve as a full-time preschool teacher at a parochial elementary school with an enrollment of almost one thousand students. The church it is affiliated with has a combined total of about twelve hundred people in attendance each week at their four services on the main campus and an additional four services at their satellite campuses.

Katherine's boss is the church and school's director of Christian education, a gentleman in his late thirties by the name of Scansen. Her new boss describes himself as "a big kid at heart!" He is often seen riding his bicycle around the massive church complex and through the halls of the school on his way to and from meetings. Scansen is not one to dress up and can typically be found wearing shorts, tennis shoes, and a T-shirt of a superhero or cartoon character. This casual and laid-back approach to ministry and work in general has been a surprise to Katherine and has taken some time to get used to.

Scansen has a passion for sharing his testimony with Katherine and other staff members on a regular basis. In small staff gatherings and semi-public settings, Scansen without hesitation, often tells of his wild life before becoming a Christian as a senior in college and the highly promiscuous behavior that he lived out in his younger years. At times he will speak of past behavior with regret, and express thankfulness to God for delivering him from that lifestyle, making statements along the lines of "I still struggle with how many young women's lives I ruined with my reckless behavior."

However, a day or two later, Scansen will make statements that seem to suggest that he misses his old way of life, by saying something to the effect of "sometimes I really wish that I could have married several of my former flames as well as my wife. I still occasionally miss my old way of life. I love my job as a DCE, but for a few years after graduating from undergrad, before I went to school to become a DCE, I had an amazing time traveling for business and enjoying myself. I still really miss that sometimes."

To some degree, Scansen's relaxed style and his frequent romanticization of his past escapades has made Katherine feel a little uncomfortable, but also slightly encouraged to not be so pious herself. Katherine writes in her journal, a month into her new teaching position, "If my boss can live a wild lifestyle, become a Christian, and continue in that lifestyle off and on for several years, then become a DCE and share parts of his testimony with the staff and sometimes mere acquaintances about how he had sex with about five hundred women, then I can be a little more relaxed about the idea of having a boyfriend at my place past 12 a.m.! Why not? Scansen was allowed to act like a wild child when he was my age, why should I have to live like a perfect angel? I'm nowhere near as messed up as he was!"

Approximately ten months later, just before the start of her second year teaching preschool, Katherine meets with Scansen, the principal of the elementary, Ms. Manning, and the senior pastor of the church, Reverend Shauspieler, to make them aware that she is twelve weeks pregnant with her first child, and that her boyfriend, Henry, is the father. Katherine is clear that she is not planning on marrying Henry anytime soon, but is completely committed to having her child and raising him or her in a loving, Christ-centered home. Scansen, Ms. Manning, and Reverend Shauspieler thank Katherine for informing them of her pregnancy, and let her know that they will be keeping this information to themselves and will be praying for her.

After Katherine leaves the office, Scansen makes his position known. "We have a duty to protect our preschool students from examples of people having sexual relationships outside of marriage. The parents that send their children to our preschool are investors, and the last thing in the world we want to do is anger our investors by allowing a single woman who is pregnant outside of marriage to teach their children. Katherine needs to be fired immediately." Unlike Scansen, Reverend Shauspieler and Principal Manning would like Katherine to remain as a teacher at the preschool. They believe that she is a fantastic teacher with a strong faith in God who is doing a courageous and Christian thing by keeping the child. However, both Reverend Shauspieler and Principal Manning ultimately leave the decision up to Scansen as he is officially Katherine's supervisor.

Two days later, Scansen walks into Katherine's classroom and speaks to her one on one. He informs Katherine that she is being let go from her position. Katherine is devastated and shocked. She responds, "So I'm trying to live out my faith and do what God's word and the Christian church teaches by having my baby and raising him or her in a Christian home, and you're firing me for that? Would have you preferred that I had an abortion and not told anyone about it? Could have I kept my job then, if I had an abortion and pretended to be perfect for you, Scansen? Basically, you're firing me because I had sex outside of marriage with my boyfriend—one of two people I've ever had sex with in my life! You are a total hypocrite who goes around bragging about his past promiscuous behavior and you're firing me because my boyfriend impregnated me? You're a total hypocrite! What am I supposed to do about health insurance now?" Scansen pretentiously replies, "I can tell you're really upset. I'm keeping you in prayer. I'll leave so you can reflect and clear your possessions in privacy."

Please thoughtfully answer the following questions:

1. What is your impression of Scansen's leadership style?
2. In your opinion, is Katherine acting in a courageous and Christian way by keeping her child and dedicating herself to raising him or her in a loving and Christ-centered home?
3. Do you believe Scansen was acting in a Christlike and compassionate manner when he decided to fire Katherine for being pregnant outside of marriage?
4. Do you think Reverend Shauspieler should have allowed Scansen to fire Katherine?
5. What is your opinion of Katherine's response to Scansen informing her that she was being let go from her position?

Adding a Lay Leader?

Bug Tatum has recently joined his fifth church in eight years. He and his second wife, Shanita, are excited for a new start. With great pride, Bug makes a point to inform his new pastor that at several past congregations he has served as a lay leader and is willing to serve as one in the future as well.

About a month after Bug and Shanita become members, Pastor Daniel notices that Bug is speaking with great authority on church policy issues, almost as if he is the chairman of the congregation or a pastor on staff. What is more interesting to Pastor Daniel is certain members in the congregation seem to be under the impression that Bug is a licensed psychologist. However, Bug has told Pastor Daniel and others publicly that he barely graduated from high school and despises institutions of higher learning and authority in general.

One morning after returning from a much-needed two-week vacation, Pastor Daniel sees Andy Willy, the church treasurer and an elder, walking out of the office. Pastor Daniel inquires how the services went with retired Pastor Louis Sparkman filling in. Andy responds, "Well it's a funny thing, Louis is getting older and he was unable to fill in for you, so he had to cancel two Sundays in a row. Thankfully Bug Tatum was able to fill in and lead the service two weeks in a row. And he did a great job! In fact, I and the other elders feel that Bug should be made a lay leader, and he can kind of serve as your right-hand man. Sort of like an assistant pastor. That way when you get sick you won't have to go to all of the trouble of finding someone to fill in for you." Although Pastor Daniel is nearly speechless, he thanks Andy for letting him know how the services went before heading to his study.

Later that day, Pastor Daniel phones Pastor Louis and learns that a man identifying himself as a church elder phoned Louis the night before each service and told him there was no longer need for a substitute pastor to show up because everything was being handled by the lay leader. Louis remembers that the man introduced himself as Bug.

Please thoughtfully answer the following questions:

1. What is your impression of Bug Tatum?

2. What is your opinion of Elder Andy Willy saying to Pastor Daniel, "In fact, I and the other elders feel that Bug should be made a lay leader, and he can kind of serve as your right-hand man. Sort of like an assistant pastor. That way when you get sick you won't have to go to all of the trouble of finding someone to fill in for you"?

3. If you were Pastor Daniel's circuit visitor giving him advice in this situation, what words of wisdom would you offer?

4. Is there any passage from the Bible that comes to your mind that might be helpful to Pastor Daniel in this situation?

Chapter 3

Dealing with Racism

Chaplain Frampton Confronts Craigly

FRAMPTON IS A FIFTY-EIGHT-YEAR-OLD ordained minister who serves as a family chaplain at the Solsbury household, in one of the oldest and most affluent communities in the city. The estate covers nearly five acres and includes the main family home, a large garden with a small chapel in the middle, two guest homes, an Olympic-sized inground swimming pool, a tennis court, a game room, an impressive library, and three worker's cottages. Frampton is privileged to live in the largest and most luxurious worker's cottage on the property.

Recently the Solsbury family has welcomed their fourteen-year-old nephew, Craigly, to stay at their home for the summer while his parents and siblings holiday in the old country. When introducing Craigly to all those serving the estate, Mrs. Solsbury said, "My dear nephew Craigly is a free-spirited young man whose shaggy hair reflects his spirit and the spirit of the times. It's a fascinating joy to witness his many moments of youthful horseplay! I do believe that you will come to love my sister's youngest child as much as I do. I look forward to see what this summer has in store for this household!"

About three weeks after the arrival of Craigly, the Solsbury family and several of their household staff have just finished evensong and are enjoying lemonade outside the entrance of the chapel. Chaplain Frampton is hearing about one of Chef Antonio Colombo's newest dessert recipes when Craigly approaches and says, "Hey Mexican Pizza! Will you make me some French toast for a midnight snack tonight? Bring it to my room by 10:30 p.m.!"

Chaplain Frampton immediately realizes what's happening. Craigly is addressing Chef Antonio Colombo as Mexican Pizza because his mother is from Mexico and his father is from Italy. "Young man!" Chaplain Frampton says sternly to Craigly, "I will be damned if I will stand here and allow you to speak to Chef Colombo that way! Apologize to him at once or you will not receive the Lord's Supper until you repent."

Craigly stares silently at Chaplain Frampton and Chef Colombo, and seconds later Mrs. Solsbury approaches and says, "What's happening here?" Chaplain Frampton responds, "Ma'am, Craigly made a racist remark to Chef Colombo. I informed him that as the chaplain, I would not allow him to take communion until he repented and asked the chef for forgiveness." Mrs. Solsbury takes a deep sigh and says, "Well, I see. I doubt he even fully knows the meaning of his actions at this tender age. Therefore, I will apologize on his behalf. I'm sorry for this. Well, no more of this unpleasantness. Let's enjoy our lemonade. Come along Craigly."

Please thoughtfully answer the following questions:

1. In your view did Chaplain Frampton respond correctly to fourteen-year-old Craigly's comments to Chef Antonio Colombo?
2. Do you believe Mrs. Solsbury handled the situation well by apologizing on Craigly's behalf?
3. Which of the Ten Commandments is someone breaking when they make a racist comment like the one Craigly made toward Antonio Colombo?

Austin, Templeton, and Martin

Austin is a fifteen-year-old sophomore in high school. Recently he has developed a passion for history and social studies. His favorite period of study is the chapter of the civil rights movement that took place in the 1960s. Austin's guidance counselor and parents have encouraged him in his study of this period. To Austin's surprise, he recently has won a scholarship that pays in full his tuition to study the civil rights movement at a historically black college during the summer before the start of his junior year of high school.

One evening after tennis practice, Austin shares the good news of his upcoming summer studies with his tennis coach, Templeton. To Austin's shock, coach Templeton does not congratulate him, but instead says, "Yeah there were a few people involved in the civil rights movement that had their hearts in the right place, but the fact of the matter is when you march thousands of people down a street you have to know that there is going to be trouble. Be careful what you believe from the professors during your summer of studies." Austin is not exactly sure what to say in response to Coach Templeton so he simply says, "Oh . . . okay. Thanks, Coach."

A few moments later Austin's father, Martin, picks him up from tennis practice. As soon as Martin sees his son walking to the car, he can tell that his son is disturbed about something. On the car ride home Austin shares what Coach Templeton said about the chapter of civil rights movement that took place in the 1960s and his upcoming studies at a historically black college. After a good deal of consideration and prayer, Martin decides to schedule a meeting with Coach Templeton to discuss his comments to Austin.

A week later the two meet after school at the cafeteria and, at first, Coach Templeton is polite and deferential. He greets Martin and says, "Hi Pastor Martin! I don't think we've had a chance to talk since Reformation Sunday last autumn! Sorry I haven't popped into church lately. How are things going?"

Pastor Martin makes small talk with Templeton for about twenty minutes before saying, "Templeton, the reason I asked to speak with you is because Austin shared with me what you said about the chapter of the civil rights movement of the 1960s, and his scholarship to study at a historically black college. I'm a little surprised because when you went through my new member class five years ago, I lectured extensively on how the civil rights leaders of the 1960s stood up against the evils of racism in our society. I thought that you agreed with that teaching . . ."

Templeton takes a deep breath and says, "Well, I may have five years ago or so. However, my eyes have been opened to the poisonous teachings of this radical culture, and how they were at work through the civil rights leaders even back in the 1960s! I feel so sorry for you that your mind has been poisoned by the media, pastor!"

After about five seconds of silence, Martin responds, "Templeton, each human being is made in the image and likeness of God. To say that one person or community is less than another is misrepresenting God's holy work in creation, and his love for all people through the person of Jesus Christ. Frankly, racism is a breaking of the eighth commandment, "Thou shalt not bear false witness." It is an insidious sin, and I believe it is one that you need to repent of."

Templeton responds, "No pastor, you need to repent of racism! You're being racist toward me!" He then storms out the cafeteria.

Please thoughtfully answer the following questions:

1. Do you believe it was wise for Martin to schedule a meeting with Templeton to speak with him about his comments to Austin?
2. In your view, was Martin's theological case against racism sound?
3. Do you believe Templeton's comment, "No pastor, you need to repent of racism! You're being racist toward me!" had any basis in reality?

T.J.'s Bizarre Perspective on Business

T.J. Calvin is a forty-year-old man who is married with three children. He owns an insurance agency and prides himself in being a savvy businessman. Since moving to town last year, T.J. has visited several churches with his family in search of just the right fit. They have recently settled into a church that has about seven hundred people in attendance each week over the span of its four weekly worship services.

One evening T.J. attends Pastor's Wednesday night Bible study and listens to Pastor Sydney discuss the practice of slavery in the ancient near east. About halfway through the lecture, T. J. interjects and says, "Yes, the fact of the matter is people in their own time simply have to follow the business practices of that time and place. We all have bosses, and we need to listen to what our bosses tell us to do. If I had lived in the ancient world or in a country in the 1700s or 1800s that allowed slavery, and owning slaves would have been the most lucrative way for me to provide for my family, then that's what I would have probably had to do. I'm guessing most of the people here would say the same thing if they were being honest and not afraid of the politically correct culture that attacks anyone who thinks for themselves."

Pastor Sydney's mother, Tilda, responds to T.J.'s comments and says, "So, did I understand you right, that you would be okay with owning slaves if it made you and your family money?" T.J. gives an exaggerated shrug and says, "Look, I'm not saying that it would have been an easy choice to make. I'm just saying that people have to make decisions in business that are applicable to their time and place that will best benefit them and their families."

Without hesitation Tilda responds, "Slavery is an abomination! For my ancestors it consisted of my people being torn away from their families and homes, stuffed in the bottom of a ship, and enduring emotional, physical, sexual, and spiritual abuse and torture! How dare you try to justify the slave trade behind the façade of people needing to make business decisions for their families!"

Pastor Sydney proceeds with the Bible study, which for its remainder, holds almost no further conversation from the participants.

Please thoughtfully answer the following questions:

1. What are your thoughts on what T.J. had to say?
2. What are your thoughts on what Tilda had to say?
3. In your opinion, do you think Pastor Sydney should have interjected in the conversation between T.J. and Tilda? And if so, what should Pastor Sydney have said?
4. In what respects is the practice of human slavery violating the fifth and eighth commandments?

Red Lines

Pastor Wexner is filled with joy as she meets her parishioners for the first time, moves into her office, and reflects on her ordination and installation services. The only item that is causing her some anxiety is the task of searching for an apartment in town that is in her price range and within a ten-minute drive of the church.

Thankfully Board of Properties Manager, Trevor Arlington, and his business partner, Jay Manchester, are more than happy to meet with Pastor Wexner and advise her on the best places in town to live. The three meet in the church boardroom and, after Trevor and Jay tell Pastor Wexner about their latest building projects and the addition to one of their stores, Jay begins drawing on the white board with a black marker. He writes down the approximate price ranges of houses, the types of amenities, and the predominate ethnic makeup of each area.

Jay then does something rather curious . . . he begins to draw red boxes around each section of town that comprises mainly non-Caucasian people. He strongly advises Pastor Wexner to stay away from these areas because, in his words, "the crime is completely out of control in these neighborhoods for the most part. And the few areas that are safe are not welcoming to white people like us. I know most of these areas are in your price range and within ten minutes of the church, but you would be much better off driving a long distance and being in a welcoming environment than putting yourself in a dangerous situation." Trevor nods his head in agreement with Jay and sips his espresso.

After the meeting with Trevor and Jay, Pastor Wexner looks up crime statistics provided by the state for the city and finds the areas that Jay put red lines around actually have very little crime at all. In fact, they seem to be safer than the areas that did not have red lines drawn around them. Pastor

Wexner finds herself speaking aloud even though she is now the only one in the room. She says with frustration and disbelief, "Did Jay and Trevor lie to me about how dangerous those areas of town were that Jay put red lines around because most of the people in those areas of town are people of color? Or are they really so brainwashed with racist ideas that they think all non-white people are dangerous, unwelcoming people? Lord, I pray that not everyone at this church shares the same racist, garbage ideas as Jay and Trevor."

Please thoughtfully answer the following questions:

1. If you were in Pastor Wexner's shoes, would you reach out to an older, more experienced pastor about the conversation with Jay and Trevor?

2. If you were in Pastor Wexner's position, would you tell Jay and Trevor you discovered through crime statistics provided by the state that the areas with red lines drawn around them are actually safer than the areas that did not have red lines drawn around them?

3. Do you believe Pastor Wexner has a responsibility to call Jay and Trevor into her office to tell them she is concerned they are harboring racist ideas about people of color?

Praying for President Hubbard

The Reverend Doctor Terrance Hubbard is serving as interim president of his alma matter, Meadow Point Christian College. He enjoys socializing with students, faculty, staff, and fellow alumni on and off campus. President Hubbard is especially delighted to hear about the dreams and achievements of his students and share with them his fondest memories as an undergraduate student at Meadow Point.

One crisp, sunny October afternoon, President Hubbard is working alongside two freshmen pre-seminary students, Jessica Collins and Allie Walker, to help put away tables and decorations at the end of the school's homecoming weekend festivities. As the three discuss Meadow Point's history and its potential for enrollment growth, Jessica casually asks President Hubbard, "Why is it that our college is almost entirely made up of white students? I mean, why is that we have almost no African American students enrolled here?" As soon as Jessica poses these questions, she feels a little embarrassed, because she senses that President Hubbard has been put on the spot.

Allie looks to be embarrassed as well. The interim administrator answers slowly, "Well, I'm nearly sixty-five years old now, and historically, or at least during most of my lifetime, Meadow Point has not really been equipped to meet the unique needs of most African American students. That's why so few African American students have applied, historically, and that's why so few have been accepted historically as well. Our cultures are so profoundly different, In many cases it would only cause heart ache to everyone involved to put African American students into a situation that is radically different than anything they have ever experienced. Likewise, it would be unfair to the students that we have here to expose them to a culture that does not have the same value systems, typically, that they grew up with and that this college cherishes. I pray that there will be a day when our two cultures will be similar enough to where a good portion of our student body is African American."

That evening, Jessica and Allie chill out at their favorite bubble tea shop and reflect on the conversation they had with President Hubbard. Allie makes the point that God loves everyone and Jesus died for every single person to have ever lived. She then quotes her New Testament professor, Reverend Doctor Richard Shuma: "God is not ageist, racist, sexist, or homophobic. Jesus Christ is the most inclusive person in the universe." Allie then says, "If Jesus is inclusive of all people, and we are a Christian college, then this college should reflect that inclusivity. Don't you agree with that, Jessica?"

Jessica agrees with Dr. Shuma's perspective as well as Allie's, and these two young women end the night by praying for President Hubbard, that his eyes would be opened. They also pray that God would give them wisdom on how to address what they see as institutionally racist policies at the college they both attend and love so dearly.

Please thoughtfully answer the following questions:

1. In addition to praying President Hubbard repent of his comments, should Jessica and Allie request a meeting with President Hubbard to voice their concerns about what he said?

2. Do you feel it would be a good idea for Jessica and Allie to first seek the advice of a trusted professor, campus human resource representative, or the campus chaplain on whether or not it is wise to schedule a meeting with President Hubbard to voice their concerns about what he said?

3. What biblical or extrabiblical writings might be helpful to Jessica and Allie in processing their conversation with President Hubbard and also in helping to respond to that conversation?

Cedric Forgives

Bowie-Knife is a sixty-seven-year-old man who loves sitting outside of his favorite convenient store and, in his words, "starting little fires!" According to Bowie-Knife's social media bio, he describes himself as follows: "I'm an old combat veteran who never served officially in the armed forces, but nevertheless, I give no quarter to the enemy, and always carry a black flag into battle. I'm ready to die for the cause!"

He is known in the community for being a teaser and a practical joker. It is often difficult for people to tell when Bowie-Knife is being serious or sarcastic. He loves playing pranks and watching how people react. Lately, Bowie-Knife's friends and family have noticed that his rhetoric has gone from silly and vaguely intolerant to downright hostile and racist.

His change in behavior becomes publicly evident one Sunday evening while he is sitting outside of his favorite convenient store. A middle-aged woman by the name of Pamela Dombreck Smith Perez walks by him with her four young children. As she is entering the store, Bowie-Knife says, "Do each of those kids have a different daddy? Obviously, none of the daddies are from this neighborhood."

Pamela ushers her children into the store and then snaps back, "Listen to me, you racist piece of crap! You're not even all white and you're judging me for being married to a man who isn't white? I went to school with your daughter and now I can see why she is so embarrassed of you! You're a piece of crap!"

After checking out, Pamela mentions to Cedric, the store owner, what happened a few minutes earlier. Cedric informs her that he heard the end of the exchange and apologizes on behalf of Bowie-Knife. After Pamela pulls away, Cedric walks outside and sits down next to Bowie-Knife. He speaks plainly to the elderly man. "Listen, we've gotten to know each other pretty well over the last year, Bowie-Knife. You know this store is my main income, and it allows me to serve as a pastor part time next door. I love you, man. And I want you to know, no matter what a person's skin color is or what religion they follow, I love everyone. But here's the thing—I can't have you harassing people as they walk into my store. I'm surprised by this because you were super friendly to me when we first met, and it didn't seem to matter to you that I was black. But you've seemed real cold lately . . . and now this with harassing that lady and her kids. What's going on?"

Bowie-Knife answers, "I've changed for the better. If you can't handle free speech, then you don't deserve my business or company. I don't have to put up with this persecution. The whole community is going to know about this!" The elderly man slowly walks away while glaring hatefully at Cedric. Over the course of the next five weeks, Cedric's once-thriving business starts to struggle as slander about him spreads. False reports are posted online and even said directly to the small business owner's face that he targeted Bowie-Knife for his political leanings and because he is white.

Soon attendance at Cedric's church begins to drop off moderately as lies about him continue to spread. Pamela Dombreck Smith Perez does her best to let people in the community know what really happened that day. Some listen and believe her and Cedric's accounts, but they are still afraid to associate with the small business owner now that Bowie-Knife and his circle of friends and acquaintances have turned on Cedric.

Eight months after the incident, attendance at Cedric's church is only half of what it was prior to the slander being spread, and his business is within a month of collapse if there is not a sudden major turnaround. One evening while sitting down for supper, he sees on social media that Bowie-Knife and one of his friends attacked a federal building and were shot dead by federal agents. Cedric is saddened by the news, but is not surprised by this report, as Bowie-Knife's behavior was becoming increasingly more radical.

However, Cedric is surprised when Bowie-Knife's daughter Kelly phones him and asks if he will preside over her father's funeral service. Cedric agrees, and one week later the local high school gymnasium is packed with people from all over the community as well as from across the nation. In fact, several national news outlets are even in attendance interviewing people about their relationship with Bowie-Knife.

At the end of Cedric's sermon, there is hardly a dry eye in the house among the two thousand plus attendees. After the service, a national news reporter approaches Cedric and asks, "Pastor Cedric, why do you think so many people loved Bowie-Knife given the horrible racist and anarchial behavior he exhibited toward the end of his life?" Cedric answers, "I think there are probably a variety of reasons why people loved him. I do not condone what he did or how he was acting recently. But I can tell you why I loved Bowie, because he is a child of God who God loved so much that he sent his one and only Son, Jesus, to die for on the cross."

Two months later Cedric sells what is left of his business and begins serving as a full-time prison chaplain in a city forty-five minutes away from his home. He continues to serve as the sole pastor of his congregation on a part-time basis and is thankful weekly worship attendance is returning to what it was prior to the slander being spread. Many people in the community have asked Pastor Cedric to forgive them since they heard him preach at Bowie-Knife's funeral. Cedric always reassures people he forgives them, but deep down he is still wounded by how he was treated by literally thousands of people in his community.

Please thoughtfully answer the following questions:

1. If you had been in Cedric's position, would have you agreed to preside over Bowie-Knife's funeral service?
2. What is your opinion of what Cedric said to the national news reporter?
3. If you were Cedric's friend or colleague, would you recommend he seek out counseling in order to help him cope with the trauma he has suffered?

Cheryle's Post

Cheryle is seventy years young and is approaching her fiftieth wedding anniversary to her high school sweetheart, Bart. The couple are proud small business owners, but they are prouder of their three children and eight grandchildren.

One evening, Cheryle watches a breaking news clip on her phone of a group of people tearing down a massive bronze statue of a person who lived almost two hundred years ago. After the statue is torn down, it is then dragged to a nearby river and cast in. This is done to the sound of cheers and applause.

Cheryle responds by writing this heartfelt statement and publicly posting it on all of her social media accounts: "Today my heart was ripped from my chest! I saw a statue ripped down and cast into the river. The statue was of Lord Riperton Applegate, a man who built numerous schools and roadways throughout our many lands. He worked tirelessly to expand our empire and our way of life to those less fortunate. Lord Applegate was a generous and kindly master. Every Christmas he gave his slaves a new wool blanket and an extra piece of coal for their woodstove. He rarely had them corrected with physical punishment, and he did his best to keep families together whenever possible. It is such a shame to see his statue and memory disrespected in this way. May you rest in peace, Lord Applegate, and may your many contributions to the world and your memory be cherished for all time!"

Cheryle's pastor, the Reverend Melisa Fisher, reads this post and over the course of the next three hours, witnesses nearly a hundred comments in response. Most are responses of outrage and disgust that a volunteer church organist would write a statement of defense for a slave owner who was known to buy and sell human beings that he would then sexually abuse and beat.

Several of the people who are outraged and disgusted with Cheryle are also parishioners of Pastor Fisher. A few vow to never speak with their one-time acquaintance again and to not return to worship in person until Cheryle steps down as the organist. They even go as far as to tag Pastor Melisa Fisher in their post, and pose these questions directly to her: "How soon will this be taken care of Pastor Fisher? Are you going to allow Cheryle the organist to spread this type of racist bigotry on the internet and then continue on as our church's organist?"

Please thoughtfully answer the following questions:

1. If you were Pastor Fisher, how would you handle this situation?
2. Do you see any way Pastor Fisher can convince Cheryle that Riperton Applegate was sinning by owning slaves and abusing them?
3. In your opinion, was it wise for people to write public responses to Cheryle's social media post?
4. What might be some healing, Christ-centered words Pastor Fisher could speak to Cheryle and her parishioners who are outraged and disgusted with Cheryle?

How Do I Love This Neighbor?

Jenson can often be seen with a smile on his face as he welcomes people into his front yard for block party barbecues every Friday in the summer months. When Pastor Steve and his wife, Melody, moved in next door, Jenson was the first to welcome them into the community with a basket of fresh vegetables from his garden and a batch of home brewed amber lager.

One evening while at one of Jenson's barbecues, Melody notices several of the guests have tattoos which appear to be a symbol of a white supremacist organization. As she looks around, nearly everyone there has very fair skin, with the exception of one African American couple who work with Jenson. Melody almost mentions this to Steve once back at home, but decides it's best not to worry him about the possibility Jenson may have a few friends who are white supremacists.

One week later as Steve naps on the living room sofa and enjoys the cool breeze rushing through the open window, he is awoken to hear Jenson yelling, "Boy, get on out of here!" At first Steve believes that Jenson must be yelling at the neighbor's dog Domino, who lives across the street and who occasionally steals food from the barbecue. Quickly Steve realizes this is not the case when he hears Jenson yell, "Get on out of here, you hoodie-wearing gang-banging punk! I don't want you around here when my barbecue gets started in an hour. If you learn to dress properly, I might welcome you over sometime. Now get!"

Pastor Steve hops off the sofa to see through the window a young African American teenager wearing a hooded sweatshirt quickly walking past Jenson's house. The teenager looks back at Jenson with a frightened look on his face as he runs down the suburban street to his home six houses away. Pastor Steve slowly walks toward Jenson and says, "Jenson, what's going on? Did I just hear what I thought I heard from you?"

Jenson responds, "Yeah! You heard me protecting our neighborhood from gang-banging hoodie-wearing punks that can't even pull up their pants! Yep, you're welcome!" Pastor Steve replies in a slow, deliberate voice, "Jenson, that child was simply walking to his home. It's none of your business or mine how he is dressed. Or anyone else's for that matter."

At this point Jenson is no longer the smiling, welcoming neighbor that he first appeared to be to Pastor Steve, as he yells, "You get the hell off my lawn and don't you ever come back, you bleeding heart liberal coward! You think you're Jesus? Go to your church and feed the people there your crap! I'm not eating it here!"

Pastor Steve slowly walks off of the property and back into his own house. He goes to his office and phones Melody to tell her what happened and ask for her advice. Melody responds by telling Steve what she noticed at the barbecue last Friday. The two agree Jenson is likely intentionally associating with people in white supremacist groups. They conclude he probably invited the African American couple from work to the barbecue to only appear inclusive and tolerant.

Please thoughtfully answer the following questions:

1. If you were Pastor Steve and Melody, how would you specifically pray for Jenson?

2. If you were Pastor Steve and Melody, do you think it would be difficult to love your neighbor Jenson?

3. If Jenson tried to make small talk with Pastor Steve and Melody in the future, do you believe they should speak the Gospel or the Law to him?

Pastor Joey Provides Encouragement

Stacey is a twenty-three-year-old graduate student who has started to date a PhD candidate by the name of Len. On their seventh date the couple is intimate, and several weeks later Stacey realizes she is pregnant. Upon telling Len the news, he promises Stacey he will support her and the child with his time and resources. Stacey believes Len and starts to become excited about the fact that she is going to have her first child the same year that she will earn her master's degree.

Stacey shares the news of her pregnancy with her father, Drew, and mother, Laci. At first her parents are supportive and even a little excited about the news of a grandchild. However, once Stacey shares a picture of Len, the child's father, with her parents, their demeanors change dramatically. Drew becomes especially disturbed and his attitude transforms completely. Drew says in a harsh raised tone, "You listen to me, Stacey. This Len is not of the same background and race as you. And this child will have a horrible life being a mixed-race child. If you want any more encouragement and financial support from me and your mother as you finish grad school, you need to schedule an appointment to have an abortion immediately."

Stacey runs out of her parents' home in tears. She drives back to campus and phones her old pastor, Joey, and shares with him what is taking place in her life. Joey listens carefully to Stacey and responds by saying, "Well first of all, I am incredibly happy for you and Len, and I am so thankful for the child that God has blessed you both with. Jesus loves the three of you very much.

"Thirdly, I am really disappointed in your dad and mom. Especially your dad for what he said. Demanding that your child have an abortion and threatening to not encourage her or support her financially unless she has an abortion because she is having a child with someone of another race is horrible. Really, it's an abomination. I want you to know that your church family and your old pastor are here for you and Len and your child. We will support you throughout this pregnancy and after your beautiful child is born."

Please thoughtfully answer the following questions:

1. What is your opinion of how Stacey's parents, Drew and Laci, acted once they realized Stacey was having a child with a person of a different race?

2. Do you agree with what Stacey's old pastor, Joey, said to her after she shared with him what was taking place in her life?

3. What are some specific ways Pastor Joey and Stacey's church family can support her, Len, and their child throughout the pregnancy and after the birth?

4. What are some biblical or extrabiblical resources that might be helpful to Stacey and Len as they prepare for the birth of their child and cope with the stress of Stacey's parents' opposition to this pregnancy?

Student Body President Dumpleton

Dumpleton is a nostalgic old soul who loves to wax poetic in the student union, breaking only to sip on a cherry soda. His university is a racially diverse enclave with students from nearly every nation on earth.

One evening while speaking to a group of international friends who inquire about the racial inequality the country is infamous for, Dumpleton states, "How racist, really, was my country sixty years ago? I mean, even my grandfather, who would be considered racist by today's standards, once allowed a person of color to use a whites only restroom at his gas station when the colored restroom toilet was broken. Does that sound like horrible racism to you? The liberal, politically correct media has blown this way out of proportion. We need to look to the future and forget about the past, bros."

That evening, Dumpleton's international friends change their minds about him, and revaluate their relationship with him. From that point on, they make a promise to one another not to associate with the student body president any further. One year later on the eve of graduation, Dumpleton takes a break from rehearsing his graduation address. As he strolls around the old college green, he spots his once-close friend, Bobby.

Dumpleton approaches him and they slowly begin to discuss sports day and the local women's swimsuit competition. Eventually Dumpleton says, "You know, brah, you surprised me. I never thought you would break off contact with me all because I'm a little racist and think that township schools should be segregated from established, primarily white schools. Did your bros get to you?"

Bobby hesitantly answers his once-close friend, "Well it was a joint decision that it was in our best interest not to associate with you any longer due to your racist beliefs. So much of what you stand for is incompatible with everything we believe in."

With that, Dumpleton returns to his dorm to rest up before his big speech. The next day right before Dumpleton approaches the stage to make his graduation address, his ex-friends spot him praying with a Catholic priest. After the graduation ceremony Bobby approaches the priest and informs him of Dumpleton's racist tendencies and says, "Father did you know that Dumpleton, the man you were praying with right before his big speech, has racist tendencies?" Father Kensington answers, "No, I did not. But I am even more thankful now that I had an opportunity to pray with Dumpleton. Because Christ knows, he desperately needs prayer."

Please thoughtfully answer the following questions:

1. If you had been in Bobby and the rest of the international student's position, would have you promised not to associate with Dumpleton any further?

2. What is your opinion of Father Kensington's answer to Bobby's question, "Father did you know that Dumpleton, the man you were praying with right before his big speech, has racist tendencies?"

3. Imagine if Jesus were to meet Dumpleton face to face, what do you think he would say to him?

Chapter 4

Death and Dying

Noreen's Situation

NOREEN IS A RECENTLY widowed fifty-eight-year-old junior high school teacher who is looking forward to retiring in the next three years. Both of her sons just graduated from college and are engaged to loving, dynamic young women. Over the last six months, Noreen has had little time to spend with her sons and soon to be daughter-in-laws. Outside of work, nearly all of her time has been dedicated to caring for her ninety-year-old mother, Elanor, who has been in declining health for some time.

On the Sunday before Christmas, Noreen entered her mother's room to find her unresponsive. She immediately phoned an ambulance and then phoned her next-door neighbor Dr. Steinkamp, who rushed over in less than a minute. The doctor informed Noreen her mother had been dead for probably about two hours, and told her she had done a fantastic job caring for her over the years, especially over the last six months.

Five days later at the visitation, Noreen is speaking with her mother's priest, Father Jackson, when her estranged sister, Carter, approaches the priest and says, "Well, as I said to you in my voicemail today Father Jackson, my sister did take care of my mother in her last days, but she also convinced her that I was not a suitable daughter or a sister. The only reason that I am being so civil with my sister right now is because she recently lost her husband and this is my mother's visitation, after all. I hope that your funeral sermon will reflect the situation accurately and be kinder to me than my sister has been. Thank you for your time and have a blessed day."

After hearing this, Noreen's heart is beating rapidly as her face becomes beet red while Carter scampers away to the other side of the room. Noreen says in a relatively calm voice, "Father Jackson, this is the first time I have heard from or seen my sister in over a decade. She threw a massive fit because my mother did not give her sole control of my dad's estate when he died. I tried tirelessly to reach Carter the last several years of my mother's life. My mom wanted desperately to see her youngest daughter and Carter absolutely could not even be bothered to answer the telephone. I always did my best to represent Carter as well as I possibly could, but I can't anymore. This is all I can take!"

Please thoughtfully answer the following questions:

1. If you were Father Jackson, what might you say to Noreen to try to comfort her as she mourns the death of her mother and tries to cope with the presence of her estranged younger sister Carter?
2. How can Father Jackson pray for Noreen and Carter in the coming months and years as they deal with a variety of feelings of grief and loss?
3. What passages from the Bible might be helpful in this situation to help bring about reconciliation between these two sisters?
4. Do you believe Father Jackson should encourage Noreen to seek licensed professional counseling services?

One Last Gift

Lewis is twenty-six years old and was ordained into the office of holy ministry last month. He is incredibly close with his parents, Arnold and Samantha, and he is even closer to his younger brother, Seth. The support and friendship of his small family has blessed Lewis profoundly as he, for the last four months, has coped with the breakup of his long-time girlfriend, Sam. He feels blessed to live under an hour from his parents and only two hours from his little brother.

An interesting fact about Lewis is he has been cutting his own hair since he was twelve years old and started cutting Seth's hair when Seth was about six years old. Lewis is amazed at how Seth refuses to have his hair cut by anyone other than his older brother, even as a twenty-year-old sophomore in college. Almost every time that Seth drives nearly two hours down for a visit, he gets a haircut from his big brother.

Death and Dying

One early Saturday morning as Lewis awakes to prepare his guest bedroom for Seth's arrival, he begins to feel a sense of excitement that his younger brother will have the opportunity to hear him preach for the first time as a pastor the next morning. Suddenly he hears his phone ringing and sees on the caller ID that it's his dad. When he picks up the phone, he hears his parents crying, and his dad says, "Lewis, you need to sit down." Lewis slowly answers, "Okay, what's wrong?" His dad responds, "There was a horrible accident. Seth was driving home from a party and just after 4 a.m. this morning, was hit by a drunk driver. He was killed instantly." Lewis goes into a total state of shock. He can't fully comprehend the news that his dad has just delivered to him. After a great deal of crying and questioning of how this tragedy took place, where it took place, and who was responsible the news slowly starts to sink in.

Seth's funeral is set for the following Saturday, and the family's home church pastor, Jake Arbor, will preside over the service and graveside committal. Lewis in some ways desires to preside over the funeral for his younger brother as one last gift to him, but he realizes that it would simply be too difficult to endure for both himself and his family.

However, there is one thing that he is determined to do for Seth. And that is to give him one last haircut. Lewis meets with the funeral director, Mr. Robert Candy, in person and explains to him that he has cut Seth's hair since his younger brother was six, and that he would like to gift his brother with one last haircut. Mr. Candy agrees to Lewis' request.

The morning before the funeral, Mr. Candy leads Lewis to Seth's embalmed body that is dressed in a brand-new suit and tie. Mr. Candy leaves the brothers alone and goes to his office down the hall. Lewis begins the process of cutting his brother's wavy hair. He speaks to him with almost more of a fatherly demeanor than that of an older brother. Lewis pauses frequently to kiss Seth's head. He speaks to him throughout the haircut. After he finishes trimming the last few hairs around his brothers' ears, he leans against his ear and says, "I'll see you again someday, buddy. This won't be the last haircut I give you, man. You are the best brother and friend a guy could have ever hoped for. I love you. I know that you are with Jesus now." Lewis then cleans up his brother's hair. He takes three locks: one for himself, one for his father, and one for his mother. He leaves the room slowly in tears, and briefly thanks Mr. Candy for allowing him the time with Seth before exiting the funeral parlor.

Please thoughtfully answer the following questions:

1. If you were Pastor Jake Arbor, what words of comfort would you offer to Lewis and his parents as they mourn the death of Seth?

2. What passages from Scripture might you point Lewis and his parents to as they mourn the loss of Seth if you were Pastor Arbor?

3. Do you think it would be wise for Pastor Arbor to recommend to Seth and his parents that they each receive professional counseling individually, and also possibly as a group, as they process the loss of Seth?

Mourning the Death of a Beloved Mother

Over the course of the last ten years, Fran has steadily lost her memory. This painful decline has been pure torture to her only son, Adrian. He comments to a close friend, "My mother was the sharpest, most brilliant woman that you could have ever hoped to know. She was the life of the party, entertaining guests on her baby grand piano for hours over cocktails and caviar! How on earth could such a vibrant woman with such strong faith in Christ decline this way?"

Tragically, after doctors have done everything within reason to save her, Fran dies at home in her bed surrounded by her family, closest friends, dogs, and books. Adrian is beyond devastated and throws himself off of her balcony. Both of his legs are broken by the fall, and his mother's doctors rush from her lifeless body to attend to Adrian.

Ten days later, Adrian delivers these words at his mother's funeral: "My dear mama, in many respects, was lost the day that this God-awful degenerative brain disorder took control of her. I miss her dearly and, as many of you know, I have been dealing with despair since I lost her. Please pray for me. Reverend Lundy, please do not forget me. Please remember me in your prayers." At this point Adrian takes his seat and Reverend Lundy slowly approaches the pulpit to deliver the sermon.

Please thoughtfully answer the following questions:

1. If you were Reverend Lundy, what Christ-centered words of comfort would you proclaim to the family and friends of Fran, and most specifically to her only son, Adrian, in your sermon?

2. If you were delivering the funeral sermon and could pick a specific passage from the Bible to preach on, which passage would it be?

3. After the funeral how would you specifically make an effort to reach out to Adrian to check up on him, if you were Reverend Lundy?

Like a Fine Wine

Evan is an elderly man who is suffering from a rare degenerative bone disease. To make matters worse, he has gone blind in his left eye as the result of an untreated eye infection from two winters ago. Lastly, Evan recently started battling a highly aggressive form of colon cancer that was detected late by his doctor.

Remarkably, the attitude of this frisky elderly man is highly positive. Each morning when nurses or doctors check on him, they ask Evan how he is doing. When responding to female medical personnel he says, "I'm like a fine wine! I'm only getting better with age. Let me know if you want a taste!" And when responding to male medical personnel he replies, "I'm not going down without a fight! It's the illnesses that should watch out. They are in trouble, not me!"

One early evening after giving Evan communion, Pastor Ryan is approached by Judy, who is Evan's long-time girlfriend. She asks to speak with him in a break room on the third floor of the hospital. Judy trembles as she tearfully says to Pastor Ryan, "Evan is on the verge of death, and I can't imagine life without him! To make matters more complicated, he doesn't really have a will in place. He named his estranged son, Rudy, as the trustee of his estate. But the guidelines he has in place are vague. It will essentially be up to Rudy's discretion on how Evan's businesses and homes are dealt with. Rudy doesn't care for me much and I'm afraid that I'm going to have to deal with a giant mess and possible legal battle with Rudy once Evan dies! I hate the thought that, instead of having time to mourn the love of my life, I will be dealing with legal fees and court appearances. What do you think I should do, Pastor?"

Please thoughtfully answer the following questions:

1. If you were in Pastor Ryan's position, how would you answer Judy's question, "What do you think I should do, Pastor?"
2. Is there a particular hymn or Bible verse you can think of that is Christ-centered which Pastor Ryan could share with Evan and Judy to give them comfort during this difficult time?

The Confession of Arby Louis Samuels

Osmond Jones celebrated his one-year anniversary of ordination into the office of the holy ministry last week. In his first year serving as a pastor, his parishioners have started to trust him. One parishioner has even requested a time of individual confession and absolution.

On a snowy December morning at the break of dawn, Pastor Jones meets Arby Louis Samuels at his office. The eighty-eight-year-old Arby slowly enters the church with the assistance of a cane made of hickory wood. The two men make small talk and Arby tells his young pastor about some of the great past football teams he watched play in person. Pastor Osmond is impressed by the stories and, as he listens to the old man, is struck by the resemblance he bears to his beloved late grandfather.

Approximately ten minutes into the conversation Arby's demeanor becomes serious. He says to Pastor Osmond, "I've been told by my doctor last week that I only have about two months to live. My wife and family have no idea. There is something else that they have no idea about that I want to confess to God and I want God to forgive me for through you. Pastor, sixty-five years ago I did something horrific. Something that I thought I would take to my grave and never tell anyone about. I'm so ashamed of it and I think about it every single day. Well, I need to tell God and I need to tell you. I had just turned twenty-three when it happened. There was a girl in a neighboring town. Only about twenty minutes from here a county over. We had gotten engaged, and then I left for my second tour of duty in the army. When I came home, I found out that she had just gotten married to someone else. A wealthy guy whose dad owned several large car dealerships. She hadn't bothered to write or call me to let me know. I found out from her mother when I went to her door.

"So . . . two months later, I followed her and her husband to a drive-in movie. After the movie they went to a secluded lovers lane lookout and . . . I pulled up behind them. I was disguised as a police officer and my vehicle was the same make and model that law enforcement was using at that time, so he started to get out his license as I approached the vehicle. When I got to the driver's side window, I pulled out my .22 . . . I had a flashlight taped to the top of it. I pointed it at them. They sort of froze like a deer in headlights. We just looked at each other for about seven or eight seconds. I shot him first, and she ran. I shot her in the back. They were both killed. And I think that you should know one other thing. When she was running toward the woods before I shot her, she yelled out, "Arby! Please don't do this! I'm sorry!" So, she definitely recognized me through the disguise. Pastor, I need Jesus' forgiveness. Will he forgive me?"

Please thoughtfully answer the following questions:

1. If you were Pastor Osmond, how would you respond to Arby's penitent confession?

2. Do you believe Pastor Osmond has a responsibility to encourage Arby to turn himself into law enforcement and confess to the murders he committed?

3. In your opinion should Pastor Osmond encourage Arby to seek out professional counseling services to deal with his guilt over the murders he committed?

4. Are there any stories from the Bible which remind you of the story Arby shared with Pastor Osmond in his confession?

Samson Is in Mourning

Samson lives in an adult foster care facility which is located inside of a four-story Victorian style mansion. His neighbors in the adjacent room are an elderly married couple named Ben and Ashley. These neighbors have become the grandparents Samson never had, but always wanted. He loves hearing their stories about how they first met while in college and their first date at a beloved local ice cream parlor. They have even told Samson about their very first kiss while waiting in line to have books signed by their favorite author.

One night Samson is horrified to hear paramedics working to save Ben's life while Ashley cries out in anguish, "Oh Jesus! Please don't let Ben die!" An hour later Ben is pronounced dead from a massive heart attack. In the months that follow, Samson is lost yet does his best to comfort Ashley, who is in an almost utter state of despair, but is comforted to some degree with the hope that Ben is now with Jesus.

A mere three months to the day after the death of Ben, Ashley also dies. The coroner rules Ashley died of congestive heart failure while sound asleep, but some in the adult foster care facility have speculated that it may have been a suicide by prescription pills. Samson all at once feels a combination of confusion, rage, despair, and thankfulness that he had an opportunity to befriend Ben and Ashley and that they had faith in Jesus. Whenever Samson hears people baselessly speculating on whether or not Ashley died by suicide, it makes him want to yell at the top of his lungs and set something on fire.

To deal with his grief over the loss of his adopted grandparents, Samson begins attending group therapy in the conference room of the house. The person leading and facilitating this group is the Reverend Dr. Seth Dublin, an experienced licensed professional counselor and pastor.

For the first session, all eight people, including Dr. Seth, sit down in a circle, and everyone takes turns introducing themselves. Each person is then asked to share why they have decided to join group therapy. When Samson has his chance to share, he proclaims, "Because my adopted grandparents are dead! I never knew my real grandparents, but they were better. They were better than my real parents too. And out of nowhere they both died three months apart. What am I supposed to do now Dr. Seth? I'm twenty-one years old, stuck in this God-forsaken adult foster care facility! This house looks like something out of a horror movie except it's painted all of these bright colors. It's completely insane! I'm stuck in here all alone without Ben and Ashley. No friends and all alone! That could be the motto of my life right now. Why did Jesus let this happen Dr. Seth? Tell me why?"

Please thoughtfully answer the following questions:

1. What words of comfort would you speak to Samson if you were Dr. Seth?
2. Are there any words from Jesus in the Gospels you would share with Samson and the rest of the group if you were Dr. Seth?
3. Are there any biblical or extrabiblical resources you would recommend to Samson as he mourns the loss of his adopted grandparents?

Looking for Support

Pastor Baron Jones describes himself first and foremost, as a crisis counselor who desperately tries to make time to serve as a parish pastor. His life for the last ten months has been filled with personal and professional crises. Hank, the sole elder, tries his best to support Pastor Baron by lifting him up in prayer and occasionally taking him out to lunch at their favorite fast food burger joint. Pastor Baron is thankful for Hank because he is essentially the only person at the congregation that gives him support and encouragement.

As Pastor Baron prepares for the most important meeting of his life with his bishop and circuit visitor, he receives a phone call from Hank's stepson informing him that Hank will be unable to attend because he fell off of a cherry picker while trimming a silver maple tree. Pastor Baron postpones the meeting and rushes to Hank's hospital bedside. The devastated pastor watches as Hank dies an agonizing death without the comfort of painkillers and with minimal medical attention in a facility that is underfunded and overwhelmed with seriously ill patients.

Hank's funeral is the most difficult service that Pastor Baron has ever led. At the close of his sermon, he remarks, "Jesus encouraged me a lot through Hank. He was a real friend. It's amazing how uplifting it can be to have someone to grab a bite to eat with once or twice a week, and just be there for each other. I'm really going to miss that camaraderie."

Less than five months later, Pastor Baron decides to retire early and occasionally serve as a pulpit supply pastor in a warmer climate. One gorgeous January evening while walking along the beach and enjoying a fine cigar, Pastor Baron begins to weep tears of joy as he thanks Jesus for the promise of the resurrection of the dead on the last day. He prays aloud, "Jesus, I know that I have asked you to tell my parents and my children that I love them and miss them. Today please tell Hank thank you for me. Tell him I will never forget how he had my back when I was being personally assaulted verbally by most of the congregation, and getting so little support except from him. Please let him know we are going to have a big party in the new heaven and the new earth. All because of your death and resurrection Jesus!"

Please thoughtfully answer the following questions:

1. If you were serving as Pastor Baron's pastor, what words of Christ-centered comfort would you speak to him as he mourns the death of his good friend Hank?
2. What would you specifically pray to Jesus for on behalf of Pastor Baron during this time of loss?
3. What specifically would you encourage Pastor Baron to look forward to if you were providing him with counsel?

The Cost of a New Sports Stadium

Ali is a migrant worker who routinely faces abuse while he works on a massive sports stadium. He and thousands of his fellow workers have never benefited from the nation's new labor laws. Countless workers have lost their wages or their housing, and some have even lost their lives. Shockingly, their families will not receive any compensation.

After half a decade of back-breaking, dangerous work, the gigantic stadium is complete. Ali decides to reward himself by purchasing a ticket to the opening game. He scrapes together just enough money to purchase a ticket in the back of the upper deck. While walking to his seat, Ali admires the fireworks and remembers the long hours he and his crew worked to perfect the private luxury suites.

Ali also remembers the day his cousin, Malik, fell hundreds of feet to his death on the second day of construction, the day that a putrid, sickening stench was filling the hot summer air, which led to the discovery of the dead body of a seventeen-year-old worker named Iman. The boy had been trapped in a crawl space while doing electrical work. Iman suffocated to death and his body decomposed for nearly a week before being located. His body was subsequently dumped into the sea without a funeral service.

Ali's father, Adnan, is a devout Muslim and his mother, Sara, is a devout Roman Catholic. They are both kind and compassionate people that love their son dearly. Sara has encouraged Ali to speak with her priest, Father Xavier, when he returns home to help cope with the trauma he has experienced over the last five years. Ali is planning on accepting his mother's advice, but is unsure of what to expect.

On a spectacular late summer evening, the two men meet for tea and hookah near a busy promenade. Ali tells Father Xavier everything he experienced while leading his own thirty-man crew in building the stadium. For the first time in Father Xavier's long career as a priest, he is absolutely speechless. After a lengthy pause the old priest begins to weep and tells Ali that he will need at least a day to pray to Jesus about what he should say concerning the horrifying ordeal Ali and his fellow workers suffered over the course of five years.

Please thoughtfully answer the following questions:

1. If you were Father Xavier, what would you say to Ali concerning the horrifying ordeal he and his fellow workers suffered?
2. Are there any words from Jesus in the New Testament you believe would bring comfort to both Ali and Father Xavier as they reflect on the horrors the workers experienced?
3. Are there any passages in the Bible or an occurrence in recent history that reminds you of this story?

An Unshakable Feeling

Nelly and Vernon annually fly to a warmer climate on New Year's Day and stay until the end of April. The sunshine, warm weather, and outdoor activities are invigorating to these high school sweethearts. They have no shortage of visitors at their beach-side condominium during the winter months as family and friends happily escape their frigid climates.

This year as Nelly sits with her best friend at the gate and waits to board her flight, she has a strong feeling this is the last time Vernon will fly away for the winter. She even has a suspicion that he may not return in the spring. Vernon has been declining slowly, but he is not in horrible health. Nelly simply has an unshakable feeling in her heart about the future.

Upon arrival, Nelly sits under her favorite palm tree and sends this email: "Hi Pastor Rodriquez, please pray for Vernon. He's feeling fine and is excited to be in the warm sunshine, but I'm worried about him. I just have this feeling that he may not have long. Maybe this is all stemming from my father dying suddenly when he was Vernon's age . . . but I don't think so. Please remember to pray for him tonight. Thanks a lot! Say hi to Steve and the kids for me. Blessings, Nelly."

The next morning as Pastor Rodriquez is reading Nelly's email, the phone rings. It's Vernon, informing her that Nelly passed away in her sleep last night. In a state of shock Vernon asks Pastor Rodriquez to preside over the funeral service. Pastor Rodriquez agrees, and Vernon quickly excuses himself to take a call from his daughter Ann, but promises to call his pastor back when he gets a chance.

Please thoughtfully answer the following questions:

1. What is your opinion of Nelly's unshakable feeling that Vernon was close to death and the email that she sent to Pastor Rodriquez?
2. If you were in Pastor Rodriquez's position, what words of comfort would you share with Vernon and the rest of his family at the funeral service?
3. Were there any passages from the Bible that came to your mind as you read this case study?
4. Do you think it would be wise for Pastor Rodriquez to recommend to Vernon he seek out an appointment with a licensed professional counselor to deal with the trauma of losing his beloved wife, Nelly?

Death Is Not a Natural Part of Life

Josie and Vicar Justin are mourning the death of their infant son, Justin Jr., who died as a result of a rare genetic disorder. They have received a great deal of support from their family and friends. Through her loss, Josie has bravely decided to start a support group for women who have suffered miscarriage or infant loss. Each woman in the group shares their struggles and shows support for one another.

Nearly every woman in the group has at one time or another been approached by a well-meaning person who has said something to the effect of "Well your little one's death was all a part of God's plan. Death is just a natural part of life. He needed your child in heaven to be his little angel."

One morning Josie quotes her husband, Justin, who is studying to become a pastor as well as his supervisor, Pastor Eric, to the support group members through a private message and writes, "Death is not a part of God's plan. Tragically death entered the world through Adam and Eve's sin in the Garden of Eden, and God was so disturbed by sin and death that he sent his one and only son Jesus Christ to die on the cross for the sins of the whole world, so that whoever believes in Jesus would have eternal life. So, no, death is not a natural part of life; it's a tragedy that was not God's plan. And any child who has died as an infant or in miscarriage is in the hands of an incredibly merciful and loving God."

Josie's message brings comfort to most of the women, and several share the quote with well-meaning friends who continue to say things along the lines of "death is just a natural part of life."

Please thoughtfully answer the following questions:

1. How would you respond to someone who told you that your loved one's death was all a part of God's plan, and death is just a natural part of life?

2. What is your opinion of the quote Josie shared from her husband and Pastor Eric with the women of her support group?

3. If you were serving as a pastor to a person who had suffered a miscarriage or infant loss, what words of Christ-centered comfort would you share with them?

4. Are there any words from Jesus in the Gospels that came to your mind as you read this case study?

Chapter 5

Engagement and Marriage

Ana and Jeff Have Fallen in Love

ANA GARCIA OWNS FIFTY-ONE-THOUSAND acres of land, five equestrian farms, six hotels, and twelve awe-inspiring homes. Each house is a one-of-a-kind architectural masterpiece located in what she calls the most beautiful region of the world. Ana has given names to each home and is blessed to have a perfect view of the sea, mountains, and forests from every window and balcony in her main residence.

One gorgeous early summer evening, Ana puts on a dazzling dress to meet close friends in a small town near her oldest beach home. She first decides to pop into her favorite bookstore and café to browse before dinner. Only a few steps into the café she notices a ruggedly handsome man in his late twenties leading some type of book study on a sofa. He is sporting a weathered sweater, khakis, and tennis shoes. In contrast, Ana is showing off her tall, beautiful figure with a low-cut glittering red dress and canary yellow stiletto heels. Her bracelets and necklace are worth far more than the establishment that she is standing in.

Ana pretends to look at romance novels as she studies this mysterious man leading a book study with grace and charisma. At the conclusion of the study the man bids its participants a kind farewell, and he makes his way toward the sophisticated, normally confident thirty-five year old. The man introduces himself as Jeffery Becker but insists that Ana call him Jeff. He tells her he is a teacher in town and he leads a book study on an ancient Roman community every Saturday evening.

The mesmerizingly attractive woman introduces herself and tells Jeff that her name is Ana and that she insists that he call her Ana. She briefly describes herself as a businesswoman without going into great details about her career. After about twenty minutes of small talk Jeff asks Ana to accompany him out to dinner that night. Ana hesitantly accepts, and then discretely texts her friends an explanation and apology for the last-minute cancellation.

Jeff takes Ana to his favorite tapas restaurant. They have an amazing time and end up talking after dinner the entire night. That morning they watch the sunrise from a local beach and say goodbye with a kiss. Over the next three weeks they see each other nearly every day, and their friends and family take notice. One Saturday afternoon, Ana tells Jeff she would like to join his book study that night. It's at this time that Jeff reveals that he is a Lutheran pastor, who is teaching a Bible study on the book of Romans each Saturday at the café.

Ana has a mixture of feelings upon hearing this and wants to know why she is just now finding out that he is a pastor. Jeff tells her that he thought if he had told her his profession right away then she wouldn't have accepted the dinner invitation in the first place, and that once Ana revealed to him that she was an atheist he was afraid to say anything. At first Ana is angry with Jeff and hurt, but the more she reflects she realizes that there are important details about herself that she has not yet shared with Jeff. It's at this time Ana goes into detail about her extraordinary success as a businesswoman, her charities, and the monumental wealth she has accumulated throughout her adult life.

Two months later Jeff tells Ana he loves her, and Ana responds with, "And I love you, Jeffery!" Eventually after almost a year of dating, Jeff proposes to Ana at the café and bookstore where they first met, and with tears of joy she says, "Yes!" They decide on a short engagement as it has been a tremendous struggle for them to not have sex while dating. On two occasions Ana was furious with Jeff that he said no, but soon calmed down and reminded herself that it went against Jeff's religious beliefs. However, there were two separate occasions when Jeff was ready to have sex, but Ana said no and told him that he would be disappointed with himself later if he violated his religious beliefs concerning sex outside of marriage.

A month into the couple's engagement Jeff is contacted by a close friend and fellow Lutheran pastor named Samuel. They talk over video and Samuel gets to the point fairly quickly. He says, "Look Jeff, I love you, bro. I'm telling you this from a place of love. I know that you and Ana are only two weeks away from your big wedding day. She's an unbelievably beautiful, generous, brilliant, and kind person, and I love her and had a fantastic time getting to know her when I visited last month. I know she respects your religious beliefs and attends church and Bible study with you occasionally, and I think that's awesome that she has shown interest in the Christian faith and in Lutheranism. But the fact is she is still an atheist and I think that could really cause some serious issues between you two once you're married. I mean, what's going to happen when you want to take your kids to church or have them baptized? What is she going to say when it comes to mission trips or tithing? What will your congregation say when they find out that she is an atheist?"

Jeff does his best to stay calm, and he slowly answers and says, "I had a feeling that you were going to bring something like this up, Samuel. So, I want to read to you what Martin Luther wrote in his writing from 1522, "The Estate of Marriage," when it comes to people who say that a Christian cannot marry someone who is not a Christian. Luther writes:

> *The fifth impediment is unbelief; that is, I may not marry a Turk, a Jew, or a heretic. I marvel that the blasphemous tyrants are not in their hearts ashamed to place themselves in such direct contradiction to the clear text of Paul in I Corinthians 7 [:12–13], where he says, "If a heathen wife or husband consents to live with a Christian spouse, the Christian should not get a divorce." And St. Peter, in I Peter 3 [:1], says that Christian wives should behave so well that they thereby convert their non-Christian husbands; as did Monica, the mother of St. Augustine.*

Samuel responds, "Jeff, Martin Luther wrote that very early on in his career when he was still looking at marriage as being purely a civil matter. As he matured in his faith and grew in his biblical understanding, he took marriage much more seriously and started to see marriage as having strong sacramental qualities. Later in Luther's career as he matured, he definitely advised Christians to only marry other Christians. You have to look at the full context."

Jeff patiently responds, "I disagree. I think Luther had it right early on in his career, in 1522, in "The Estate of Marriage." A Christian has the freedom to marry a non-Christian. I love you, bro, and I hope that you fly in for the wedding."

Please thoughtfully answer the following questions:

1. Do you have an opinion on the concerns Samuel brought up to Jeff, his close friend and fellow Lutheran pastor?

2. What is your opinion of the excerpt from Martin Luther's "The Estate of Marriage" from 1522 that Jeff used to defend his engagement to Ana?

3. After Jeff read the excerpt from Luther, what did you think of Samuel and Jeff's closing remarks in their conversation?

4. Can you think of a way both Jeff and Samuel are correct in their beliefs on this matter?

The Advice of TNT

Babcock is a lay leader at his home congregation. He is married but attends worship nearly every week alone, and helps out wherever the pastor or the elders need him to. As of late he has been attending a Bible study at a megachurch on the outskirts of town, and will occasionally share updates with his home church pastor, Rev. Lopez. Over the last several months Babcock seems to have a refreshed zeal for life as a result of his time at the weekly megachurch Bible study under the direction of Bible study leader TNT.

Late in the afternoon on Ash Wednesday, Babcock knocks on Rev. Lopez's study door and asks if they can talk for a few minutes. Rev. Lopez agrees and they sit down for a chat. A few minutes into the conversation Babcock says, "My new Bible study leader, TNT, has completely and utterly changed my life. He has flipped everything upside down in my life in just three short months! I mean that in a good way. Reverend Lopez, I know that you had to get a bachelor's degree, and then go to seminary after that and stuff, but TNT doesn't have all kinds of fancy degrees. He's just following his heart! And that's what he wants me to do too. He wants me to follow my heart. He knows that my wife, Jen, doesn't go to church, and he also knows that she hasn't been in the mood to make love to me a lot lately due to her depression. So, TNT has recommended that I divorce Jen. And follow my heart to a brighter future. He believes strongly that is what God wants. Once the divorce is finalized, he is going to have me register in the singles dating service at his church, so I can find just the right woman. Someone who is with me at church and Bible studies and meets my romantic needs as well. Don't you think that's great news, Reverend Lopez?"

Rev. Lopez responds with, "Listen, Babcock . . . I have to lead the Ash Wednesday service in a few minutes. How about we talk more over dinner after tonight's service?" After a brief pause Babcock responds with, "Okay, I guess I can find time for that." Rev. Lopez continues on and says, "Good. Please promise me that you will not file any type of divorce paperwork or contact a lawyer. At the very least give me an opportunity to speak with you about some of the advice that TNT has been giving you . . .let's look at that advice in the light of the Scriptures and what our church teaches. Because I am strongly of the opinion that Jen has done nothing that would justify you divorcing her . . . okay, let's talk more over dinner after the service."

Please thoughtfully answer the following questions:

1. If you were in Rev. Lopez's position, what passages in Scripture would you point Babcock to when discussing this matter with him over dinner?
2. In your opinion, would it be wise of Rev. Lopez to recommend Babcock no longer attend the megachurch weekly Bible study that is taught by TNT based on what has been shared?
3. From what you have read, do you believe Babcock would benefit from meeting with a licensed, professional therapist on a regular basis?

Rodney Barker's Upcoming Wedding

Rodney Barker is nearing his thirtieth birthday, and is planning on announcing his engagement to Ruby Keller on his big day. In fact, he will be introducing her for the first time to his family and friends at his birthday party, which is also doubling as a Halloween party. At this point, all Rodney has revealed to anyone about Ruby is that she is a little bit older than him but has an incredibly youthful spirit. When Rodney's friends learn he is engaged to an older woman they are all surprised, because Rodney typically has dated women several years younger than him. But across the board everyone agrees that they just want Rodney to be happy, and they are thrilled he has finally found someone to settle down with.

On an unusually hot October night Rodney walks through the doors of his favorite restaurant with a lady dressed as a glow in the dark peacock. She appears to be approximately eighty-five to ninety years old. But as it turns out she is only seventy-four years old, and is in fact none other than Rodney's fiancée, Ruby Keller!

Rodney's family is in shock and somewhat horrified. Everyone is polite, and it seems that most people are forcing themselves to smile as Rodney introduces his bride-to-be to groups of friends and family. The evening becomes especially awkward when Rodney introduces Ruby to his grandmother Alice, and the two ladies realize that they were in the same high school class together. Moments later the awkwardness is nearly unbearable when Rodney asks his father, Andrew, if he would perform the wedding ceremony, and if they could go ahead and schedule pastoral pre-marriage counseling sessions sometime in the next week. Rodney's mother, Heather, quickly excuses herself upon hearing this request. Pastor Andrew pauses for a few moments and says something to the effect of "Yeah . . . I'll have to check my calendar but maybe I can find time this week."

Please thoughtfully answer the following questions:

1. Should Rodney's engagement to a woman forty-four years his senior concern his family or friends?
2. Is there anything unethical, unfair, or unscriptural about Rodney's engagement to a woman so much older than him?
3. What type of questions and concerns might you have if you were Rodney's parents, Pastor Andrew and Heather?
4. Would you share any of your questions or concerns with Rodney and/or his fiancée, Ruby Keller?

Some Advice for Buxton?

Daphne is a forty-three-year-old yoga instructor who has recently started attending weekly worship with her husband, Buxton. Pastor Albert is thankful that God has answered his many years of prayers and is looking forward to getting to know the couple better through a new small group Bible study he is hosting at his home starting next week.

The day before the start of the new Bible study, Pastor Albert gets a knock on his open office door. He looks up to see Daphne and invites her to sit down for a cup of coffee. The two begin chatting and Daphne says, "I'm sorry I didn't make an appointment, this was sort of spur of the moment. I thought, hey, I'm going by here after yoga anyway, I might as well stop in and say hi to Pastor Albert and talk for a bit!"

Pastor Albert responds, "Well, that's nice of you. I'm always happy to meet with people and talk about life." Daphne takes a deep breath and then starts to tear up and says, "Well . . . actually I've been thinking about this for a while. I need your help. You see, Buxton and I are really in trouble. He has lost most of his passion toward me and is working a ton. Meanwhile my sex drive is through the roof. I know that you two are kind of buddies and occasionally watch football games together. One of the big reasons that I started attending worship is because I was hoping that you could talk to him and tell him that he needs to make sure that he is taking care of my needs each day. I mean, that's his responsibility, right? I've been faithful our entire marriage, and I don't want to sin by not being faithful to him, but he needs to make love to me more often . . . I'm afraid that if he doesn't start pursuing me more, I will fall into sin. Will you please talk to him for me, Pastor Albert?"

Please thoughtfully answer the following questions:

1. In your opinion how should Pastor Albert respond to Daphne's request to speak with her husband, Buxton, about her desire to have him take care of her needs each day?
2. Do you think it would be wise for Pastor Albert to inform Daphne that he would like to discuss this topic further during marriage counseling sessions which include both Buxton and her in his office?
3. What biblical or non-biblical resources might Pastor Albert reference during his marriage counseling sessions with Buxton and Daphne?

Aunt Ruth and Aunt Ellen Give Unsolicited Advice to Their Niece

Cindy is a stunning twenty-five-year-old woman whose wedding day has arrived. She is ecstatically happy to be marrying her best friend, Donte. In fact, the young couple have lived apart and not been intimate for the last three months to make their wedding day and honeymoon more special. Over two hundred of their closest family and friends are gathered at their church and will join them for their reception.

All that today is missing is Cindy's late mother, Tina, who passed away five years ago of breast cancer. However, Cindy is thankful her mother's two older sisters, who are twins, Ruth and Ellen, are in attendance to act as a source of support and to stand in the stead of their younger sister as they celebrate with their niece.

Approximately twenty minutes before the start of the ceremony, Aunt Ruth and Aunt Ellen knock at the bride's dressing room door and request to speak with Cindy alone. Her bridesmaids exit the room, and the elderly unmarried aunts gift their niece with a painting they had commissioned by a local artist. It depicts Tina looking down with joy from heaven on her daughter as Cindy walks down the aisle with her father, Mike. This brings all three women to tears of joy.

As the ladies begin to collect themselves Aunt Ruth says, "Now, we must give you the excellent advice that we heard our mother give your mother on her wedding day to your father, Mike." Aunt Ellen adds, "And without a doubt, your mother would give you this exact same advice if she were here in person."

Aunt Ruth continues on, "Yes, that's right. Now what you must understand, Cindy, is each man has needs. And you must do your best to meet Donte's needs, but you must also understand that no one woman can meet all the needs of their husband. So, he has the right to occasionally take a lover while away on a business trip, or extended vacation, and you have the right to demand that he be discreet with his occasional indiscretions."

Aunt Ellen then adds, "Yes! Yes, that is a reasonable agreement that all married couples would be wise to adhere to. And, who knows, maybe at some point you also will decide to discreetly take a lover of your own while on a working vacation or at a favorite night club?"

Cindy is overwhelmed by what she is hearing and answers, "What!? None of this sounds like something that grandma would have said, and I know my mother would not want you saying any of this to me! Especially right before I walk down the aisle! That's not the type of marriage that Donte and I are going to have. We are committed to each other and plan on being faithful to one another and will keep our vows before God."

The twins stand up, and Aunt Ruth says, "Well, there will come a day when you will cherish our experience, and I have no doubt you will seek out our wise counsel for your marriage and, when the time comes, for the raising of your children as well."

Cindy begins shaking with anger as she bursts out of her seat and says to the aunts, "Neither of you have ever been married or have had children! You're coming in here and telling me that I need to cherish your experience on marriage and raising children? I really want you to leave the room now because I need to get ready. I love you both, and I'm glad you're here, but I need to be alone for a few minutes. I'll see you in a little bit. Thank you for the beautiful painting." And with that the twin sisters scurry out the door to the sanctuary, as Cindy cleans up her tears and touches up her makeup and writes herself a note to speak with her pastor about the conversation with the aunts. But, of course, Cindy will first share what just happened with her bridesmaids as soon as they come back in the room.

Please thoughtfully answer the following questions:

1. What is your opinion of the marriage advice Aunt Ruth and Aunt Ellen gave to their niece?

2. Do you feel Cindy was too strong in her rebuke of her aunts' marriage advice and lecturing?

3. If you were Cindy's pastor and she came and related the odd conversation with her aunts to you, what pastoral words of comfort might you share with her?
4. What Bible passages might be comforting to Cindy after the strange, unsettling conversation with her aunts on her wedding day?

Thank You, Tattle!

Tattle describes himself to friends and acquaintances as a gay transgender pirate. Some friends are confused by this definition, but very few question it to Tattle's face. What there is no confusion about is Tattle is a generous person who loves to throw a great party. In fact, Tattle frequently opens his four-thousand-square-foot penthouse and rooftop to old friends and new acquaintances to use as a wedding and reception venue free of charge. His only demand is that they have the time of their lives!

As guests arrive for Tim and Mary's wedding rehearsal, Tattle offers Father Morton a glass of twenty-three-year-old scotch. As the two men sit at the bar Tattle remarks, "Father! You know it's a good bottle of scotch when it's older than the bride and groom!" Everyone at the rehearsal seems to be having an amazing time, except for Mary's mother, Charlotte, who says to Mary in the restroom, "Honey, if your father and I had known the man who was allowing you to use his home for the wedding and reception was an openly gay man who is rumored to have hosted orgies in this very spot, then we may not have agreed! I know he is your friend and he seems very generous, but I do not want to be closely associated with anyone who is rumored to use hard drugs and who throws wild sex parties!"

Upon hearing this Mary begins to cry and says, "Oh Mom, Tattle is one of our best friends! He has been so incredibly kind to Tim and me. And he was one of the first people to show up at the hospital when I miscarried last year. He held my hand and Tim's hand for an hour. And because he is allowing us to use his place, this is saving you and Daddy so much money! Aren't Christians supposed to love everyone? Didn't Jesus love everyone and eat and drink and go to parties with tax collectors and prostitutes? He enjoyed being closely associated with people who did wild things. Shouldn't we be the same way as followers of Jesus? I'm not perfect! Tim isn't perfect! But Tattle loves us anyway! He's our friend, Mommy, and we love him even though he isn't perfect. Will you please do the same?"

Please thoughtfully answer the following questions:

1. What is your impression of Tattle?

2. What is your opinion of the concerns Charlotte brought up to her daughter Mary?

3. Do you believe Mary made any good points when responding to her mother Charlotte's concerns?

4. If you were Father Morton and Charlotte brought the same concerns to you that she brought to Mary, how would you respond?

Look at Barnabas and Debbie

Burbank was raised by his father, Stan, and from the time Burbank was born until the age of eighteen, his father was married and divorced eight times. The woman who was the closest thing to a mother to young Burbank was his father's long-time girlfriend Steph. Sadly, Steph died when Burbank was only thirteen years old. Her untimely death rocked Stan's world because she was the love of his life. Interestingly Stan said in her eulogy, "I never once had the opportunity to propose in the seven years that Steph and I dated!"

Starting during his sophomore year of college, Burbank begins to court a young beauty by the name of Alice Montgomery. He is stunned by the solid home environment she was blessed to be raised in. Alice's parents met in law school and are both devout, practicing Catholics who put a high priority on family time with Alice and her six siblings. Burbank has been amazed by Alice's family from the first time that Barnabas and Debbie visited Alice at college and took her and Burbank out for dinner at a nice seafood restaurant.

After two years of dating, Burbank converts to Catholicism and soon after approaches Barnabas and Debbie to request permission to ask for Alice's hand in marriage. They happily give Burbank permission. With tears in his eyes Burbank says, "Since I came from such an unstable home environment, and never really had a good marriage modeled for me by my dad and one of his wives, I thought that you were going to hold that against me and deny me permission to ask Alice to marry me."

With great compassion, Barnabas and Debbie both reassure Burbank that they know he will not repeat the sins of his father, and that they will do their best to continue to model a good marriage for him and Alice to aspire to. One day later Burbank proposes to Alice at the top of the clock tower of their university, and Alice happily accepts.

Please thoughtfully answer the following questions:

1. What is your opinion of how Barnabas and Debbie treated Burbank?

2. If you were Barnabas and Debbie, how would you encourage Burbank and Alice to grow in their faith in Jesus?

3. If you were a Catholic priest providing premarital counseling to Burbank and Alice, what advice would you give them as they prepare to enter holy matrimony together?

The Future Mrs. Binx?

Johnny Binx and Heather Craig are in the middle of a whirlwind romance! Dinner and dancing at Johnny's mother's country club, late night swims in the neighbor's pool while the entire household is away on vacation, and of course foot massages while binge-watching their favorite show.

Johnny is delighted with how things are going so far, but he isn't ready to pop the question just yet. Heather has confided in her closest friends that she is expecting Johnny to propose on Valentine's Day over dinner at the country club. One month later Heather continues to wait with bated breath for a person that she calls "the man I didn't know that I needed!" to propose and for a short engagement to begin.

Two years later Heather is still waiting, and one early morning she gives Johnny an ultimatum, saying, "I spoke with my pastor about this. I told her that you are perfectly happy just living together! And Pastor Heba suggested that I give you the choice. You can either get serious, propose marriage, and commit, or we are done. I'm so much more than just some sex object, Johnny! Marriage is a sacred act, and I'm ready to be married! Are you ready to be married, Johnny?"

Please thoughtfully answer the following questions:

1. What is your impression of Johnny and Heather's relationship?

2. What do you think of the advice Pastor Heba gave to Heather concerning her future with Johnny?

3. Do you think there are any passages from the Bible which would be good for Heather and Johnny to read together?

4. If you were Pastor Heba, would you encourage Johnny and Heather to attend counseling together in order to work on their relationship?

Will Kev Listen?

Kev drinks five pots of coffee and smokes two packs of cigarettes a day. His secret addiction was recently discovered by his fiancée, Toto. She now realizes why her soon-to-be husband has acted so nervous lately. Toto was starting to believe Kev was jittery about the wedding ceremony and big night.

A solemn pledge is made by Kev to Toto that no more than two cups of coffee will touch his lips each day, and he will give up cigarettes completely starting immediately. This pledge is soon broken as Kev smokes three packs of cigarettes in Toto's mother's bathroom the night before their wedding. After a massive verbal fight that spills out into the front yard, the wedding is called off by Kev, who claims that Toto is trying to control him.

An hour later, Toto rushes to Rev. Lopez's house to confide in him and his beautiful wife. Toward the end of the conversation, Toto says, "Reverend Lopez, you walked alongside us through marriage counseling. Please, if Kev is going to listen to anyone it will be you. Will you try and talk some sense into him? He isn't answering my calls or text messages. Will you go to his apartment and tell him how much I love him? Tell him I don't care if he keeps smoking. Just as long as he tries to get off of cigarettes eventually. And if this has anything to do with our wedding night, tell him not to be nervous. He's going to do great! I can't wait!"

Please thoughtfully answer the following questions:

1. If you were Rev. Lopez, would you go to Kev's apartment to speak with him and, if so, what would you say to him?
2. If you were in Rev. Lopez's position, what concerns might you have about Kev and Toto's relationship?
3. What are some ways Rev. Lopez and his beautiful wife can point Kev and Toto to Jesus' unconditional love and forgiveness?
4. Are there any Bible passages that come to your mind which might be beneficial for Rev. Lopez to share with Kev and Toto at this time?

Desiring a Change

Jerry, Jerome, and Milford are all in their late forties, and have been close friends since they met in grad school. They make a point to meet for dinner at least once a month at a restaurant they have never tried before. Each man shares about his joys and struggles in his relationships and careers. Lately each friend has felt that something is missing in their lives and has desired a change.

One evening while enjoying barbecue, Jerry reveals that he is engaged to his long-time girlfriend, Kay; Jerome announces that he and his wife, Bella, are considering a separation once their youngest child, Bobby, finishes his freshman year of college; and Milford is excited to share that he and his beloved wife, Vista, are preparing to retire early and move out west to start their own coffee shop and antique business.

As a pastor, Milford tries his best to be compassionate and considerate to his close friend Jerome during this difficult time while gently encouraging him to seek out reconciliation and professional couples therapy with Bella. This is the last time the three men are together in one place, as Milford dies two years later in a freak car accident.

After his death Jerry and Jerome begin meeting for double dates with their wives every second and fourth Friday of the month. Both men are eternally grateful for the friendship and gentle, Christ-centered relationship advice Milford gave them at various times in their lives. They never forget to thank God for Milford and his beloved wife, Vista, when they bless the food before dinner. It is also their tradition to toast Milford and Vista at the beginning of each get-together.

Please thoughtfully answer the following questions:

1. What is your opinion of the advice Milford gave to Jerome concerning his marriage to Bella?
2. Does this story remind you of any stories from your own life?
3. What passages from the Bible might be helpful for Jerry and Jerome to meditate upon as they mourn the loss of their close friend Milford?
4. What are some ways Jerry and Kay and Jerome and Bella could reach out to Vista and encourage her as she mourns the loss of her beloved husband, Milford?

Chapter 6

Missions

We Are Not Really Equipped . . . (Part 1)

BEVERLY VILLAGE CHURCH IS located in an economically thriving bedroom community. About five years ago this congregation was considered rural and medium sized. But with an economic and developmental surge in the area, it is now considered suburban and on the edge of being categorized as a large congregation. They have a thirty-acre campus with plenty of beautiful green space and a large preschool and kindergarten with a total of two hundred and ten students, with ten full-time teachers and ten part-time teachers.

Over the last year, sizable groups of people from various immigrant communities have gathered on the outskirts of the church property to play cricket matches and enjoy a wide variety of home-cooked authentic meals from all over the world. Most of the members of Beverly Village Church are aware of these gatherings and find them to be interesting, but have no desire to join in the cricket matches or contribute their own favorite home-cooked meals to the festivities.

However, in the last ten months, Pastor Harry, who is head of mission and outreach, has been participating in the cricket matches and meals on a weekly basis. He brings this up in nearly every Bible study and sermon he leads, and in the last month approximately fifty to sixty parishioners have been joining him at the festivities and have even started to bring home-cooked dishes of their own to share with their new friends at the events. To the delight of Pastor Harry and the congregation members who have joined him, several of their new friends are enrolling their children in either the preschool or kindergarten. A few people have even started joining in weekly Sunday worship at Beverly Village Church.

Pastor Harry feels absolutely elated by the interactions that he and some of his parishioners are enjoying with their new friends. In fact, it is his turn to attend the monthly elders' meeting while Senior Pastor Terrance Hubbard is out of the country on vacation, and he cannot wait to share his excitement with his elders. As Pastor Harry walks toward the boardroom, he notices it is oddly quiet, and as he enters, to his surprise, he sees Pastor Terrance along with the entire board of elders already seated with serious poses.

Pastor Harry says hello to everyone and then leads the group in an opening devotion. As soon as the devotion ends Pastor Terrance stands simultaneously with Head Elder Craig Avon. He says in a solemn tone, "Pastor Harry, the reason that I had to end my out of country vacation and return early without my family was so that I could be here this evening, and inform you that I and the entire board of elders appreciate your outreach efforts to the people who have been playing cricket and preparing meals on the church property. However . . . we as a church are not really equipped to cater to their unique needs. That area of the property is nearly two hundred yards from our bathroom facilities and kitchens. We do not want the unsightly appearance of portable toilets on our beautiful property. And our kitchen facilities are overbooked already; it is an impossibility for these folks to cook in either of our kitchens. We frankly do not have the funds currently to install a structure with multiple bathrooms and a working kitchen on that end of the campus. And even if we did . . . having two hundred to four hundred people competing in cricket matches, barbecuing, and in some cases eating picnic style on the ground only five to six yards away from a busy road is an insurance nightmare. This well-intentioned experiment has run its course and needs to end now. Since you have made contact and built relationships with some of these folks, I will let you break the news to them. Tomorrow Board of Properties Manager Rob Growling will install a security gate, no trespassing signs, and security cameras on that end of the property."

Pastor Harry responds, "Pastor Terrance, thank you for sharing your thoughts with me and the elders tonight. Would you reconsider the situation if I were to pay for an aesthetically pleasing, permanent shelter house structure with restrooms and a kitchen for that area of the property out of my own salary?" Pastor Terrance quickly and firmly answers, "At this time that is not a possibility. I, the elders, and the board of properties manager together have made our decision. It is final."

After a long, reflective pause, Pastor Harry responds, "I have never given you or anyone at this church an ultimatum of any kind. But tonight,

I am going to do that because I feel so strongly the decision to expel the immigrant people from our property is being done out of fear for what is not familiar to some at this church and in this room. We can either continue to welcome these beautiful people onto our campus for meals and cricket matches, or you have lost my services as the pastor of mission and outreach of this church." With only a moment of hesitation, Pastor Terrance says, "Well, would you please give me and the elders a moment to discuss your demand?"

Less than ten minutes later Pastor Harry is called back into the board room, and Pastor Terrance stands up and says, "We have discussed your demand, Pastor Harry, and I and the other elders have voted unanimously to reject your demand and accept your resignation. Thank you for your faithful service to God's people here at Beverly Village Church and in our community in general. You will be missed. You and your family's health insurance will last through the end of the month, and we have decided to pay you three months severance as a thank you for your service here. Please have your office cleared out by the end of the week. God speed."

Please thoughtfully answer the following questions:

1. In your opinion, was it reasonable for Pastor Terrance, the elders, and the board of properties manager to decide the immigrant people cooking on the property and playing cricket needed to be expelled from proceeding with their activities due to a lack of restrooms and kitchen facilities and out of safety concerns and possible lack of insurance coverage by the church for such activities?

2. What are your thoughts on Pastor Harry's offer to pay for an aesthetically pleasing, permanent shelter house structure with restrooms and a kitchen for that area of the property out of his own salary, so his new friends could continue to meet at the church for a time of friendship and community?

3. What is your opinion of Pastor Harry's ultimatum to Pastor Terrance and the elders?

4. In your opinion, did Pastor Terrance and the elders respond in a Christlike way to Pastor Harry's ultimatum?

We Are Not Really Equipped . . . (Part 2)

Within two weeks of Pastor Harry leaving his position as pastor of mission and outreach at Beverly Village Church, he has already planted a new church named New Beginnings, a mere ten-minute drive to the north. His congregation worships in a public junior high school gymnasium in the middle of a recently constructed upper-middle-class subdivision. The school has also agreed to rent their practice football field and a shelter building with restrooms to New Beginnings each Sunday.

A majority of the people from various immigrant communities who were playing cricket on the green space at Beverly Village now play at the school's football field. Many of these people are also visiting New Beginnings from time to time for worship, Bible study, vacation Bible school, trunk or treat, food festivals, and other events. In addition, about a quarter of the people who were worshiping at Beverly Village Church have decided to go with Pastor Harry and become members at New Beginnings. As a result, a number of young families in the subdivision are taking notice of this growing community and their welcoming, outgoing presence.

Six months into New Beginning's launch, both of their weekly services, Bible studies, and a majority of their outreach events are well attended. The congregational leadership team is forming a building committee and laying the groundwork for a permanent structure less than a two-minute drive from where they are currently worshiping.

Pastor Harry's boss, Bishop Reverend Doctor Earl Gordon, invites him out for coffee to discuss the success of New Beginnings. The two men have a friendly and relaxed conversation for several hours, and as they are getting ready to leave Bishop Gordon says, "You know I've received several phone calls from your old colleagues at Beverly Village, Terrance and Craig, and they aren't happy about the success of New Beginnings. They feel like you have stolen some of their members. But I have your back, Harry. They should have supported you and followed your example of opening up the church to the immigrant communities that were coming to them.

"I was struck by the fact that Terrance said to you, 'We as a church are not really equipped to cater to their unique needs.' So often we ask, 'Where can we meet new people? How can we reach out to people and share Jesus' love with them?' Well, here was a case where people were coming to Beverly Village, and Beverly Village basically acted like they didn't want them. But it was clear to everyone that you loved those people, Harry. Your love for them reminds me of Jesus' love for people on the outskirts of society in Luke's Gospel. Folks have taken notice of how you care about people, Pastor Harry, and they are following your leadership. I want to congratulate you on your success and encourage you to always remember to give Jesus the glory."

Please thoughtfully answer the following questions:

1. In your opinion, did Pastor Harry show resiliency in planting a congregation not long after he left his former position at Beverly Village Church?
2. What do you think of Pastor Harry's choice to plant a church a ten-minute drive away from his former church?
3. Do you agree with Bishop Gordon's words of support and affirmation addressed to Pastor Harry?

Justin's First Mission Trip (Part 1)

Justin Stanford is a young man with an aptitude for languages and a strong work ethic. He has recently turned nineteen years old and can hardly believe that it has been six months since he graduated from high school. Justin has been working at a factory and doing roofing in order to save money for college and to volunteer as a Christian missionary and English teacher.

Eventually a good opportunity arises for Justin to teach English and to serve as a missionary eight thousand miles away. The young man is a little nervous because, to this point, he has not traveled outside of his home country, but he feels good about the fact that he will be traveling through his denomination's international missions organization. Once he arrives, Justin will be connected to other missionaries from his area of the world who will help him get acclimated to a new culture and workplace that will be his new home for the next several months.

The country he is moving to is restrictive of Christianity, but its government encourages its citizens to learn English. Justin works with a short-term mission coordinator named Jackie in preparation for his arrival in his new home for the next several months. Jackie connects Justin to Martha. Through a brief email, Martha shares her phone number with Justin and instructs him to call her on a pay phone once he arrives at the airport, and she will then give him instructions on which ferry boat to take from there.

Justin and his family are concerned by the brief and unprofessional nature of Martha's email, so Justin sends a reply asking if he could have a backup phone number in case Martha is unavailable, and he also requests the address of the hotel he will be staying at.

Martha responds sharply, "Those pieces of information are not needed," and she is adamant that all Justin must do is arrive at the airport, purchase a charge card for the pay phone and give her a call, and she will instruct him on what to do and where to go next. At that point several members of Justin's family voice concerns about him continuing with the trip, but Justin insists that he has already made a commitment to serve for three months and that he feels it is his duty to keep his commitment.

Please thoughtfully answer the following questions:

1. From what you have read, what do you think of Jackie's and Martha's abilities as administrators?
2. Do you believe Justin and his family were right in being concerned by the brief and unprofessional nature of Martha's email?
3. If you had been in Justin's position, would have you continued with the trip? Why or why not?
4. If you were Justin's pastor, what Christ-centered words of wisdom would you speak to him before he leaves to serve as an English teacher and missionary?

Justin's First Mission Trip (Part 2)

After a one-hour connecting flight, Justin hops onto a fifteen-hour nonstop flight. Upon arrival he follows Martha's instructions and purchases a charge card and dials the number she gave him. Each time a robotic sounding voice answers, "We are sorry. The phone number you dialed no longer exists. Please hang up and try your call again."

After four tries, Justin heads straight to a money exchange booth where a polite gentleman is happy to assist the young, jet-lagged traveler. Sadly, he has the same result and asks, "Um sir, do you have another phone number that I could possibly try?" With a hint of panic Justin answers, "No, this is the only number that I have. This is the only number that I was given by my organization. It's the only number that they gave me."

Moments later Justin has the exact same result with a kind female flight attendant. Justin then approaches five middle-aged well-dressed businessmen, who assist him with the latest technology. When the call does not go through after three or four tries and it is clear Justin has no address or backup phone number, one of the men says, "You might need to go to your country's embassy." Another businessman then adds, "It sounds like the organization that you're with doesn't have its act together, mate. We're sorry. We would stay and help you get to the embassy, but we have a flight to catch. We are late for it already." As the men walk away, they say, "Best of luck, mate! Hang in there!"

Exhausted with jet lag, hungry, moderately panicked, frightened, and over-stimulated, Justin contemplates taking a flight home the first chance he gets. But instead, he decides to pray and to keep praying to Jesus for help. Soon an overwhelming sense of peace comes over Justin, and he decides to clutch his luggage tight and take a nap on an airport bench and rest.

Please thoughtfully answer the following questions:

1. If you were in Justin's position, how do you think you would have reacted to the phone number that Martha gave you not going through?
2. What are your impressions from what you have read of the missionary organization that Justin is serving through?
3. Are there any stories from the Bible that remind you of this situation?
4. If you had met Justin at the airport, how would have you tried to help him in a pastoral, Christlike way?

Justin's First Mission Trip (Part 3)

After a short nap of approximately thirty minutes, Justin wakes up slightly refreshed and asks himself the question, "Who can I call back home that will be awake at four thirty in the morning? Grandma! She hasn't even gone to bed yet! She is awake reading mystery novels and listening to doo wop music!"

Justin heads straight for the information desk and with their assistance phones his grandma, eight thousand miles away. To Justin's joy, his grandmother answers and he says, "Grandma! I am so glad to hear your voice! I'm stranded at the airport. The number that Martha gave me is the wrong number. It doesn't exist anymore."

Grandma is horrified and says, "Oh my gosh!" Justin catches his breath and continues, "Yeah, it's ridiculous! You need to call Pastor Arbor and Dad and ask them to get ahold of Jackie Seed at Center International Missions, so they can tell her that I am stranded at the airport. I'm standing at the help desk. Here, I'll give you the phone number to the help desk as well. Please have them call me back here."

Thirty minutes later a lady at the help desk hands Justin the phone, and a voice on the other line introduces herself and says, "Hi Justin, I'm Dara! I'm your new boss. I hear that you're stranded at the airport." Justin replies politely, "Yes, good to meet you, Dara. Yes, I am." Dara continues, "Okay, well do you see the coffee shop to your left?" Justin responds, "Yes, I do." Dara answers, "Alright, well go over there and wait and in about an hour a gentleman named Bon will meet you there with his wife Mav and they will take you to your apartment."

Approximately an hour later, a pale man with a long ponytail approaches Justin and says, "Hi, I'm Bon. Are you Justin?" Justin happily answers, "Yes, I am. It's great to meet you. I tried calling Martha's number multiple times and it didn't go through." Bon responds, "Oh that's weird. I had my phone on me the entire night."

Justin follows Bon to a waiting taxi and hops in the front left passenger side where he meets Mav, as the car goes flying down the road at eighty-five miles per hour. Bon begins to tell Justin that, once he reaches his new, permanent apartment in about a week, he will be housing with a gentleman in his late twenties named Duke who is a devout atheist and is living abroad to simply teach English.

At this time Mav asks Justin to show her the number that Martha gave him to call. Seconds later Mav says, "Oh, this is Martha's old phone number! How did this happen? I can't believe she made that mistake!"

Moments later the three board a ferry boat that takes them to Justin's temporary apartment where he is told he will be staying during his week of training. From the outside the building looks rough, and the group of people standing outside of the complex do as well. As Justin walks up the eight flights of stairs with his new acquaintances, he is unsure of what his accommodations will be. As they enter his apartment a wild dog barks from the neighbor's barred door.

Upon entrance Justin is relieved to see a spacious, well-furnished two-floor apartment. He says good night to Bon and Mav and lays down on his bed and begins to calculate the amount of time he has before he can go home. Justin then says a prayer of thanksgiving to Jesus and falls asleep soundly.

Less than two days later Justin is asked to move out of his apartment to make room for a new missionary named Kaylene. Justin is then asked to sleep in the English Center in a classroom each night on top of a hard table with a mat, blanket, and pillow. An hour later Duke arrives for training and is also asked to spend the night in the English Center in another vacant classroom a top of a hard table with a mat, blanket, and pillow.

That evening at around two in the morning, Justin struggles to sleep as he hears the sound of sirens going off and people arguing on the busy street below and neon lights glaring through the windows. Suddenly Justin hears the steel door to the English Center opening. Dressed only in his underwear he grabs a lamp to defend himself, as he imagines someone is breaking in. The lights go on and standing in the entranceway to the center is a doe-eyed lady with fair skin and a tight ponytail. She is dressed conservatively and is holding hands with a shy gentleman who stands almost six inches shorter than her.

Justin says in a calm but firm voice, "Hello, what's going on? Is everything okay?" The awkward-looking woman stares at Justin and says methodically, "Hi, I'm Martha. You must be Justin. This is my fiancé, Dan. We were just dropping by to see if the new staplers and paper clips had come in yet. Yeah . . ." Justin responds slowly in disbelief, "Hi, nice to meet you both. I don't know if those items have arrived yet . . . I have no idea."

Minutes later Martha and Dan leave the English Center and Duke emerges from his room and asks if that was Martha and Dan at the door. Justin tells him it was and informs him why they were visiting. Duke responds, "That's not why they were here. No way! That makes no sense. I can't believe this group has us sleeping on tables. They have me travel two hours for orientation and they can't even put me up in a hotel? This is not the way that you treat people. Especially as a Christian organization. When I first came to this country four years ago, I was on fire for Christ, but I am a borderline agnostic now because I have had so many bad experiences with this particular Christian missionary group. I still have some faith in Jesus, but only a little."

Please thoughtfully answer the following questions:

1. If you were Pastor Arbor, would you reach out to young Justin to check on his well-being?

2. What are your impressions of Justin's first few days as a missionary and English teacher?

3. What is your opinion of what Duke shared with Justin when he said, "When I first came to this country four years ago, I was on fire for Christ, but I am a borderline agnostic now because I have had so many bad experiences with this particular Christian missionary group. I still have some faith in Jesus, but only a little."?

4. What book of the Bible would you recommend to Justin to read during this challenging time?

5. What book of the Bible would you recommend to Duke to read during this challenging time?

Beth Is in Shock

Beth is twenty-three years old and is close to graduating college. When she was in high school one of her favorite habits was attending church and youth group on a regular basis. Actually, the highlight of the summer before she started college was a weeklong mission trip to a neighboring country to help dig wells and paint a large school building in a rural village. Each night her fellow missionaries would worship with the villagers, and for communion ladies would bring the bread straight from the oven and would draw wine directly from the barrels and quickly bring both to the pastor to consecrate. These formational faith experiences of high school made an eternal impact on Beth.

During her last semester of college, she has felt a great deal of stress. Her bachelor's degree does not afford her many career opportunities. Therefore, she is wrestling with the decision to either apply for an entry level position in her hometown and live with her parents for a year, or to begin applying to graduate schools to hopefully gain a better career in the long term. The stress of these decisions has been enhanced by the prospect of massive student loan repayments that will start to come into effect shortly after graduation.

This stressful time has caused Beth to pray often and get back in the habit of attending church on a regular basis, which has stirred up great memories of living out her faith in Christian community as a high schooler. One day after a campus chapel service Beth shares a little of her story with Sandy, the campus pastor, and she suggests Beth consider international mission work on a long-term basis. This suggestion by Pastor Sandy both excites Beth and ignites her imagination. She begins picturing some of the places and people that she could possibly get to know through mission work.

A mere six months after Pastor Sandy made her suggestion, Beth flies to one of the oldest countries in the world and begins her eighteen-month missionary term. She is met at the airport by Polly, a second-career long-term embedded missionary who has no desire to ever return to her home country other than for the occasional visit to spend time with her aunt. The two ladies begin to make an effort at bonding on the crowded bus ride to Polly's apartment.

Beth is shocked to hear Polly say casually, "Most of my family is now dead, and I have no contact with my father. He abused me as a child and I want nothing to do with him. Being a missionary has been about sharing Jesus with people, but it's also been about escaping the extreme trauma that I suffered back home. Some people can't deal with how isolated you are here as a missionary from other Christians and people of a similar background, but I absolutely love it. I want to be primarily left alone and not bothered. I do my work, spend a little time with a few friends, and live my own life. After you spend the week with me and I get you introduced to the location of the school you'll be teaching at, super markets, an outlet clothing store, bus stops, etc. . . . don't expect to see a ton of me. I'm a very private person. I hope you're good at making friends."

As Beth follows her main contact into this strange and new place a mid-sized apartment complex, she is amazed at how beautiful the lobby is. Upon entering Polly's apartment, the furnishings impress her, and so does the view of the river from the sixteen-hundred-square-foot, two-bedroom, two-bath home. As Polly shows Beth to her room, she says something to the effect of "I'm technically not only your tour guide over the next week, I'm also your boss officially. So, make yourself at home but remember you're moving out in a week."

Six and a half days later, Beth arrives at her new apartment on the other end of the city. She is accompanied by a friendly translator named Tennie. The two ladies step out of the taxi and are overwhelmed by the stunning heat and humidity along with the aroma of fried foods, raw sewage, and motor oil. They approach a building with a brutalist style of architecture that appears to be around fifty years old. Beth stares at the barred windows as she walks through the narrow, dimly lit hallways to the elevator. It's obvious that this building has seen better days, but Beth is doing all that she can to stay positive.

Finally, Tennie and Beth arrive on the fifth floor and are met by one of the apartment managers, who hands over the apartment key and some basic paperwork. Tennie translates for the manager and says, "Welcome to your new home. Remember you are a foreigner here and we want you to be safe. Be careful walking around at night. Always double lock your doors. Make sure you have a cell phone. And call me if there is an emergency."

Beth thanks him and enters the apartment with Tennie. She is amazed at how basic her apartment is. The kitchen has a tiny refrigerator and a stove with only one working burner. The furnishings are dated and uncomfortable. There is no television and the walls are bare, without artwork. Finally, she enters the bathroom to find a little sink and a squatter potty with a shower hose hanging almost directly over it.

Ultimately, the feelings of culture shock, jet lag, exhaustion, disappointment, loneliness, and homesickness get the best of Beth. She bursts into tears and throws herself into her translator Tennie's arms. Over the next thirty minutes Tennie consoles Beth. Once she is done crying for the moment, Tennie graciously insists on taking Beth out to lunch and shopping.

Please thoughtfully answer the following questions:

1. Do you feel Pastor Sandy was wise in her suggestion to Beth that she consider international mission work on a long-term basis?
2. What is your overall impression of Beth's boss, Polly?

3. If you were in Beth's position, how would you feel after your first week of your eighteen-month missionary term?

4. If you were Pastor Sandy and were communicating with Beth, what Bible passage might you encourage her to read as a source of comfort and strength?

5. What extrabiblical writings might you recommend to Beth as she adjusts to life as a long-term missionary?

Where Is Hobbs?

Hobbs is a twenty-five-year-old woman who has recently experienced the trauma of a divorce. As involved as she was in church activities when she was married, her time commitment to church functions has doubled since becoming single. In fact, Hobbs has considered that this may be the perfect time for her to realize her dream of becoming a full-time foreign missionary.

On her first day back at work following the Christmas break, she is summoned into her boss's office and is dispassionately informed she is no longer employed. No reason is given and a security guard escorts her out after she clears off her desk. This unexpected firing is, in Hobbs's mind, a sign from God that it is time to pursue her dream of foreign missionary work.

With great enthusiasm, Keenum, her senior pastor, rallies several boards, committees, and essentially the entire congregation to spiritually and financially support Hobbs as she prepares to serve as a foreign missionary nearly eight thousand miles away. While settling into her new role as an English teacher at a private school and also at an English center inside of a state-run church, she is overwhelmed by the cards, care packages, and encouraging video messages she receives within the first six months of her service.

As Hobbs approaches a year in the field, she notices the encouraging mail and videos have steadily declined in the last six months. However, Pastor Keenum as well as her long-term mission coordinator are impressed with her service and have strongly encouraged her to sign on for not only one more year, but two more years of service. They reassure her she will continue to be supported not only spiritually, but financially as well. After three weeks of prayer and contemplation she agrees with only slight hesitation and enjoys a one month visit back home, where enough money is contributed to her fund mainly by her home church and a few other congregations to support her basic living expenses for another year.

Toward the end of her second year of service, Hobbs has grown closer to her students and colleagues than she ever thought possible; however, she misses her mother, younger sister, nieces, and nephews dearly. But thankfully she is going to have a one month visit back home with everyone in a few days and will not have to spend a great deal of time fundraising for the upcoming year.

Hobbs is picked up at the airport by Stacey, a once-close friend from church who she has lost contact with since becoming a missionary. After Stacey embraces Hobbs with an awkward hug, she begins to make small talk and says, "Isn't it amazing about Pastor Keenum accepting the call to the church in his home town? I hear they have almost three times as many members as we do, and are doubling his salary. Isn't that great?"

Hobbs is slightly in shock as her ears ache and she battles to focus while fighting jet lag after an uncomfortably long flight. So, she timidly responds, "Yeah, Stacey, that's great . . , when did this happen?" Stacey giggles and says, "Oh, they must not have stopped by your house to say goodbye! Last Sunday was actually officially his last day. Pastor Keenum has already moved. I hear his new house is amazing!"

Over the course of her visit home, Hobbs finds out that likely the new associate pastor, a disc golf junkie by the name of Brae, will become the new senior pastor. To her amazement she also learns that her congregation has cut their support toward her down to one quarter of what it was the year before.

This sends Hobbs into a near panic as she spends almost the entire trip attempting to raise the needed amount from a variety of other churches in the area. She reaches almost ninety percent of her needed funds. Yet, she still is in need of another ten percent, so she reluctantly accepts a sizable no-interest loan from her younger sister and brother-in-law. Hobbs boards her flight exhausted, frustrated, and with the memory of her mother's cries as they said goodbye playing in her head.

Over the next six months, Hobbs officially becomes the senior missionary in her group as her dear friend Jodie decides to return to her home country after fourteen years of full-time service. This means Hobbs is now one of the main contact people in her group for new missionaries and visiting administrators. As she reflects on the relationships that have been formed in the first two and half years and how needed she is, Hobbs feels torn in different directions.

On the one hand she misses her family back home tremendously. Because of the busyness of life and work the only family member or friend that has been able to visit her has been her mother. As a result, she feels pressure to leave foreign missionary work and return home to her family. On the other hand, she has made ten close friends, built decent relationships with dozens of others, has fallen in love with many aspects of her new home's culture, and enjoys talking with friends about Jesus. Yet there are days when Hobbs feels so burnt out and exhausted, she quietly plays with the idea of not serving as a missionary any longer but instead working a purely secular job where she currently lives. She would just live a typical Christian life and talk to people at work and in her close circle about Jesus when opportunities presented themselves.

At the urging of good friends in her adopted country as well as the long-term mission coordinator, she decides to commit to another year of foreign missionary work. Although she is receiving meager spiritual and financial support from the congregations and friends that promised strong support when she first began her journey, Hobbs knows she is serving with the purpose to learn, grow, and share the good news of Jesus' love with others.

Two and a half years later, Hobbs decides it is time to return to her home country permanently. She is completely burnt out, penniless, and experiences reverse culture shock on a nearly daily bases for the first three months she is home. And where is home now for Hobbs? She lives in the basement of her younger sister and brother-in-law's modest home and works part-time at a T-shirt pressing company.

Every time Hobbs would return home for a visit while serving as a missionary, she felt it was as if she had died and all of her friends had gone on living without her: starting and growing families, obtaining promotions and graduate degrees, taking fantastic vacations, and building great wealth. Now that she is home permanently those feelings have been magnified ten times.

Over the next several years, Hobbs slowly starts to get her life back. After three years at the T-shirt pressing company, she attends a wonderful university where she earns her master's degree with a focus on the culture and people that she served as an English teacher and missionary for five years.

One hot late July morning, Hobbs boards a plane with her new husband, Chase, and flies to the country that she lived, worked, cried, and laughed in and thinks about every single day. As she visits familiar friends and recognizes how much is the same yet has changed, she has trouble believing it was ten years earlier that she first arrived as a foreign missionary in this place.

Please thoughtfully answer the following questions:

1. Do you think Pastor Keenum had a responsibility to inform Hobbs he was accepting a call to another church given the fact he was one of the people who encouraged her to sign on for two more years of service after her first year in the field?

2. What is your opinion of Hobbs's home congregation cutting their support for her down to one quarter of what it was the year before at the end of her second year, and not informing her until she arrived home to visit her family?

3. If you had been Hobbs's pastor, what comforting words from Jesus would have you spoken to her as she struggled to get her life back upon returning home?

4. What practical steps could Hobbs's home congregation have taken to help her adjust to reentering everyday life in her home country?

A Mini Vacation with a Nomadic Capitalist

Alexander Breeze is a self-described "nomadic capitalist" who has lived in eight different countries for two years or more. Mr. Breeze is in the process of trying to heal from a nasty divorce and custody battle that will hopefully be ending in less than a week. He is exhausted, but is looking forward to a miniature vacation to an outlying island with his friends from church set to begin the day of the ruling. Mr. Breeze expects the ruling will be favorable to him as his attorneys have presented irrefutable evidence that he is the most stable and healthy parent of the two. He expects to be awarded full custody of his daughter Stella.

As Alexander steps off of his yacht with his friends from church, he receives a call from his lawyer. His attorney informs him the judge has ruled that since neither Alexander or his ex-wife, Bebe, are citizens of the country that the separation and eventual divorce took place in, then it should be up to their home country's judicial system to decide who is awarded full custody of six-year-old Stella.

Alexander is in a state of utter shock as his attorney breaks the news. He tosses the keys to the luxury villas to his friends from church, and down the boardwalk he goes while listening to his attorney explain the details. Alexander eventually yells out, "Stuart! Stuart! How can this be? When this process started two years ago, we were guaranteed by the judge a fair and clear ruling on this matter as long as both parties presented their cases in a timely manner! Both parties did just that! I paid millions to have this resolved, and the judge just decides two years in that he isn't qualified or it isn't appropriate for him to rule on this case because Bebe and I aren't technically citizens of this country? I've been the CFO of my company for almost six years. Bebe and I both have platinum visas through my company. What is this, some type of sick game the judge has been playing with us for the last two years? I don't believe this—it's inexcusable!"

After Alexander calms down, he joins his three church friends in the villa. They go out to dinner and Alexander generously pays for dinner and ice cream. Early the next morning as the four enjoy a soak in the jacuzzi, Alexander tells them about the latest development in his legal battle for full custody of Stella. Everyone is initially supportive until Alexander tells Missy that this unexpected decision by the judge means he will have to start over in his legal battle for Stella, which means a great deal more in legal expenses.

Therefore, his promise to fully fund her needed missionary expenses for the entire next year is not possible anymore. Alexander goes on to say that he will do his best to fund half of her needed missionary expenses for the next year, but he won't know about that for certain for another week or two.

Missy responds to the news with, "Wow! Here I am only three months from my fundraising deadline, and you drop that on me. After I babysat Stella two times a week for you for the last year, while you worked late and went out with your friends? Fully funding me is only a very small percentage of your income. You could easily afford it. Easily! And everyone here knows it! I'm out of here!"

Missy storms out of the tub, and Alexander walks towards her saying, "Missy, I really don't think you're being reasonable. Please try to see it from my perspective." Missy responds, "You try to make yourself out to be some type of wealthy generous Christian patriarch, but you're nothing more than a sly, manipulative snake. I've wanted to say that to you for so long and this is finally the right time! Goodbye, I'm taking the next ferry boat home."

A week later, Pastor Hal asks his parishioners, Alexander and Missy, to meet with him to discuss the conflict these two once-close friends are now having. Alexander happily agrees to meet, but Missy insists that there is nothing to discuss until Alexander fulfills his promise to fully fund her needed missionary expenses for the next year. She refuses to meet with Pastor Hal and Alexander until a full payment is made.

Please thoughtfully answer the following questions:

1. What is your opinion of Missy's response to Alexander breaking the news to her that he will no longer be able to fully fund her needed missionary expenses for the entire next year?

2. Do you feel Alexander is in any way in the wrong in this situation?
3. What is your opinion of Missy's refusal to discuss the conflict with Pastor Hal and Alexander until Alexander fulfills his promise to fully fund her needed missionary expenses for the next year?
4. How would you handle this situation moving forward if you were Pastor Hal?
5. What Bible passages might be helpful to Pastor Hal in addressing this conflict?

Correcting Pastor Skip

Donnell High School has been vacant for the last four years. The city was petitioned to save the buildings from demolition due to the campus's historical significance. Initially the campus was going to serve as an apartment complex, but fell through at the last minute. And then a ghost investor attempted to purchase the buildings to turn them into an adult only hotel, but Light House Church stepped in and outbid the ghost investor for the campus.

Pastor Kev has recently accepted a call straight out of seminary to Light House Church to plant a congregation at the massive former high school. He was informed by the senior pastor, Skip, that the church will be named Ray of Light—a satellite campus of Light House Church. As Pastor Kev tours the campus for the first time he is accompanied by Pastor Skip and Chairman of the Congregation Ronald Houseman. He is overwhelmed by the massive size of the five-building complex, and thinks to himself, "Why would we need so much space for this church plant?"

As the three men roam the endless hallways, Pastor Skip says in a commanding, matter-of-fact voice, "Kev, you are the skipper of this church plant, but I'm the general of this naval fleet. If you don't have what it takes to steer this ship into steady waters then we can and will replace you. There is a bright shining star by the name of Johnny Binx who would love an opportunity to be the skipper of this vessel! He's learned a lot from me already. So just remember no one is irreplaceable, so make the most of your opportunity, young man, or you will be replaced."

Pastor Kev interprets Pastor Skip's comments as a veiled threat. He says little in response because he is afraid of offending Skip and possibly having his call rescinded. He desperately needs this work to support his wife, son, and two daughters. His student loan repayment process will begin soon as well, so he is utterly determined to make this situation work.

However one year into his first call, Pastor Kev is exhausted and on the verge of complete burnout. He has received almost no encouragement from Skip, but has heard plenty of demands. Kev has reached out to his bishop about being placed on a call list, and the bishop has denied his request and firmly stated, "You need to give this call at least another six months. Pastor Skip is an experienced vision caster. Give him a chance to work his magic. You can learn a lot from him. You'll learn he's a great guy once you get to know him."

As Pastor Kev reflects on his bishop's words, he considers either joining another denomination or possibly leaving the ministry altogether. Kev's wife, Jen, suggests they take the kids out for dinner and a movie to get their minds off of things. As they head to dinner, they sit at a stoplight next to the Ray of Light campus. Kev glances over to see Pastor Skip with approximately five or six scantily dressed women and Skip's close friend and pupil Johnny Binx; the same Johnny that Skip occasionally threatens will replace Kev if he doesn't do a good job. Skip and Johnny lead the crowd of women into the church's main entrance.

Kev and Jen are concerned about what they just saw. They pull into the parking lot of the church and discuss what they should do. Kev phones his bishop and explains the situation to him. His bishop just happens to be finishing up a meeting at a church only six blocks away, so he heads right over. Pastor Kev and Bishop Pete enter the massive complex, and they call for Skip but receive no response. Eventually the two men enter the gymnasium, and they witness a scene of hedonism. Pastor Skip and his friend Johnny Binx are engaging in sex acts with a crowd of women.

Pastor Pete yells, "Pastor Skip! This is a church! In the name of Jesus Christ, I command you to stop! And you, sir, whoever you are you need to stop as well!" At this time Bishop Pete and Pastor Kev turn their backs as the women and Johnny Binx clothe themselves and exit the church in a hurry. Pastor Skip shows little repentance or explanation for his actions, and instead says, "The heart wants what the heart wants. What you saw were consensual acts between grown adult people. No one was harmed." To which Bishop Pete responds, "No Pastor Skip, you harmed your ministry today! Each person involved in that scene showed disrespect to this church and each member of the congregation of Ray of Light. You totally misrepresented Jesus Christ today."

Please thoughtfully answer the following questions:

1. What is your opinion of Bishop Pete's handling of the entire situation overall, and his correction of Pastor Skip?
2. What words of encouragement and guidance would you offer to Pastor Kev at this time?
3. As you reflect on this story does it remind you of any stories from the Bible?

Ridley Returns

Ridley spent a year of junior high school in a completely foreign country with his parents and two siblings. His parents were serving as missionaries, and, as Ridley puts it, "Me and my brother and sister were along for the ride basically. We didn't have a lot of choice in the matter. Dad and Mom technically asked our opinion, but I always felt like they pressured us to say yes, and agree to go along. My younger sister doesn't think so, but my brother who was a few years older than me completely agrees with my perspective."

At the age of thirty-nine while on an extended business trip, Ridley decides to add a stopover on his flight home, so that he can visit the place where his parents served as missionaries nearly twenty-six years earlier. Almost eerily the rustic street with austere style apartments and office buildings has changed very little. The main street outside of the apartment complex that had a carnival atmosphere seems nearly identical to middle-aged Ridley.

The state-run church looks frozen in time as Ridley walks through the open doors and into the lobby. Ridley requests a tour of the church, and the receptionist informs him the pastor will be back from dinner shortly and would be happy to show him around. Approximately twenty minutes later a pastor in his early thirties approaches him and says, "Hello, I'm Pastor Sammy; it's a pleasure to meet you." Ridley responds, "Hello, I'm Ridley. Thanks for agreeing to show me around. My parents use to help at this church as missionaries years ago."

With almost no hesitation Pastor Sammy says, "Your parents were George and Laci! And you are Ridley! We still have a picture of your whole family hanging in the fellowship hall!" Over the course of the next three hours pastor Sammy shares with Ridley that he first heard about Jesus from him in a Sunday school class at the age of seven. Sammy also remembers a time when an older student threatened to place a curse on him in the name of the devil, and Ridley stuck up for him and rebuked this student in the name of Jesus.

With astonishment Ridley listens to Sammy tell him that as a little boy he only felt comfortable hearing stories about Jesus from him, because all of the adults at the church seemed old and scary. Sammy even goes as far as to say that he does not believe he would be a pastor today had Ridley not told him about Jesus so many years earlier.

At the end of the evening Pastor Sammy and Ridley exchange contact information and promise to keep in touch, and Sammy says, "Thank you, brother, for the wonderful impact that you had on my life. I learned so much from you." Ridley responds, "Well, you're welcome, but you had a much greater impact on my life. I'm sure that I learned far more from you, brother, than you ever learned from me."

Please thoughtfully answer the following questions:

1. What is your opinion of Ridley's assessment that his parents pressured him and his siblings to go with them to serve as missionaries?
2. What do you think of the words Sammy and Ridley shared with one another at the end of the evening?
3. In your view, specifically how did Ridley impact Sammy's life?
4. In your view, specifically how did Sammy impact Ridley's life?

Chapter 7

Pastoral Counseling

Elizabeth's Younger Brother

ELIZABETH DILLION IS A wealthy widow, who enjoys volunteering as the treasurer of the church she attends. When not volunteering, Elizabeth is passionate about gardening and renovating her great house and two guest homes on her estate. Her nearly decade-long renovations are nearly complete and Elizabeth is planning a grand ball to celebrate. This ball will also be an opportunity for her church community and friends at the club to meet her world-renowned younger brother, Zach, a good-looking young man who seems to have no shortage of financial resources.

One week before the grand ball, Elizabeth requests a meeting with Pastor Ford. Right from the start the meeting has an incredibly serious tone. About twenty minutes into the meeting Elizabeth says, "I requested this meeting with you this afternoon to discuss my brother Zach. Well, he's a troubled young man. And now he's back in my life. One month ago, I saw the lights on in my east guest home. And when I went to the door, I saw that Zach had moved in without my permission. I didn't have the heart to ask him to leave. And to be frank I'm frightened to ask him to leave. He's dangerous, and I believe that he is capable of almost anything. He's lived all over the world, and nearly every person he's ever dated has either gone missing or has died an untimely death under enormously mysterious circumstances. Last night over dinner, Zach told me that he is searching for just the right person to draw him back into the dating game. And that he is sick of traveling and wants to live in my east guest home for a very long time. He said that he's excited about all of the dating opportunities that my grand ball will provide. I'm not sure of what I should do. Pastor Ford, do you have any suggestions for how I might handle this awkward situation with my brother?"

Please thoughtfully answer the following questions:

1. If you were Pastor Ford, what advice might you give to Elizabeth on how to handle this awkward situation with Zach based on the information she has provided?
2. Before the end of the conversation, would you ask Elizabeth to provide more context concerning her statements about Zach's past relationships ending with the person either going missing or dying an untimely death under enormously mysterious circumstances?
3. Based on what Elizabeth has shared concerning her brother Zach, do you believe Pastor Ford should advise her to contact the authorities concerning her brother?

A Change of Scenery?

Evan is a twenty-three-year-old man who for the last four years has worked long hours at a local factory. His main duty is to move steel coils on the night shift. This is difficult and dangerous work for him that he is becoming resentful of. Evan's work situation is not helped by the fact his mother and father have pressured him to continue to live with them at their home, stating, "Evan, you simply cannot handle the responsibility of living on your own and paying your own bills. Emotionally you are no further along than you were as an eighteen-year-old senior in high school. You need us to care for you."

Recently, Evan has confided in friends at work during break time, and they have strongly encouraged him to move out of his parents' house and into his own place near work. His supervisor Ken has even taken the liberty to put him in touch with his home church pastor, Reverend Anthony Bosco, a pastor with over forty years of parish ministry experience.

Early on a Thursday morning, Evan and Pastor Bosco meet at a local diner to have breakfast and to discuss Evan's struggles with his parents. The two talk about work and some of their favorite movies for about the first half an hour, and then Evan starts to explain his situation by saying, "I love my parents . . . but I've started to realize that they have been taking advantage of me for most of my adult life. They've told me time and time again that I'm too immature to live on my own, and that I need to live with them or I will mess up my life so badly that I will end up homeless. I make good money at the factory, but almost 70 percent of it goes toward paying them rent. Just for my little bedroom and my own full bathroom. They hardly ever let me have friends over to visit, and I have to have the TV off by 9:30 p.m. every single night. For what I've been paying them over the last four years, I could have bought a nearly new three-bedroom, two-bath home and basically had it paid off by now.

"Most days my mom will come in my room at 10 a.m. without knocking after I worked twelve hours the night before and start running the vacuum and humming old songs. Basically, she's just trying to get me out of the house for the day. She doesn't want me around. She only wants me to officially live there so I'll pay her rent. I risk my life four, sometime six, nights a week at work to earn that money. I pay most of it to them. They have access to all of my accounts and sometimes take extra out if I forget to clean my room, and they won't even let me get six hours of sleep each day. I've had it!

"I need a change of scenery and a change of life. I'm thinking about selling everything that I have and going out west. Just taking some basic supplies, buying a young stallion, and riding it bareback through the mountains just like the pioneers or the Native Americans did. They had the right idea! Get back to the basics. No TVs, internet, phones, or factory jobs. None of it! Jesus and his disciples didn't have any of that modern stuff either. They only had basic supplies and walked places most of the time, I think. Just good old-fashioned living. Don't you think that's how God wants us to live? Simple and off the grid, sort of? Don't you think that's what God wants me to do, Pastor Bosco . . . live off the grid out west? Riding bareback through the mountains, while camping out by fires at night . . . swimming in creeks and lakes each day? Don't you think that that is what God wants me to do, sir?"

Please thoughtfully answer the following questions:

1. Based on the information Evan has given, do you believe he has legitimate concerns about how his parents are treating him?

2. If you were in Pastor Bosco's position, would you encourage Evan to stay in his parents' home and continue working at the factory, move into his own place near work and continue working at the factory, or would you encourage him to sell all of his possessions and move out west to live a simple, off-the-grid lifestyle?

3. What biblical passages or extrabiblical resources might you point Evan to in an attempt to help him navigate this situation with his parents and his possible move to a completely new way of life out west?

Ben Needs Prayer

Triad is a forty-five-year-old person that identifies as non-binary and feels like a big kid at heart. They live in a condominium with an acquaintance that they met online. Their roommate is a determined young graduate student named Ben Lindon. The two have a friendly but not exceptionally warm relationship. For the last three months, every Friday evening while Triad is at work Ben goes out of his bedroom window and crawls on the roof over to Triad's open bedroom window and enters in. Ben then proceeds to read through Triad's personal diary while lying on their bed. This has become Ben's most treasured hobby and often gets him through the long work week, knowing that on Friday night he will have an opportunity to read Triad's latest personal diary entries.

Early on a chilly Sunday morning, Pastor Crestmont finds a particular prayer request note from a person who occasionally attends worship. The note is uniquely intriguing and yet creepy, as it reads, "My roommate hasn't been journaling anything good lately in their personal diary. Please pray that they start writing some good stuff in there again. I go to all of the trouble of getting into their room to read it, and lately it has been boring. I need some good stuff to read each Friday night to get me through the work week. Thanks a lot, Pastor! I appreciate you praying for me! Love, Ben Lindon."

Please thoughtfully answer the following questions:

1. If you were Pastor Crestmont, how would you respond to Ben's prayer request?
2. Do you think it would be wise for Pastor Crestmont to meet with Ben and discuss the prayer request in person?
3. In your view, is Ben breaking any of the Ten Commandments by entering Triad's room and reading their personal diary while lying on their bed?

Max Is in Need of Some Friendly Advice

Max is a thirty-year-old single man who has recently moved to a new state to work as a structural engineer at the main employer in the county. He is struggling to adjust to the culture and work ethic of his new home. However, his transition has been made easier by the welcoming nature of the church that he has been attending since he arrived. In fact, Max is looking forward to having lunch with his new pastor in the historic downtown on Saturday.

Max arrives on Saturday about twenty minutes late for his lunch appointment with Pastor Washington at the Old Green Egg Café and Theater. But Pastor Washington is just happy to see Max and is looking forward to getting to know him better. For about fifteen minutes they talk about family, work, the historic downtown, and the area in general, until Max says, "Pastor, I would like to ask your advice on something . . . I feel a little bit bad about this since we just sat down for lunch, but if you don't mind, I would like to tell you about something, and hear what you think . . . is that okay?" Pastor Washington responds, "Of course, you can tell me whatever you would like, and I will give you the best possible advice that I can give."

Max then laughs nervously and says, "Okay thanks . . . so I've only been in town for less than two months, and I don't have a lot of friends yet. So yesterday, my buddy at work, a guy named Rick, asked me to go with him to this old-school arcade. And I just thought we would check out this arcade and maybe get some fast food. So, he takes me to this arcade and they have all of the classic games, and we are having fun. And then after an hour Rick says, 'Hey, my buddy owns this great little restaurant about a block away. You want to go?' And I say, 'Yeah! Sounds great. I didn't even have a chance to grab lunch today.'

"So, we start walking down this old alleyway and then this bouncer meets us at this back door and he takes us to this little private room. And the service is top notch! Champagne on ice, a silk tablecloth, a candelabra that is all lit up, and the oysters and lobster were unbelievable! But . . . around this time I started to get a strange feeling . . . like maybe Rick and I had different expectations about what this evening was supposed to be. I mean, I just wanted to hang out and have a guys' night at the arcade, and I think maybe, I don't know, he might have wanted some type of date?

"Well, the next thing I know after dinner we are jumping in this limo. Rick just left his car at the arcade and this limo is driving us all around the lake. And I didn't want to be impolite and ask too many questions about where we were going or anything because Rick was being incredibly nice. He paid for everything! All of the arcade games, the amazing dinner, the limo, everything! He's a really nice guy.

"Finally, after almost forty minutes of driving us around, the limo driver pulls into this secluded lane that had a perfect view of the lake, and he parks. Then he says over the little intercom system, 'We've arrived, gentlemen.' Then he starts playing this strange old music that my parents listened to on their anniversaries and date nights . . . at that point I was so freaked out that I just busted out the door and started running down the road. I eventually hitchhiked back to my apartment in town.

"I didn't sleep at all last night, and I'm still totally shaken up from everything about last night. It was a six-hour adventure that I still can't wrap my mind around. The thing is, what is it going to be like walking into work on Monday? Is Rick going to be awkward around me because I got out of the limo and ran down the road? I mean, Rick has been at the company forever, and is really well liked and has tons of influence. I don't want to be on his bad side. Do you think I should try and talk with him and clear the air? What do you think that I should do, Pastor Washington?"

Please thoughtfully answer the following questions:

1. If you were in Pastor Washington's position, what words of encouragement would you try to offer to Max during this time of transition and stress that he is facing?

2. Do you think that it would be wise of Pastor Washington to read the Twenty-Third Psalm to Max as a way to comfort him with the promises of God's love and care in the face of trials?

3. In your opinion, would it be wise of Max to try to call Rick and let him know that the reason he ran out of the limo and hitchhiked home was because he was feeling uncomfortable with the situation?

What Did Pastor Tyson See?

Tyson is an associate pastor at a medium-sized suburban congregation. His colleague Pastor Skip has recently accepted a call on the other side of the country. Now that Tyson is the sole pastor of a church with nearly four hundred members in worship each week, he is feeling slightly overwhelmed and is planning on relying on his full-time secretary, Violet, to help him manage his day-to-day tasks and stay organized. Thankfully Violet is incredibly capable and has a mountain of experience as the congregation's full-time secretary.

On Saturday evening, Pastor Tyson looks out the parsonage kitchen window and notices that some of the lights have been left on in the church office. He decides to do the ecologically responsible thing and walk over to turn them off. As he enters the building he is overcome by the strong scent of cinnamon candles. He also hears the musical stylings of a famous jazz musician playing over a stereo in Pastor Skip's now vacant office.

Hesitantly, Pastor Tyson opens the office door to find Violet, the full-time church secretary, sitting on the floor with Sam, the head elder, on a bright orange bed comforter, feeding one another strawberries dipped in chocolate. They are both fully clothed, but the lights are off and there are five or six candles burning, along with two glasses of red wine, next to an empty wine bottle on the floor.

Before Pastor Tyson has an opportunity to say a word Violet says, "Oh hi, Pastor Tyson! It's so good of you to stop by. Sam and I were planning out a surprise birthday party for my brother-in-law. Yes, we are trying to keep it a secret so we met here in Pastor Skip's old office. Please don't tell anyone. We want it to be a big surprise. Thank you!"

Please thoughtfully answer the following questions:

1. What would be your immediate response to the situation if you were Pastor Tyson?
2. Do you believe that anything unethical was taking place between Violet and Sam?
3. How might this situation involving Violet and Sam affect the congregation as a whole?

A Memorable Holy Week

Pastor Hue is seventy-one years old and is nearing his forty-five-year anniversary of his ordination into the office of holy ministry. In September he will retire from full-time parish ministry and his duties as circuit visitor. Hue is looking forward to traveling around the country with his dear wife, Tammy, spending more time with his kids and grandkids, and occasionally serving as a guest pastor at congregations near his home.

However, on this rainy Monday morning all he can focus on right now is taking some time to rest and catch up on sleep after an exhausting Holy Week. In the span of the last eight days, Pastor Hue has led multiple services on four different days, led a late night to early morning prayer service on Holy Saturday, led three services on Easter Sunday, and helped prepare breakfast that day as well. He is exhausted and needs some rest!

As he sleeps on the sofa and warms himself by the wood stove with his favorite cat, Alfredo, Tammy hesitantly wakes him up and says, "Hue, I'm sorry, honey, but a man named Rodger Rogue from St. Paul keeps calling for you and leaving messages saying that he urgently needs to talk with the circuit visitor. He says it has something to do with the health of their pastor. I thought it was worth waking you up for. I'm sorry." Hue answers, "Okay, no problem, honey. Thank you for letting me know."

After Pastor Hue grabs a large cup of tea, he calls Rodger Rogue back and, immediately after saying hello, Rodger has this to say: "Hello, Circuit Visitor Pastor Hue. I'm the head elder over at St. Paul. We have a serious concern regarding the health and abilities of Pastor Art Johnson. Do you know him?"

Pastor Hue answers with a sense of irony, "Do I know him? We graduated from undergrad the same year together and seminary the same year together as well. He actually married a distant cousin of mine on my mom's side of the family." Rodger answers hurriedly with a sense of surprise, "Oh wow, well we think his health is rapidly declining. There have been signs for months now, but over Holy Week our worst concerns were confirmed. He read the same exact sermon word for word like a script without looking up once for Palm Sunday, Maundy Thursday, Good Friday, and Easter Sunday. Thankfully not everyone in the congregation noticed because not everyone was at each service. Many people only came to the Easter Sunday service this year. So, if we act right now and have him go on sabbatical while he gets medical treatment, hardly anyone will have to know that he read the same sermon for each service during Holy Week!"

Pastor Hue takes a deep breath and responds, "Well, has Pastor Johnson been to the doctor yet?" Rodger answers, "You see that's just the thing, Pastor Hue. I'm afraid Pastor Johnson is more stubborn than an old angry mule! I spoke to him along with the other elders last night for almost three hours, and he refuses to go and see the doctor, and he's even claiming to have read different sermons for each service. He's in complete denial! We are at our wit's end on what to do here. We need your help. Would you please talk with him for us?" Pastor Hue slowly responds, "Yes, I'll speak to him. Of course. I'll call him as soon as I get off the phone with you and try to arrange a lunch appointment with him for sometime either today or tomorrow."

Please thoughtfully answer the following questions:

1. In your opinion, is the head elder of St. Paul, Rodger Rogue, acting responsibly by sharing with Circuit Visitor, Pastor Hue, that he and others think Pastor Johnson's health is rapidly declining?

2. If you were Pastor Hue, and took seriously what Rodger shared, would you recommend to Pastor Johnson he go on a sabbatical or even retire so he can better focus on his health?

A Late-Night Phone Call to a Friend

Evan is a twenty-four-year-old former factory worker who moved into the area last year from the eastern part of the country. He is striving to live an off-the-grid lifestyle that is self-sustaining and filled with the simple pleasures of life.

Over the last month, Evan has felt lonely. It has been an adjustment not going into work each day at the factory. Sure, he loves riding bareback on his horse Gypsy, swimming and bathing in fresh bodies of water, taking naps under pine trees, cooking breakfast on his pot belly stove in his yurt, and not having to worry about being late for work or bosses yelling at him, but something is missing.

One day while making his monthly trip into town to get supplies, he notices a sign in the hardware store window for a new church near his campsite. Evan decides that this might be a great opportunity to get back in the habit of going to church and to make some new friends at the same time.

Five months later Evan makes an early morning phone call to his friend back east, Pastor Anthony Bosco, and tells him an alarming story, saying, "So I saw a sign for a church near my campsite and thought this would be a good opportunity for me to get back into the habit of attending church and maybe make some friends, and at first everything seemed great. The pastor introduced himself, and he sort of reminded me of a younger version of my Grandpa Jake. His name is Harley . . . Pastor Harley. The congregation seemed nice too. Nearly everyone in the church is related to Pastor Harley, which is impressive because they have like a hundred members!

"Right away all kinds of people were saying to me, 'You're family now, Evan. We are responsible for you.' And they were giving me the best seat at the church picnics and baking me all of this delicious food the first few months and everything was awesome! Then they told me I needed to start signing up as an usher and a reader for every service. And they told me it was important that I start supervising the youth retreats. So, I did everything they asked and I think I did okay.

"But I started noticing that Pastor Harley wasn't really talking to me anymore, and I was getting seated in the back at the church picnics and stuff. I started to feel lonely again, and I was feeling a lot of pressure with my extra duties at the church. So, one Saturday night I drank a bottle of whiskey by my campfire, and I accidently slept in and missed the church service. I was supposed to usher, serve as a reader, and supervise a youth event that day. I really messed up!

"The next thing I know, Pastor Harley and the elders were at my campsite investigating what happened, and they figured out that I slept in because

I was drunk. So, the next week during the church picnic Pastor Harley announced to the entire congregation what I had done, and they asked me to stand up on the edge of the property for my punishment. The next thing I knew Elder Samson was using an old power hose to blast me with water. I fell on my back and couldn't believe what was happening! People were laughing at me! These people are my friends and they are laughing at me while I'm being power sprayed with a hose!

"When they finally stopped after like ten minutes, I got up and was laughing, and I said, 'I'll never do that again!' Pastor Harley made sure that I knew that this was his will, and this not only needed to happen to teach me a lesson, but also it was a part of the initiation process. Now that I think about it, I have never heard Pastor Harley mention Jesus or anything about the Bible or the creeds. He's always just talking about his will and his vision. Don't you think that's sort of weird, Pastor Bosco?"

Pastor Bosco pauses for a few moments to reflect. He knows Evan has seriously struggled with alcohol addiction for several years, and he realizes this entire situation with the fire hose could be completely made up. Evan has made up outrageous stories in the past.

However, something about the way Evan is telling him the story seems to come across as real, and he wants to believe his friend Evan and put the best construction on things, so he says, "Well, Evan, it is never appropriate to turn a power hose on someone in front of a large group of people because a person has accidently slept in and missed an event. So that alone is reason to not go back to this church. Secondly, the basis of any cult is the will of one person. And it sounds like this Pastor Harley is basing his actions and teachings on his will and not God's will. Thirdly, I know you are looking for a Christian church to attend, and if you never hear this Pastor Harley mention Jesus, the Bible, or the creeds, those are all further indicators to me that this is not a Christian church and you should no longer attend it.

"Jesus Christ stood on the teachings of the Law and the Prophets of the Hebrew scriptures. Jesus did not show up out of nowhere; instead he appeared to God's people in the land that God had given his people, and he obeyed his Father's will and showed the world his Father's love. Jesus loves the people of the world. He teaches us to treat others the way that we would want to be treated.

"I think it is fair to say no one would want to be publicly humiliated with a power hose. That is not a Christlike example of treating someone the way that you would want to be treated. From what you have told me, this Pastor Harley sounds like a cult leader and this church sounds like a cult. Evan, my advice to you would be to get out of there and not go back."

Please thoughtfully answer the following questions:

1. If you were Pastor Anthony Bosco, would you be inclined to believe Evan's story even though you knew Evan has seriously struggled with alcohol addiction for several years and he has made up stories in the past?

2. What is your opinion of Pastor Bosco's assessment of Evan's story and his advice to Evan moving forward?

3. Do you think that it would be wise of Pastor Bosco to visit his friend Evan out west sometime soon to say hi and see how he is doing?

Dinner at the Rockingham's

Rodney Rockingham is an accountant who is entering his forty-fifth year of marriage to his wife, Ivy. Almost every night for the last decade after Ivy falls asleep, Rodney has snuck out the back door and walked across the street and had a sexual encounter with his neighbor Blossom in her she-shed.

After a great deal of prayer and careful consideration, Rodney decides to confess to the affair with Blossom at a dinner with his wife, and their pastor, the Reverend Paul Benton, and his wife, Kay. At first hearing the news, Ivy believes that Rodney is having some type of psychological breakdown or perhaps is trying to tell a nonsensical joke. Eventually, it hits Ivy that Rodney is actually informing her of this affair in front of their pastor and his wife at a candlelit dinner.

Ivy, who is in a state of shock, quickly goes to the car and drives to her sister's home three hours away. Pastor Paul attempts to speak to Rodney about his confession, but finds himself unable to do so due to mild chest pains. Kay immediately phones an ambulance, and Pastor Paul is transported to the emergency room. About thirty minutes after arrival the doctors inform Kay that her husband experienced a mild heart attack and will need to be in the hospital for at least a week. It is also highly recommended that Pastor Paul avoid stressful situations and take an extensive leave of absence from work or possibly retire altogether.

Please thoughtfully answer the following questions:

1. Once Pastor Paul begins to recover, would you recommend he ask a fellow pastor or his bishop to reach out to Rodney and Ivy to see if they would be willing to go through marriage counseling with a pastor other than Paul?

2. If you were giving pastoral advice to Rodney and Ivy, would you suggest they consider moving to a new area of town in order to not be

constantly reminded of the affair between Rodney and Blossom every time they pass her home and she-shed?

3. What Bible passages would you recommend Rodney and Ivy study together if they go through marriage counseling?

4. If you were Pastor Paul's pastor, would you advise him to follow his doctor's medical advice?

The Man with Red Sunglasses

Haley, Melanie, and Autumn are grad students who share a beautiful two-story house in a vibrant neighborhood near campus. One evening they decide to host a party for a dozen of their female colleagues.

Halfway through the evening the conversation turns to the serious and tragic topic of numerous sexual assaults that have taken place on and near campus over the last year and a half. This topic hits close to home for all of the women at the party, as each one of them either knows someone who has been assaulted by possibly the same perpetrator or was in the approximate area within minutes of where one of the assaults took place. As the women reflect on what they saw firsthand or heard directly from eyewitnesses, a similar person continues to be described.

Each woman describes what sounds like the same man near a number of the crime scenes either right before or after the fact. This man had dark, thick hair, was dressed almost entirely in black, wore red sunglasses, and stood around six feet tall with a slim, athletic build. A number of the women have met this man before, but not a single one can recall when or where they were first introduced to him.

In each case he was at a party and was naturally socializing with guests. What makes the description of this mystery person all the creepier is not a single one of the women can recall his name even though at least three of the women are certain he told them his name.

Twenty minutes later, the ladies arrive at the local police station as a group and give statements to several on-duty officers. Three of the ladies who met the man and conversed with him for several minutes give separate detailed descriptions to three different sketch artists, and each sketch turns out almost exactly the same.

Four months later, Haley and Melanie are both contacted by a female attorney who informs them that a suspect has been apprehended and is set to stand trial in just over a month. The attorney believes that their testimonies could be key in obtaining a conviction. However, as Haley and Melanie look at footage of the man arrested, they are both doubtful that he is in fact the man they spoke to the night of the assaults near the crime scene.

Over the next three days the ladies wrestle with whether or not to testify against this man they doubt is the same person they spoke with, but the police and the prosecuting attorney's office seems to be certain it is the same person. At the encouragement of Haley's parents, they seek out the pastoral advice of Haley's grandfather, Emit, , who still serves full time as a pastor at the age of seventy-five.

Emit advises the ladies that, if they have serious doubts about whether the man in custody is the same man that they met and spoke with, then they should make that known to the police and the prosecuting attorney's office. What's more, they should not go against their consciences by testifying that this is the man dressed mostly in black with red sunglasses.

Please thoughtfully answer the following questions:

1. What is your opinion of the advice Pastor Emit offered to Haley and Melanie?
2. What words of comfort might you speak to Haley and Melanie if you were in Pastor Emit's position?
3. Do you think that there are any passages from the Bible that might be helpful to Haley and Melanie during this difficult time that Pastor Emit could read to them?

Pablo Speaks Up

Pablo Delgado serves as a history teacher at a large inner city high school. His state has one of the most segregated public school systems in the country. Taxpayer dollars almost exclusively stay in the communities where a taxpayer lives. Therefore, a wealthy community will have fantastic, updated school buildings with an abundance of the latest technology, teaching materials, extracurricular activities, and a low teacher-to-student ratio.

In contrast, an economically struggling community will have an inadequate facility with a scarcity of outdated technology, teaching materials, few if any extracurricular activities, and a high teacher-to-student ratio, which in effect creates a semi-private public school system in a state that rewards children whose parents can afford a home in an affluent community. It is within this system of benign neglect toward the poor in mostly rural and inner city communities that Pablo serves.

Nearly every Sunday during the fellowship hour and from time to time at Bible studies, Pablo tries his best to tell his brothers and sisters in Christ how segregated the public school system is in their state. People will listen to him to a point, but ultimately it is difficult for many of them to grasp what he is saying, as the majority of these people have only experienced well-funded public education in their suburban enclave. The lack of empathy and response by his brothers and sisters in Christ frustrates Pablo sometimes to where he feels like crying. It saddens him that people he loves dearly could be so blind on such a vital issue of injustice in their own state.

On a crisp autumn day, Pablo meets with his pastor, the Reverend Sherrod Blitzer. The two men try to make small talk as they sip their drinks and nibble their food. Pastor Blitzer struggles to make conversation, as this is only the third time he has spoken at length with Pablo, who is one of five hundred members in his congregation. Halfway into the meal Pablo shares with his pastor the frustrations that he has experienced when trying to speak with fellow parishioners about how segregated his state's educational system is.

And toward the end of the conversation Pablo says, "I'm strongly considering going to the seminary to earn my masters of divinity degree to become an ordained pastor. I've been praying about it a lot. I know it will be a lot of work, but I'm ready. My faith in Christ is strong, and, as a pastor, I will have influence as an administrator and teacher to address systematic forms of segregation and bigotry in our society.

"Also, at the seminary I will have an opportunity to influence my professors and classmates and their families by sharing my unique experiences. Poor people in rural and inner city settings are just as loved by Jesus as people in wealthy suburban places. The church and the world as a whole need to hear that. Pastor, do you think that I should consider attending the seminary?"

Please thoughtfully answer the following questions:

1. What is your opinion of Pablo feeling frustrated about his brothers' and sisters' in Christ lack of empathy and response to his testimony of the place of public education in their state?

2. In your view, are the reasons Pablo named to Pastor Blitzer for considering attending the seminary valid?

3. If you were Pastor Blitzer, how would you respond to what Pablo shared with you about feeling frustrated with his fellow parishioners and his question, "Pastor, do you think that I should consider attending the seminary?"

Chapter 8

Prison Ministry

The Healing Power of Artwork

MOSHE IS A THIRTY-ONE-YEAR-OLD man who has been incarcerated in prison for the last eight years of his life after being convicted of armed robbery and fleeing the police. However, he is thankful his country's prison system is designed with the goal of rehabilitation in mind as opposed to punishment. In prison Moshe has learned to read and write, care for a community garden, and paint murals. In fact, his favorite style of artwork is psychedelic.

One Thursday evening as Moshe finishes his two-month project of painting a mural at the entrance of the dining hall of Jesus and the apostles eating breakfast together on a beach, he takes a big puff of his cigarette and thanks God for the opportunity to relax and heal through painting while sharing his faith with the guards and inmates in the community.

Upon completion of the mural, the entire prison community comes together to celebrate the unveiling of Moshe's new mural with cake and a single glass of sweet wine for each prisoner, administrator, and the majority of guards. Toward the end of the celebration, a prisoner by the name of Bibi approaches Moshe and says, "I love your painting! It is beautiful! I always thought that Jesus was simply a wise teacher, but after looking at your painting and seeing the love and joy that is on his face and his followers, it has made me interested in knowing more about him. Would you please tell me about Jesus?"

Moshe is initially stunned because so few of his fellow prisoners have asked him about Jesus in the eight years he has been in prison. Moshe answers with a smile and says, "Yes, Jesus is God in the flesh. God took on flesh and became a human being. He paid the price for the sins of the whole world through his death on the cross and his glorious resurrection on the third day. Jesus is close to us. He is not far away. He is with you wherever you go. God also saves a person through the waters of holy baptism, when a person is baptized in the name of the Father, the Son, and the Holy Spirit. Bibi, have you ever been baptized before?"

Bibi answers, "No, I haven't," to which Moshe responds, "Would you like to receive the free gift of salvation through the waters of holy baptism?" Bibi looks intensely at Moshe and responds, "Yes, but where can this happen?" Moshe explains the situation to a guard, and moments later they are being led to a shower facility where in front of several inmates and guards Moshe baptizes Bibi in the name of the Father, the Son, and the Holy Spirit.

Please thoughtfully answer the following questions:

1. Does it seem to you Moshe is being treated humanely in prison?
2. What did you think of Moshe's description to Bibi of who Jesus is?
3. Does Bibi's baptism by Moshe put you in mind of any stories from the Bible?

An Unforgettable Summer Holiday

Hubert is on summer holiday in a country over five thousand kilometers away from his home. He has a love for animals and is documenting various forms of farming and herding while exploring a different culture. Thus far, everyone he has come across has been welcoming, and villagers will on occasion invite him into their homes for dates and honey along with some hot tea. The young holiday traveler is even invited to spend the night from time to time. Hubert always accepts the invitation, as a night indoors on a guest sofa or rug once every two weeks is a welcome change from camping outside on the hard ground.

One warm Saturday afternoon as Hubert is photographing a herd of wild, ornery goats, he is suddenly approached by a tribal leader, who is accompanied by roughly three dozen armed men. One of the men steps forward and clearly explains to Hubert he is trespassing on the ancestral property of the tribal leader and that there will be a fee and a punishment. As Hubert apologizes and promises to leave promptly and never return, the armed men encircle him and confiscate his camera, currency, and passport. Hubert is then blindfolded and led away from the area.

Four hours later Hubert is exhausted and confused as he is quickly forced to hike up a mountain. Eventually his blindfold is taken off and he sees a cave that is serving as a primitive prison cell. He is given a drink of hot water and then is locked away in his cell. A few minutes after entry, Hubert spots a person in the corner smoking a long pipe. They begin to converse and as it turns out the man is originally from a city approximately ninety-five hundred kilometers from Hubert's home and is a city that Hubert has always wanted to visit.

That night, Hubert and the man build a charcoal fire and eat a basic vegetable soup that one of the prison guards brought for supper. To Hubert's shock, the man who appears to be twenty years his senior is only five years older than him. His cellmate shares this mystifying story: "Next month will mark two years since I was captured by the tribal leader and his garrison of armed men. The years have fallen away like crumbs from my mouth. I came to this country with my college roommate, Roy. I had recently been ordained as a minister and had been at my first call a mere six months, and Roy was a rising star in the world of journalism.

"We were going from village to village and from time to time would strike up conversations about Jesus with the families that invited us into their homes. Roy would sometimes film the conversations. Eventually there was a baptism in a village near the tribal leader's main camp, and it was at that point that he and the armed men seized us.

"After three months in this cell, the tribal leader and his men came to Roy and me with this proposition: 'We need men to help us fight a neighboring tribe that wants our land. They are cruel and want to enslave our children and rape our women. If you join us and fight them with us, we will grant you freedom.' Roy happily accepted their offer and was armed and trained that entire week. He was desperate to get out of here! I declined the offer for reasons of conscience. I do not believe in participating in violence.

"A mere two weeks later, most of the tribe returned but Roy had been killed in combat. They brought his body back and buried him at the edge of the mountain. They even allowed me to deliver a short sermon, and at the time they claimed that they would take Roy's service into consideration when determining my release date, although I am skeptical I will ever be released from here. The last words that Roy ever spoke to me were, 'Jin, don't forget to love your captors. They need Jesus' love more than anyone. I love you, my friend.'"

After Jin finishes sharing his story of captivity with his new cellmate, Hubert looks straight at him and says, "Thank you for sharing your story with me, Jin. I can't imagine how difficult the last two years of your life have been. I'm sorry to hear about the death of Roy. I wish that I could have met him; he sounds like he was a truly talented journalist and a great man. I want you to know that I have hope that we will be released from here eventually. In fact, I think that we should pray that it will happen soon. Also, would you prefer that I call you Jin or Pastor Jin?" After a brief pause Jin responds, "I have not been called Pastor Jin in nearly two years. I would appreciate you calling me Pastor Jin. Thank you."

The two men spend several hours praying to Christ for a safe release. One month later they are awoken by the tribal leader and several of his guards, and remarkably are set free. Their passports are returned respectively, but neither man is returned their currency. As they are departing, the tribal leader hands Pastor Jin the passport that belonged to Roy and says, "We are letting you two go because Roy fought with us. Roy would have wanted you to be free, and you are friends with Hubert so we will let him go too. Make sure you never step foot on my ancestral land again."

Please thoughtfully answer the following questions:

1. If you had been in the position of Roy, would have you taken the opportunity to fight with your captors for the chance to earn your freedom?
2. What is your opinion about Pastor Jin's decision not to fight with his captors against the neighboring tribe based on the fact he does not believe in participating in violence?
3. What do you think of Roy's last words to his friend and college roommate: "Jin, don't forget to love your captors. They need Jesus' love more than anyone. I love you, my friend"?
4. Had you been in Hubert's position, do you think you would have encouraged Jin to pray with you, that you both would be released soon?
5. If you had been in Jin's position, do you think you would have appreciated Hubert calling you Pastor Jin?

See You Soon

Yoshi is a parish pastor who also serves as a prison chaplain at a maximum-security facility. He leads a Bible study with twelve inmates each week and also has a time of individual confession and absolution with each person before the Bible study.

This Wednesday is particularly difficult for Yoshi, as it is likely the last time he will see his friend Crawford before Crawford is executed in less than a week by the state for the quadruple murder of a family thirty-nine years ago.

As the two friends sit down in a small room with a guard about eight feet away, Crawford looks at Yoshi and says, "I know that I am going to face Christ soon, and I want to have a clear conscience and confess my sins. But as God is my witness, I did not murder that family. It's true that I broke into the vacant house down the road from theirs, and I was sleeping in it that night, but I had nothing to do with the murder of that family. I know that God knows the truth, so I'm at peace in a sense about dying, and I'm realistic that the governor won't halt my execution. On the other hand, I want to live and keep learning about Jesus with my friends and try to make a difference in here by telling people how much Jesus loves them. Thank you for being a great friend, Yoshi. I know that I will see you again on the last day. This isn't goodbye, it's see you soon."

Please thoughtfully answer the following questions:

1. What is your impression of the words Crawford spoke to his friend, Yoshi, in likely their final conversation before Crawford's execution?
2. If you were Pastor Yoshi, how would you respond to what your friend Crawford said to you?
3. Are you able to think of any words of comfort from the Bible that Yoshi could share with Crawford before he is executed?

Puppet Treasures Attending Chapel

Puppet is a fifty-five-year-old man who treasures the privilege of attending weekly chapel services. One evening while making a batch of toilet wine, his cellmate Elliot suggests something rather intriguing. "Puppet, you should make extra wine this time and sneak some down to the chapel for communion. You make the best wine in the house!" Puppet is inspired and flattered by Elliot's suggestion.

Five days later, Puppet approaches Father Martinez with a batch of toilet wine that was made with a lot of hard work. Puppet says, "I've been making toilet wine for thirty years. The inmates love it and so do the guards. They say it's better than that store bought stuff on the outside from vineyards. I snuck some down here for holy communion. I would be honored if you would bless it for holy communion during the service."

Father Martinez smiles and responds, "Puppet, thank you for making this wine. I appreciate your hard work and creativity. But I don't think it's a good idea to use your toilet wine for holy communion for tonight's service. I don't want to see you get in trouble with the guards for sneaking this stuff down here."

Puppet understands Father Martinez's perspective and agrees. A few minutes later the chapel service begins and is truly moving to each one of the inmates and Father Martinez. A number of guards in attendance are proud of Puppet because of how much he has grown in his faith in Jesus over the last two years. It seems that with each chapel service Puppet has grown friendlier and more joyful.

Please thoughtfully answer the following questions:

1. If you had been in Puppet's position, would have you taken Elliot's suggestion seriously to sneak some of your extra toilet wine down to the chapel for communion?
2. Do you think it was wise of Father Martinez to tell Puppet that using his toilet wine for holy communion was not a good idea in order to avoid Puppet getting in trouble with the guards for sneaking it into the chapel?
3. If you were a guard who was proud of how Puppet had grown in his faith, how might you encourage him to continue to grow in his faith in Jesus?

Should They Continue to Serve as Prison Chaplains?

Gregory and his wife, Jacqueline, serve as chaplains in the most dangerous adult female correctional facility in the country. Before leaving for work they spend about an hour praying to God the Father for safety each day. This ministry has been the most challenging and draining experience of their lives, but they feel strongly that God has put them in this position to show the inmates and guards the love of Jesus Christ.

One frigid November night, alarms ring out and the sound of gunfire echoes in the halls as prisoners take over the facility. Gregory knows that Jacqueline is on the other side of the prison leading a small group Bible study. He rushes into the hall and takes off on a full sprint to his wife. Once in the classroom, he is tackled by several inmates and is forced into the corner with Jacqueline and four guards. They are held in that spot by knife point.

Seconds later a gang leader by the name of Centipede orders five of her members to put one of the guards in the middle of the room and rape him.

The violent sexual assault lasts twenty horrifying minutes. Over the next hour and a half, each guard in the room is raped repeatedly by the six armed inmates. Finally, the sexual violence comes to an end when an armed swat team breaks down the door and fires tear gas into the room and forces the prisoners to the ground by overwhelming force.

An hour later Gregory and Jacqueline start to recover from the effects of the tear gas and struggle to process the horrifying scenes of gang rape they witnessed. The two chaplains finish their police statement and both tell the officer they are thankful to have not been raped and that they will be praying for the guards who were assaulted. The officer interviewing Gregory and Jacqueline says, "You were both lucky. The gang was planning on raping you two last. Had the swat team been a little later you two would have been gang raped. God was watching out for you for sure."

Over the next month Gregory and Jacqueline take a leave of absence to receive psychological care as they deal with the trauma that they have experienced. During this time, they discuss whether or not they want to continue serving at the same facility as prison chaplains or possibly stop serving as prison chaplains altogether. In addition, they also seek out the wise counsel of their family, friends, and church family, and of course spend a great deal of time in prayer to God the Father asking for his guidance.

Please thoughtfully answer the following questions:

1. If you were Gregory and Jacqueline's pastor, would you advise them to start serving at a new prison or to possibly stop serving as prison chaplains altogether after their traumatic experience?
2. What Christ-centered words of comfort and compassion would you speak to Gregory and Jacqueline if you were their pastor?
3. As you reflect upon this tragic event, are there any passages from the Bible you are reminded of?
4. If you were Gregory and Jacqueline's pastor, would you encourage the couple to receive long-term mental health treatment to help them cope with the trauma that they have experienced?

In Need of Love

Tyler is a foster care kid, and today he has officially aged out of the system on this his eighteenth birthday. He packs a duffle bag full of clothes and toiletries and begins walking on a bike path toward a suburban area that was the closest thing to a stable environment for him as a child. After eleven miles of walking, he approaches the brick ranch-style home where he lived from the age of five to the age of six. It was his home for just over thirteen months with Ms. Wonda and Mr. Jake. They were the closest thing to parents that he can ever remember, yet he has no idea what their last names are.

Tyler knocks on the door and is met by a young woman. He asks for Wonda and Jake and she tells him that she has no idea who Wonda and Jake are. Tyler tells her that he used to live in the house when he was little and that he would love to see his old bedroom. The young woman responds, "I wouldn't feel comfortable with that. Sorry." She then slowly closes the door and locks it.

With only a few dollars in cash and nowhere to sleep for the evening, Tyler begins to make his way to the main street. Eventually he spots an outlet toy store and decides to go in to look at the newest video games. Once inside he sees a large candy section at the entranceway and throughout the store there is nearly every type of toy imaginable. As he hears announcements over the loudspeaker that the store will be closing in fifteen minutes, Tyler starts to slightly panic, as he is afraid to sleep out on the street.

Tyler quickly walks into the storage area and hides behind some large boxes. About forty-five minutes later he hears employees saying good night and locking up the store. Tyler comes out of the storage area and begins exploring. He helps himself to a wide variety of candy and begins playing with innumerable toys and video games. Tyler has only a few memories of ever visiting a toy store and being gifted with a toy or candy as a child. Yet now on his eighteenth birthday, as he is officially an adult, nearly every type of toy and candy imaginable is at his fingertips.

After a night of indulging the depths of his childlike imagination while playing with toys and feasting on a small mountain of candy, Tyler does his best to clean up the mess and any traces of his personal party. He then grabs some superhero bedsheets and pillows and crawls into a small cubby hole in the back of the storage facility. He sleeps almost the entire day, and then at night plays with toys, rides bikes around the store, plays new video games, eats some baby food for nourishment, and steals a little cash from a register. He then cleans up after himself and retreats back to his cubby hole apartment for the day. Tyler repeats this process for nearly a month.

One afternoon, Tyler awakes to see two police officers and several store employees standing at the foot of his cubby hole with shocked and completely serious looks on their faces. The older officer says to him, "Son, you need to get up and come with me." Tyler cooperates and he is handcuffed and taken down to the police station, where the owner of the outlet toy store presses the following charges: two counts of criminal trespassing, felony theft from a cash register, shoplifting merchandise, menacing, and harassment. If convicted on each charge, he could face up to a combined total of twenty years in state prison.

Tyler stands before the judge in court the next day. His court-appointed attorney advises him beforehand he should plead guilty to each charge, and as a result, the judge might have mercy on him for taking responsibility for his actions. Tyler follows his lawyer's advice and the judge instead decides to make an example of him, sentencing him to the entire twenty years in prison. He is quickly transported to an old Gothic-style stone prison where he is housed in general population with some of the most violent inmates in the state.

A few days after arriving, Tyler is given the opportunity to meet with a prison chaplain named Pastor Yoshi. Tyler is lonely and frightened so he happily accepts the opportunity. He tells Pastor Yoshi essentially his entire life story. How he has no memory or idea of who his biological parents are. His journey through the foster care system, which placed him in fourteen homes throughout the course of his young life, and how Ms. Wonda and Mr. Jake were the closest things to parents he ever experienced, yet he knows so little about them, including their last names. And of course, his month-long stay in the toy store and eventual arrest and incarceration.

Please thoughtfully answer the following questions:

1. If you were Pastor Yoshi, what words of comfort would you speak to Tyler?
2. Are there any comforting words specifically from Jesus in the Gospels that come to your mind that might be good for Tyler to hear?
3. In your opinion how should Pastor Yoshi encourage Tyler and pray for him as Tyler adjusts to life in prison?

A Dream of Space

Kenzie dreams of taking a commercial flight into outer space. However, she is currently serving a five-year sentence in federal prison for identity theft. She is looking past her present circumstances and is letting her fellow prisoners and the guards know that one day she will be orbiting the earth in luxury aboard a first-class commercial flight into outer space.

After three years and six months in prison, Kenzie is granted parole. She quickly moves back in with her mother, Peg, and lands a job at a fast-food restaurant only one mile from the prison. Every extra cent she earns is put into a special savings account that is set aside for her flight into outer space. After a year of living like a pauper, it soon becomes clear to Kenzie that, with her current salary at the fast-food restaurant, she will not be able to save enough to visit outer space.

Kenzie decides to contact her friend, Father Baker, the man who served as her chaplain in prison. She sits down for a milkshake with Father Baker and seeks his wise counsel. Kenzie says in an optimistic, youthful tone, "Well, I have this dilemma, Father Baker. I'm saving up to take a first-class flight into outer space, but my job at the restaurant doesn't pay enough to save up the money that I need for the trip. I basically have three options. One, I could search for a better job that would pay more, but with my record I doubt any good companies would hire me. My second option is I can start an online fundraiser to raise the money. The third option is I could work with my brother and his friend to build my own rocket ship to fly into outer space. Well, and there is a fourth option, I could go back to stealing identities to get the money, but I think Jesus probably doesn't want me to do that. Right, Father Baker? What do you think is my best option, Father Baker?"

Please thoughtfully answer the following questions:

1. If you were in Father Baker's position, what advice would you give Kenzie once you learned of her predicament?
2. What are some concrete ways Father Baker can encourage Kenzie to follow Jesus in her daily life?
3. Is there a person or persons mentioned in the Bible that remind you of Kenzie?

The Terror of Bentley

Bentley has been housed in solitary confinement for the last two weeks of his life. He was transferred out of the general population after he and several members of his crew were involved in a brutal fight with a rival gang in the yard. Bentley has a high level of expertise in martial arts, so he escaped the battle with only minor cuts and bruises. Unfortunately, however, several members of his crew died from their injuries.

Bentley has treasured his time alone in his cell because it has given him an opportunity to plan his revenge on the rival gang that took two of his soldiers. One of the guards that stands watch outside of Bentley's door is a young man named Spencer. He has noticed the hardened inmate plotting and stewing for the last two weeks. This frankly terrifies Spencer as he knows Bentley's reputation and, from time to time, he awakes in the middle of the night suffering from night terrors about Bentley.

Spencer decides to seek out the spiritual advice of the pastor who confirmed him ten years earlier, Pastor Clayton. The two men sit in the sanctuary on what happens to be a day off for both of them. They briefly catch up over small talk, and then Spencer says, "Pastor Clayton, I know I haven't been to church in a long time, but I need your advice. I sometimes guard the door of an inmate who is hardcore. He has a lot of power and most of the inmates and guards are terrified of him."

Pastor Clayton interjects, "Are you terrified of this inmate, Spencer?" Without hesitation Spencer responds, "Absolutely! You would be too if you were anywhere near him! Just looking at him freaks most people out. He's a straight up psychopathic nightmare! And I'm almost certain he is planning the death of four inmates of a rival gang that killed two soldiers of his gang in a yard brawl a few weeks ago. I've seen him sliding messages under his cell door to people who work for him. I can almost guarantee he is planning murders. If I say anything to my supervisor and Bentley finds out then he could easily have me murdered. But if I say nothing to warn my supervisor or the warden then I could have at least four inmates' blood on my hands, and that scares me because I don't want to have to answer to Jesus for that on the last day. I don't want to go to hell for not saying something, but I also don't want to get murdered for saying something. Do you have any advice on what I should do, Pastor Clayton?"

Please thoughtfully answer the following questions:

1. If you were Pastor Clayton, what words of advice might you offer to Spencer as he contemplates what to do in this difficult situation?
2. Can you think of any biblical or extrabiblical resources that might be helpful to Spencer during this time?
3. What would you ask from Jesus in prayer on Spencer's behalf if you were Pastor Clayton?

Fasting as a Protest

Vimla is preparing to embark on a fifteen-day fast in the privacy of his cell to protest the sexual abuse many of his fellow prisoners are subject to on a daily basis. The prison warden has threatened Vimla with force feedings if he refuses meals. Nonetheless these threats have only strengthened the old teacher's resolve.

Five days into his much-publicized fast, Vimla savors a glass of ice-cold water as journalists flood the warden's office with requests to interview the teacher, who is admired around the world. In a moment of desperation, the warden phones the most senior prison chaplain, Pastor George Wyandot, and requests he speaks with Vimla and try to convince him to end his fast. Pastor Wyandot agrees to meet with Vimla and listen to what is troubling the teacher. The seasoned prison chaplain also agrees to express how concerned the warden is about Vimla's physical well-being during this fast when an opportunity arises in their conversation.

After a captivating three-hour meeting with Vimla, Pastor Wyandot leaves the cell declaring that he is joining the great teacher in his fast to protest the sexual abuse that prisoners are subject to in the prison. The normally deferential Pastor Wyandot goes straight to the warden's office with a fire in his eyes. He demands that he immediately address the sexual abuse taking place in the prison or there will be hundreds of prisoners, and people outside of the prison, fasting in protest. The pastor says in closing to the warden, "May you listen to the truth. In the name of Jesus Christ. Amen."

The warden, who is normally brash and filled with confidence, is frightened to his core by Pastor Wyandot's appearance and his words. The shocked warden gives his word he will launch a thorough investigation into the claims by Vimla of sexual abuse against prisoners inside of the federal penitentiary.

Please thoughtfully answer the following questions:

1. What is your impression of Vimla?
2. What is your opinion of the fact Pastor Wyandot decided to join Vimla on his fast to protest the sexual abuse being perpetrated against many of the prisoners?
3. After Pastor Wyandot left Vimla's cell, what stuck out to you about his meeting with the prison warden?
4. Are there any stories from the Bible that remind you of this case study?

A Missing Person

Deon has spent the last two years in prison and is yet to be charged with a crime or speak with an attorney. In fact, none of his family members or friends have any idea where Deon is. Many people believe he was murdered or he possibly moved out of state to start a new life.

One hot July morning, Bishop Xavier Jefferson is having lunch with an inmate in the cafeteria of a county jail when he sees a familiar face—a face he has seen on missing person flyers posted all over the county. It's Deon Williams, the young man whose parents spoke at the bishop's church last year asking for prayers and help passing out flyers for their missing young adult son.

The bishop excuses himself and approaches the young man, who has aged badly in the two years since he went missing. The bishop says, "Hello, I'm the bishop, Xavier Jefferson. I'm a pastor and I'm friends with your parents. They are searching for you, Deon."

Deon quickly responds, "Thank God! You've got to help me, Pastor Jefferson! I was pulled over when driving to my friend's house to play video games on the white end of town. The officer pulled me over and told me to step out of the vehicle. He said he smelled marijuana on me, which, it's true, I smoked a bowl about an hour earlier, but that was it. I swear! He cuffed me and took me here to jail. They said they were going to let me have a phone call, and speak with a lawyer, and charge me so that I would have a chance to go to trial, but none of that's happened yet. All that I do every day is build furniture. I haven't been paid a dime for my work. I think I'm being treated this way because I'm black. I really don't think the jail would treat a white person so cruelly. You have to help me! Please tell my parents that I'm alive! And please pray to Jesus that he will rescue me from this place!"

Please thoughtfully answer the following questions:

1. If you were in the same position as Bishop Xavier Jefferson, how would you respond to Deon Williams's plea for your help?

2. Are there any stories from the Bible that remind you of this story?

3. How would you specifically pray to Jesus on behalf of Deon if you were Bishop Xavier Jefferson?

Chapter 9

Raising Children

Uncle Judas

BETH IS AN OPTIMISTIC sophomore in college who is thrilled to be serving as activity coordinator of her dormitory. She often speaks about her single relative, Uncle Judas, who raised her after her parents died in a tragic car crash. The majority of the ladies in Beth's dorm are intrigued to hear stories about the famous Uncle Judas—his upbringing in one of the oldest cities in the world, his accomplishments as a businessman, chef, painter, musician, linguist, actor, comedian, and a devoted uncle to his late younger sister's daughter.

To the delight of the campus community and most of Beth's dormitory, the news is delivered that Uncle Judas will be visiting the faculty, staff, and students during the second semester. The entire campus is abuzz with conversation and excitement leading up to his arrival. Finally, the long-anticipated evening has arrived and Manor Hall is overflowing with onlookers and press. Suddenly Uncle Judas slides onto the stage and tosses his top hat into the crowd and gives the audience an introductory bow.

Almost immediately several young ladies try to rush the stage while screaming hysterically. They are held back by security, and Uncle Judas begins his concert, which lasts for over two hours. After the show, the president of the university invites several faculty members, along with Beth and Uncle Judas, to his home for a late-night dinner.

University President, Dr. Reverend Allan Fermann, is intrigued to hear about Judas's foundation dedicated to ending world hunger. In fact, Judas has a passion for the poor in general and begins to share about his desire to adopt an impoverished child from every country of the world to raise as a single parent while traveling internationally and performing as a comedian and fulfilling his various business commitments. He says confidently, "I'm planning on purchasing my own fleet of jets so that all my children can travel with me in comfort. I will hire nurses, teachers, chefs, and nannies to accompany me so that the children may have the proper care and opportunities that they deserve. We will travel around two hundred days a year together and explore God's creation."

Please thoughtfully answer the following questions:

1. In your opinion, what issues might arise for Uncle Judas if he were to adopt a child from every country of the world and attempt to raise each child as a single parent?

2. Do you believe it is feasible for Uncle Judas to raise a massive family of children as a single parent while traveling around the world performing as a comedian and taking care of business concerns?

3. What, if any, pastoral advice do you believe would be appropriate for President Dr. Reverend Fermann to offer Uncle Judas concerning his future family plans?

Two Mindys

Mindy volunteers to help with nearly half of the events her church sponsors. She is highly extroverted and seems to always have a smile on her face. Lately, Pastor Elmont has noticed certain members becoming emotional when speaking about Mindy and essentially claiming they do not believe the church could survive without her, and a few people are going as far as to say that they are not sure if they would personally survive without Mindy. These types of comments are concerning to Pastor Elmont as well as to several elders and church council members.

One Wednesday afternoon while eating lunch in her office with her husband, Tommy, and daughter, Violet, there is a faint knock on the door. It's Layla, the congregation's recently retired custodian. She tells Pastor Elmont that she is noticing a large number of members are starting to speak of Mindy as an absolute authority on raising children and theology. This development became most apparent to Layla when she was correcting her granddaughter with a stern, slightly raised voice, and a fellow parishioner and close friend by the name of Catherine stopped her in the act and said, "You know Mindy would never speak to her children or grandchildren that way. She would sit them on her lap and gently explain the situation to them. You should start attending her Bible study. Her parenting skills and reading of Scripture are second to none."

One week later, Pastor Elmont receives a late-night call from Sheriff Adler requesting a chaplain at a crime scene. Pastor Elmont agrees and a few moments later is texted the address from Sheriff Adler. What pops up on the screen is disturbing to the veteran pastor. It's the address of her highly respected parishioner Mindy. She hurries to her home and sees crime scene tape wrapped around the property, two ambulances on site, a dozen law enforcement vehicles, and a coroner's truck near the entrance.

Sheriff Adler informs Pastor Elmont that Mindy has been taken into custody on suspicion of murder of her husband Richmond, but he offers Pastor Elmont the opportunity to speak with her parishioner for a few moments if she would like to. Pastor Elmont agrees only if Mindy would like to speak with her.

A few moments later, there is a brief conversation in the back of a police cruiser. Pastor Elmont starts off by saying, "Mindy, anything that you tell me is confidential, but I don't know if this vehicle has cameras in it or not, so you should be aware of that." Mindy responds while shaking, "I know, Pastor. I'm going to tell you what I'm going to tell my lawyer, the detectives, and the whole congregation. It was self-defense. Richmond has had a serious problem with alcohol for decades. It's been a secret, and I would have reached out for help but I didn't know how to. I know that I always look so put together at church, but at home my life is messed up. I basically have been living two separate lives for years. If I hadn't shot Richmond tonight, he would have killed me and the kids. No doubt! No doubt at all!"

That night as national media descends on the sleepy bedroom community, Mindy and Richmond's three children are put into the care of their Aunt Zella. The next morning, shortly after Mindy was charged with first degree murder, her sister Zella phones Pastor Elmont and poses two questions to her: "Where should I tell my two nephews and my niece where their father is? And secondly, where should I tell them their mother is?"

Please thoughtfully answer the following questions?

1. If you were Pastor Elmont, what advice would you give Zella concerning what to tell her two nephews and niece about where their father is and where their mother is?

2. In your opinion, should Pastor Elmont make any type of announcement to the congregation concerning the tragic death of Richmond and/or the charges that have been brought against Mindy?

3. Do you think it would be wise for Pastor Elmont and her parishioners to avoid watching media coverage of the murder trial?

4. If you were visiting with Mindy in prison, what pastoral words of comfort might you offer her during this difficult time?

5. If you were visiting with the children of Mindy and Richmond, what words of comfort might you offer them as they mourn the loss of their father and miss their mother?

Coach Alexiou

Pastor Alexiou is the head coach of a local high school football team. His group is young, inexperienced, and undersized. Thankfully though, they are an athletic and intelligent group that is coachable, with good attitudes. The conference that Coach Alexiou's team competes in is composed of ten schools that all have traditionally run a ground and pound style offense that relies heavily on a strong physical defense.

However, Coach Alexiou and his assistants believe strongly in coaching to their team's strengths and working with the players they have as opposed to the players they would like to have. Therefore, the decision was made before the start of the season that the best bet for success on the field would be to run primarily a five wide style offense, one that allows the quarterback to throw the ball quickly to his fast wide receivers and requires his undersized offensive line to stay on their blocks for only two or three seconds on average.

Midway through the season this strategy has worked relatively well as his team is three and two heading into their homecoming game with their cross-town rival. Unfortunately, many in the community are not happy about the new style of offense the first-year head coach has implemented, even though the team is vastly improved from the season before and has already won two more games than they did the entire last season. Coach Alexiou and his whole staff and team are determined to stay focused on their opponent for the week, and to continue to encourage one another with positivity.

Late in the third quarter, Coach Alexiou's team is down fourteen to zero on homecoming night. The passing game has not worked all game, and the only play that has gone over twenty yards was a quarterback scramble. Now their rival has the ball and is five yards away from scoring another touchdown. Surprisingly a bad snap leads to a turnover, and Coach Alexiou sends his determined offense back onto the field.

The first pass is dropped by the wide out and the second pass only goes for two yards. As coach calls the next play, he hears a man who is distantly related to one of his players yell from behind the bench, "Run the gosh darn ball! Run the gosh darn ball! Enough of the cute little screens and slants! Get back to the basics! We are a traditional run first program! That's how we won state my junior year!" Suddenly another fan yells, "Old Coach Hancock must be rolling over in his grave to know that his state championship program is being turned into a pass happy bunch of dandies! I feel sorry for these boys that they have to be coached by somebody like you, Coach Alexiou!"

The play is called. It's a double reverse pass. A forty-yard bomb is caught by a foreign exchange student named Chen who only learned about American style football for the first time five weeks earlier. After making the catch Chen, runs another fifty-three yards to the endzone for a touchdown! Coach Alexiou and his whole team erupt as they swarm Chen with hugs and congratulatory high fives. Sadly, several disgruntled adults in the crowd yell xenophobic comments like "Now the hero of our team is a little foreigner who doesn't even know what football is! Yeah, Coach Hancock is definitely rolling over in his grave tonight!"

The final score of the game is twenty-one to ten, and Coach Alexiou is tremendously proud of his players and staff after this loss. They competed with one of the best teams in the state the entire night. Sadly, as the team walks into their locker room, the distant relative of a player who was yelling at Coach Alexiou earlier in the night charges at the first-year coach, screaming, "I'm going to teach you that we need to run the ball at this school! I'll teach you the hard way, Alexiou!"

Right before the disgruntled fan can land a punch, one of Coach Alexiou's assistant coaches' uncle knocks the fan out. This uncle who landed the punch did so while holding his eighteen-month-old grandson. Quickly a sheriff's deputy who is working security and crowd control rushes over and starts to investigate the scene.

Once inside the locker room, Coach Alexiou addresses his team and staff and tells them how proud he is of their good sportsmanship, hard work, and perseverance. He encourages the team to stay positive and allow the loss to be a learning experience. Lastly, Coach Alexiou apologizes that the players had to hear negative and downright xenophobic comments from certain fans during the game, and he also apologizes that they had to witness the violent confrontation between the disgruntled fan and the uncle of the assistant coach. The whole team and staff understands and tells Coach Alexiou they are fine and are already looking forward to the next game.

Please thoughtfully answer the following questions:

1. What is your impression of Pastor Alexiou's coaching philosophy and style toward his staff and players?
2. If you were a parent, would you want your child to play for a coach like Pastor Alexiou?
3. What is your opinion of the behavior of the uncle of the assistant coach who held his eighteen-month-old grandson while protecting Coach Alexiou?
4. What is your reaction to Coach Alexiou's post-game speech to his players and staff following a tough loss to their rival?
5. Are there any words from Jesus, specifically in the Gospels or Bible passages in general, which you think might be of comfort to Coach Alexiou following the loss and the harassment from certain fans?

Should Anything Be Said to Ms. Emily?

Tutz Rhine is a five-year-old with moxie. Her mother, Lacey, describes Tutz as "an adorable princess scamp! She's a feisty blonde just like her mother, and her mother before her. It runs in the family!" The majority of Tutz's teachers and classmates find her antics hilarious. Whether it be teasing a teacher about kissing her fiancé when he delivers lunch or throwing a water balloon at the head of a custodian from the top of a jungle gym, her antics bring a lot of laughter to St. Mathew's Church and School.

A normally slow-paced Tuesday afternoon receives a shot of adrenaline when Deputy Paul from the sheriff's department visits the students in the auditorium for a special talk about safety when crossing the street. At the end of the talk, children encircle Deputy Paul for an opportunity to ask him questions about his job. Suddenly Tutz walks up behind Deputy Paul and kicks him in the calf for no apparent reason.

Tutz's teachers are horrified by this behavior, and they insist that Tutz apologize to Deputy Paul. She does and moments later the preschool director, Emily, is informed about what took place by Ms. Josie. Emily shows only slight concern and essentially plays off the entire happening as Tutz acting playful after a long morning. The pastor of St. Matthew, the Reverend Keiko Hersh, is disturbed and concerned about this latest incident involving Tutz. She requests that her parents be informed immediately.

As Pastor Hersh listens from her office to Ms. Emily explain the situation via phone to Tutz's parents, she is disturbed at how minor Ms. Emily is depicting the incident to have been, especially in light of the fact that a five-year-old boy named Scott was suspended for two days less than a week earlier by Ms. Emily for kicking a door.

Pastor Hersh senses that Ms. Emily has a pattern of showing favoritism to female students and staff members, while treating male students and staff members rather coldly. She has tried to give her the benefit of the doubt in her first six months as the pastor of St. Mathew's Church and School, in part because Ms. Emily's family has a lot of influence in the community.

Pastor Hersh sees the church and the school as being closely connected, and in fact, she strongly feels that the school is an extension of the church, and, in reality, the church's most vital ministry. She understands that the entire staff is helping to raise the students of St. Matthew's School, and Pastor Hersh sees that as a massive responsibility that she does not take lightly. She views herself as not only the shepherd of the church, but of the school as well, and to some degree, as a de facto school superintendent.

For the remainder of the day Pastor Hersh ponders how she should address the favoritism that she believes Emily is showing toward the female students and staff at St. Matthews, and the cold and at times harsh attitude she seems to show the male students and staff. Eventually Pastor Hersh decides to phone her circuit visitor, Pastor Cam, to get her advice on the situation.

Please thoughtfully answer the following questions:

1. Based on what you have read, what is your opinion of Emily's performance as a preschool director?
2. In your opinion, do you believe Pastor Hersh is overreacting?
3. If you were Circuit Visitor Pastor Cam, what advice might you give Pastor Hersh?
4. Are there any words of Jesus in the Bible that come to your mind that might be good for Pastor Hersh and Emily to reflect upon together?

A Wide Variety of Youth

Pastor Cam and Heather, the director of Christian education of St. James, are preparing to drive twenty youth group members six hundred miles south on the church bus to the National Youth Conference. The ages and maturity levels of these young people vary drastically. There are four people as young as thirteen on the trip and three students as old as nineteen.

After checking into their hotel, the group arrives at the conference and are welcomed by hundreds of young adult volunteers. The first five days are packed with a community service project, where several of the youth from St. James build a large gazebo in a public park under the direction and supervision of a structural engineer.

Lunch is at an excellent barbecue, Mexican, or pizza place each day, and every night nearly twenty thousand youth and approximately seven thousand adult volunteers flood into the professional sports stadium and hear from inspired speakers on a wide range of topics from "Standing Up against Bullying in the Name of Jesus" to "Considering a Calling from God to be a Church Worker." Each night they are then led in worship by a famous Christian rock group or rapper.

On the fifth night of the conference, all twenty-seven thousand people celebrate the Lord's Supper together and receive the body and blood of Jesus Christ for the forgiveness of their sins. After the service, Pastor Cam and Heather have a concluding late-night pizza and conference wrap-up party in their hotel dining hall.

Ronnie shares about how he met a student from the other side of the country who is also saving up to buy a dirt bike for his fourteenth birthday. Cindy shares about how nervous she is to enter her freshman year of high school. Yet thankfully, she was comforted to hear CC, the keynote speaker on night three, share how scared she had been to enter high school at the same age. "It feels good to know that other people can relate to the same fears and anxieties that I have," Cindy explains.

Nineteen-year-old Stacey shares how she recently started dating a graduate student named Kyle. They met while she was taking a class at the local university during her senior year of high school. She was eighteen and he was twenty-four at that time. Now that she has turned nineteen and is working a part-time job while in college full time, Kyle would like her to move into his apartment. Stacey concludes by saying, "And we might start trying for a baby during my senior year of college. That way the baby will be due around the time that I graduate. It's really important to Kyle that we have a baby in the next few years. I hope my parents are okay with it. They actually haven't met Kyle yet."

Please thoughtfully answer the following questions:

1. If you were Pastor Cam and Heather, how would you respond to what Stacey shared with you, and the St. James youth group that varies drastically in age and maturity levels?

2. What might be a way Pastor Cam and Heather can emphasize the beauty and sanctity of marriage to their youth group with positivity and encouragement?

3. Are there any Christ-centered passages in the New Testament that would be good for Pastor Cam or Heather to read to the St. James youth group at the end of the conference wrap-up party?

Confirmation Sunday and After

Pastor Henderson has a confirmation class of ten eighth graders, and only one of his students has parents who attend worship on a regular basis. However, all of the students' parents want Palm Sunday to be a perfect confirmation Sunday. Each eighth grader has their own page in the bulletin complete with their baptismal verse, confirmation verse and testimony, where they completed their service project, and a professional headshot photo.

After the confirmation service, each student spends almost an hour taking photos with family members, friends, Pastor Henderson, the school principal, Mr. Bach, and finally a serious group photo and a silly group photo of the ten confirmands. Naturally, each family has rented their own private event center to celebrate their child's special day, complete with food from a catering service and of course, many fine gifts.

Five years later, Pastor Henderson sits down with the newly hired director of Christian outreach, Skyla, and begins looking through the directory with her to help familiarize her with each family in their congregation. When Pastor Henderson starts to specifically search for youth between the ages of eighteen to thirty years old, he is in shock at how many of these people have not been to worship in at least four to five years.

The veteran pastor is a little bit embarrassed by this and says to Skyla, "A big part of your job, and what needs to become a bigger part of my job, is to meet people in our community where they are and build relationships with them. We no longer live in a time when most people feel a responsibility or a need to attend worship or look for a church when they move into a new community.

"Sadly, the story here at this particular Lutheran congregation has been that the majority of parents place paramount importance on getting their children baptized and confirmed, but then we never see them again . . . except for maybe if they need a place to get married that is aesthetically pleasing and has good acoustics. That's the sad truth. The parents are dropping the ball big time, and I have done a horrible job of holding them accountable."

Please thoughtfully answer the following questions:

1. What is your opinion of what Pastor Henderson shared with Skyla about the parents of their congregation not making worship a priority for their children once confirmation Sunday is complete?

2. How might Pastor Henderson do a better job of encouraging confirmation students and their parents to not treat confirmation Sunday like a graduation celebration from worship and essentially all church gatherings?

3. If you were in Skyla's position as the new director of Christian outreach, how would you work with Pastor Henderson to encourage the confirmands and their parents to continue following Jesus long after confirmation Sunday is over?

4. Are there any passages from the Bible that come to your mind as you reflect on this case study?

Kids Cook Supper Sunday

Director of Christian Education, Darren Alberta, has created a fun event for families called "Kids Cook Supper Sunday." The premise is simple: Let the kids cook a supper for their parents, grandparents, and any adult member who has a big appetite. The menu is completely up to the kids, and Darren is happy to purchase all of the needed grocery items to make this the most delicious supper St. Thomas Lutheran Church has ever experienced.

At five forty-five in the evening, a mere two weeks prior to Christmas day, dinner is served! Marshmallow pancakes drenched in chocolate syrup, cinnamon cereal in bowls of highly caffeinated soda, French toast stuffed inside of hot dog buns with butter and maple syrup, and a side of classic potato chips. All washed down with ice cold glasses of chocolate milk. Eight-year-old Nathan Kellerman leads everyone in a blessing of the food. This meal is a hit! The adult members of St. Thomas Lutheran Church laud this meal as a sugary feast, and a new annual tradition is born at the church every second Sunday in December.

At the conclusion of the candlelight Christmas Eve service, Mr. and Mrs. Kellerman approach Rev. Lopez and let him know that their twin boys, Nathan and Ethan, now expect to be allowed to prepare a sugary supper every Sunday. And they encourage Rev. Lopez to consider ending the new annual tradition of Kids Cook Supper Sunday. Rev. Lopez carefully listens and tells Mr. and Mrs. Kellerman that he will take their suggestion into consideration.

However, after some more thought Rev. Lopez believes there is no harm in continuing the new tradition, as it was so well received by the congregation. He feels that Nathan and Ethan simply need to be given clear boundaries by their parents on what they can and cannot eat. He believes that the Kellerman's must drive home the idea to their eight-year-old twins that a sugary supper is a once-a-year treat.

A month later, Rev. Lopez and Darren Alberta receive an email from their bishop that reads, "Hey brothers, just wanted to give you both a heads up that I've been getting phone calls from some of your parishioners complaining that your Kids Cook Supper Sunday is giving the children in the congregation unhealthy nutritional expectations and habits. Please give me a video call to discuss this further at your earliest possible convenience. Thank you and Lord bless, Bishop Lincoln."

Please thoughtfully answer the following questions:

1. What is your opinion of Kids Cook Supper Sunday?
2. If you were Rev. Lopez and Darren Alberta, would you stand firm in your support of Kids Cook Supper Sunday?
3. Are there any words from Jesus in the Gospels that come to your mind as you reflect on this case study?
4. Do you believe Mr. and Mrs. Kellerman and possibly others are right to be concerned Kids Cook Supper Sunday may give children unhealthy nutritional expectations and habits?

Dealing with a Toxic Situation

Elly Birdie has two daughters who are currently on the run from law enforcement, yet she feels qualified to lecture fellow members of her church and the school board on how to raise their own children. Her husband, Trevor, has recently discovered that Elly was married five times before they met and never disclosed this to him while they were dating or going through premarital counseling with Pastor Skip.

Every Wednesday night at six o'clock, Elly holds proper manners and housekeeping workshops in her sister-in-law's living room. Ten elderly women and one young lady who has recently started college arrive early and drink a cup of Elly's famous jasmine tea. At least one lady in the group feels that she has been coerced by Elly into attending the workshops under the threat of false rumors being spread about her first marriage.

The lady who feels coerced into attending has brought her concerns to Pastor Skip in private and said, "Elly frightens me. She is manipulative and highly influential in our community. Several other ladies in the proper manners and housekeeping workshops feel the same way that I do, but they are terrified to say anything. She makes people tell her their secrets and then she tries to destroy anyone that crosses her. Will you please do something about Elly's horrible toxic behavior, Pastor Skip?"

Please thoughtfully answer the following questions:

1. From what you have read, what is your impression of Elly Birdie?
2. What is your opinion of what was shared with Pastor Skip by the lady who feels coerced by Elly?
3. If you were in Pastor Skip's position, how would you respond to the request to deal with Elly's horrible toxic behavior?
4. If Pastor Skip reached out to you for advice on how to deal with this situation, what would you say?
5. Are there any words from Jesus in the Gospels that come to your mind as you reflect on this case study?

A New Beginning

For five years Knoxy has attempted to support his wife and three children on winning lottery tickets. He currently is drowning in debt and feels as if he has nowhere to turn. Knoxy has contemplated suicide and bravely has turned to his family and friends for help, who have recommended that he check himself into a hospital for care. Knoxy courageously follows their advice.

One afternoon while lying in a hospital bed and watching a gardening show on television, Knoxy decides to start a restaurant that grows its own ingredients in a local garden. One year later his business is thriving, as he trains his three children in the art of organic gardening and shares with them the secrets of hospitality and smart business practices.

Knoxy has given up gambling with the help of God and is slowly paying off his debts. His children and wife, Pam, are all tremendously proud of Knoxy's transformation. While giving an interview to a local foodie magazine, Knoxy says, "I want to thank Jesus for blessing me with such a wonderful and supportive family! It's an honor to care for them and set a good example for my three beautiful children. Also, my pastor, Pastor Alexiou, deserves a lot of credit for encouraging me, praying for me, and always reminding me that I can start new each day in Jesus' unlimited grace and forgiveness. Glory be to Jesus Christ!"

Please thoughtfully answer the following questions:

1. What is your opinion of what Knoxy shared with the local foodie magazine?
2. If you were Pastor Alexiou, would you encourage Knoxy to spend time with a licensed professional counselor each week?
3. If you were Pastor Alexiou, how would you encourage Knoxy to continue living a life that is centered on Jesus, as he faithfully lives out his calling as a husband and a father?
4. Is there a specific book of the Bible you would recommend to Knoxy to study on a regular basis?

Edith Is a Great Parent

Edith has done her best to raise her four grandsons as a single parent. The sixty-one-year-old's meager salary with basic health benefits does not allow her and the boys many luxuries. Occasionally Edith's boss, Mr. Saulsberry, goes out of his way to promise her the opportunity to interview for a promotion or earn a raise in the near future. However, those opportunities never arise.

Ten years later, all of Edith's grandsons are successful in their careers and personal lives and, most importantly, they still love Jesus. One evening while watching and listening to her oldest grandson, Damien, conduct a world class orchestra in the playing of Handel's *Messiah*, Edith is moved to tears at God's mercy on her and her grandsons that she loves as dearly as her own children.

This night is made all the more remarkable when she runs into her pastor, Rev. Lopez, during intermission, who says to her, "Edith, I know that sometimes people in the community may have looked down on you for being a single mother, but I want to congratulate you on the fantastic job that you did raising these young men. You encouraged your daughter-in-law to not have an abortion and, in each case, you stepped up and raised the child. I applaud and congratulate you. You are a true spiritual daughter of the blessed Virgin Mary."

1. What is your impression of Edith?

2. What do you think of Rev. Lopez's words of encouragement to Edith during intermission?

3. Does this case study remind you of any stories from the Bible?

Chapter 10

Rural and Small-Town Ministry

Julian's New Home

JULIAN WAS BORN AND raised in one of the largest cities in the world. He enjoyed a privileged upbringing with all the benefits of a top-tier private education and access to world-class museums, parks, restaurants, and medical care. His family's penthouse had views of the city's harbor, and nearly every week in the summer Julian's parents took him sailing in that harbor. He is eternally grateful his parents worked incredibly hard, yet kept family time a priority over their career ambitions. Most importantly of all, Julian's parents raised him to know that he is a baptized child of God who is loved unconditionally by Jesus Christ.

During his junior year of college, he began seriously considering attending seminary to become a pastor. His campus pastor encouraged him to visit the seminary that he attended. Julian did just that, and after a great deal of prayer and consideration, he applied to his pastor's alma mater and was accepted. His parents were proud of him but still would have been had he gone to medical school, law school, tried his hand at acting, or decided to pursue almost any other field of interest.

The first two years of seminary were filled with a substantial amount of work in the classroom, along with residential field work at a local congregation, an institutional module, and a cross cultural module. For Julian it was a busy twenty-four months of studies, making some great friends with classmates, and preparing for his internship/vicarage. When speaking with the seminary's vicarage placement director, Julian requests he be placed at a rural congregation. He wants to experience life and ministry in a setting profoundly different than anything he has experienced up to that point in his life.

Julian gets his wish, and for his vicarage year he is placed at Old Prairie Church. One hot July afternoon, he loads up his car and drives over one thousand miles to begin his internship. As he approaches the church and sees an old brick home next door, it occurs to him that this is the first house he has seen in the last ten minutes. As he pulls into the church's stone parking lot, he begins to stretch his legs as he studies the simplistic v-shaped wooden structure of the church. The building appears to be on the edge of disrepair with a roof, windows, and some siding that need replaced.

Suddenly, a shrill voice calls out from the direction of the old brick house, saying, "Hello, Julian! I'm Pastor Karl Lentner. I'm your vicarage supervisor. How was your trip?" Julian quickly answers the elderly man while firmly shaking his hand and says, "Oh, it was good. It went by quickly. I stopped halfway and spent the night at a motel. It's a pleasure to meet you." Pastor Lentner then picks up one of Julian's bags and says, "Alright, let me take you to your room in the parsonage."

The elderly man struggles to carry the fifty-pound bag as he leads Julian to the front door of the brick house. An old screen door is propped open, and a weathered wooden main door is pushed forward revealing a house that appears to have had almost nothing updated in the last fifty years. As Pastor Lentner leads Julian up the narrow staircase to the second floor he says with pride, "The church celebrated its one hundred and fiftieth anniversary last year. This house was built five years after that. So, she looks pretty good for being about one hundred and forty-six years old. Wouldn't you agree?" Julian nervously laughs and answers, "Yeah, she looks great for a hundred and forty-six." The old pastor is delighted with his vicar's response and says, "If you're impressed now wait till you see the view from your room."

They enter a nearly bare room with a ten-foot-high ceiling and wallpaper from Julian's grandparents' generation. It has two large windows looking out at the church and a cow pasture in the distance. "Well, this is it!" says Pastor Lentner with a smile. "This view never gets old. I hope you find the bed comfortable. The dresser isn't much but you will have room for the new leather couch we ordered you. My room is down the hall on the left. And the restroom is downstairs next to the kitchen. Oh, before I forget, let me grab you a fan."

That evening as coyotes howl in the distance, the entire church gathers outside of the parsonage for an old-fashioned ox roast to welcome Vicar Julian. Gunner Thompson plays his guitar by the campfire and leads people in classics like "Amazing Grace" and "Go, My Children, with My Blessing."

Just before midnight, Julian decides to retire to bed. He says good night to the thirty parishioners that are still enjoying the festivities.

As the new vicar drifts off to sleep and enjoys a cool breeze rushing through his open bedroom windows, out of nowhere he hears rifle blasts. He hops out of bed and sees from the window Gunner Thompson dancing around while firing a rifle in the air yelling, "I'm just an old jack rabbit! I can't help myself tonight!"

At this point, a large F-350 truck with massive tires pulls up beside Gunner and his crew. They jump in the truck bed, and the monstrous vehicle begins to do donuts while Gunner continues to fire his riffle into the air. After about three minutes, the truck peels off onto the road and disappears into the night. The last few partygoers warm themselves beside a dying fire and comment to one another, "The boys sure do have an ornery side to them," and "I'm glad that they still know how to have a good time after all of these years. Don't ever change, boys."

The next morning Julian awakes to the sound of a wild rooster crowing in the yard at the break of dawn. Thankfully he manages to get back to sleep for several more hours before breakfast. As they enjoy a remarkably good cup of coffee, Julian makes a point of mentioning to Pastor Lentner the theatrics of Gunner and his crew late last night. Pastor Lentner responds, "Yeah, I was impressed by their passion! They bring a lot of joy to every celebration. Listen, Trinity is a congregation about forty miles to the north of here. They've been without a pastor for about a year, so they have asked me to be their vacancy pastor. I agreed now that I have a vicar to help out around here. You'll be preaching up there at Trinity every week in the winter. Sorry I didn't tell you sooner. I think you'll love it."

It is an understatement to say that Julian is in a state of shock at how his first two days of vicarage have gone. Yet he is optimistic that as he gets to know the congregation better, he will feel more comfortable and confident about his vicarage year moving forward. His optimism is reinforced by an encouraging phone conversation with his campus pastor, who says, "There is no such thing as a typical vicarage year. Every experience is unique. Just keep your eyes focused on Jesus as you faithfully serve God's people at Old Prairie Church and Trinity."

Eleven months later Julian is relieved to be less than a month away from the end of his vicarage year. He is borderline exhausted, and for every good experience and relationship that he has enjoyed over the last year it seems that he had at least one experience that was unpleasant. So, it is to Julian's surprise that, one early Saturday morning after he finishes teaching a men's Bible study, Pastor Lentner, Head Elder and Chairman of the Congregation

Frank Thompson, and Circuit Visitor Reverend Ted Hargrove sit down with him and present him with an interesting opportunity.

Head Elder Frank Thompson leads off the conversation. "Vicar Julian, your character, leadership, dependence on Jesus, and ability to roll with the punches over this year has been an inspiration to everyone at Old Prairie and Trinity. You never once complained about having to bunk in the same house with your supervisor, Pastor Lentner, or threw a fit about having to drive through harsh, snowy conditions to preach and lead worship at Trinity every week in the winter. And personally, I'm so grateful for the patience and love you have shown my son Gunner and his whole crew over this year. Before you got here, they hadn't been in worship since confirmation. Now they are here almost every week and hardly ever miss one of your Bible studies! Well, I've said enough. I'll let Pastor Lentner take it from here."

With a real sense of conviction, Pastor Lentner says, "I wholeheartedly agree with everything that Elder Thompson just stated, Julian. You know, I'm no spring chicken. I'll be seventy-four in a few months, and I would like to transition into an emeritus role soon. What I, Circuit Visitor Hargrove, and Elder Thompson would like to ask you is, would you be open to receiving a call to Old Prairie and Trinity and serving as a dual parish pastor after you finish your last year of seminary? Now, don't answer now! Pray about it. Everything seems to just fit. You have great integrity, you're a strong preacher and administrator, you don't mind serving congregations that don't have a lot of members and are rural . . . and we could help you, too."

There is a brief pause and then Circuit Visitor Hargrove adds, "Old Prairie has a large endowment, and they would be willing to build you a brand-new parsonage if you came here as the pastor. Also, the district would pay off any remaining school debt that you still owe. If you're interested, the seminary would have to, of course, approve this call. But I don't see that being a problem. Think about it, Julian. Pray about it and get back with us in the next two months."

Please thoughtfully answer the following questions:

1. Would have you been in a state of shock after your first two days of vicarage had you been in Julian's place?

2. What is your opinion of Julian's campus pastor's encouraging words of "There is no such thing as a typical vicarage year. Every experience is unique. Just keep your eyes focused on Jesus as you faithfully serve God's people at Old Prairie Church and Trinity"?

3. If you were Julian, would you prayerfully consider the interesting opportunity Pastor Lentner, Head Elder and Chairman of the

Congregation Frank Thompson and Circuit Visitor Reverend Ted Hargrove presented?

A Tiny Church

Karl is a non-denominational pastor in a town of just over eight thousand people. He planted a church about five years ago that initially had around twenty members. Today it has grown to almost two hundred members. The church structure is designed to resemble the early church depicted in the book of Acts: there are regular community meals; whenever someone is sick, they are lifted up in prayer; and there is an effort to help the poor.

One Sunday after worship a young couple named Cane and Mary approach Pastor Karl with a unique story. Cane says, "We are so glad to have found this church! Mary and I recently moved into town and have been searching for a church through ads in the newspaper. The place we visited last week had a really compelling write-up in the paper so we thought we would check it out. It was strange because the address was a vacant parking lot on the outskirts of town near an old industrial park. When we got out of the car, we couldn't figure out where the church was supposed to be, then all of a sudden someone calls us over to this old ticket booth, and that was the church. It didn't have any type of sign or anything. We squeezed in and there were two people sitting inside and a middle-aged lady pastor leading worship. So, all together it was the five of us. The sermon wasn't bad, but overall, it was a super weird experience."

Mary then adds, "Yeah, we are not going back there again. I don't understand why the people wouldn't just have a worship service in their house. Why worship on the outskirts of town near an old industrial park in a tiny, unmarked ticket booth? It doesn't make any sense."

Please thoughtfully answer the following questions:

1. If you had been in the position of Cane and Mary, would have you entered the old ticket booth on the outskirts of town for worship?
2. Do you think it would be weird to worship with such a small group of people inside of a tiny structure like a ticket booth?
3. If you were Cane and Mary, would you consider making a return visit to the church that gathers in the ticket booth?
4. Do you think it would be wise of Pastor Karl to encourage the young couple to reflect on their experience in the light of any particular passages from Scripture?

Where Is Levi From?

Levi is a world class artist who has gained notoriety in one of the epicenters for artistic expression. His work is inspired by the people he meets while playing the flaneur. Levi moved away from home at the age of nineteen when he dropped out of art school, and he has no desire to ever return. His girlfriend, work, and new family and friends are all located where he currently resides.

To Levi's shock, one beautiful spring morning he finds himself digging through his papers to locate his passport. As his last remaining close relative, his father, Sampson, died suddenly of a heart attack the day before and has left his moderate estate to his estranged son. Once Levi arrives in his country of birth, he hitchhikes an hour and a half to his father's farmhouse. It is here that Levi was raised with his older sister, Julia, and twin brother, Mike, who both died in a car accident when Levi was sixteen.

Once at his father's home, he finds the key under the decorative milk jug on the porch and enters a home that has changed little in the last twelve years. Levi walks up the narrow steps to his old bedroom that he finds to be exactly as he left it. The only difference is there are dozens of envelopes lying on his old bed. Levi opens one envelope at a time and reads a letter for each month he has been away. Every letter is from his father and is overflowing with love and a yearning to once again see his estranged son.

That evening, financial details are finalized with his father's attorney, and there is only one more meeting for the day. The pastor Sampson had requested to preside over his funeral is scheduled to meet Levi at the funeral home to discuss details of the service and burial with the funeral director and Levi. Pastor Plymouth and Ted, the funeral director, try to make small talk with Levi after they both first offer their condolences.

Pastor Plymouth awkwardly asks, "Have you had a chance to catch up with any friends or family since you've been home?" Levi slowly answers, "I've lost touch with most of my old friends. My dad was my last remaining relative here. Growing up, I lived in the middle of nowhere, my parents worked in opposite directions, my siblings and I all went to different schools, and we switched churches several times. We didn't really live super close to anything of any real significance. So, when I was asked where I was from, I would say one town because it was about twenty minutes from my high school, and then when my brother Mike would be asked about where he was from, he would answer another town because it was about twenty minutes or so from where he went to high school. And my sister Julia just wanted to distance herself from the whole area. Sometimes my parents would tell people that we identified as being from the city where we went to church at the time. So, in a way, I did not identify with this area as being my home even when I was growing up here. But sometimes I did, I guess."

Please thoughtfully answer the following questions:

1. If you were Pastor Plymouth, how would you respond to what Levi said in response to the question, "Have you had a chance to catch up with any friends or family since you've been home?"
2. What words of comfort would you speak to Levi if you were Pastor Plymouth as Levi prepares for his father's funeral service?
3. Are there any words from Jesus in the Gospels that might be good for Levi to hear during this difficult time?

The Future of a Historic Congregation

St. Timothy Lutheran Church is approaching its one hundred and seventy fifth anniversary celebration! Festivities include a community wide picnic, a special guest preacher who is world renowned, a hot air balloon show, bounce houses and carnival rides for children, a contemporary Christian concert, and a performance by a choir that will sing traditional hymns in German and in Norwegian.

In the span of seven days, over eight thousand people join in the festivities at St. Timothy. The congregation is surprised by their state with a beautiful historical marker recognizing St. Timothy's historical contribution to the state over the last 175 years on its anniversary. Local television stations, newspapers, and internet bloggers are in attendance to record the unveiling of the marker.

In the two years following the anniversary celebration, life returns to a slower pace, and Bo Wilford, the chairman of the congregation, notices that attendance is declining at the Saturday night service as well as at both Sunday morning services. Seven years earlier approximately twelve hundred people worshiped at St. Timothy each week. That number currently has shrunk to approximately four hundred people.

This decline in attendance has concerned Bo and most of the elders. They are fearful if this decline continues, eventually St. Timothy will not be able to afford a full-time pastor and will be forced to share a pastor with their sister congregation, St. Titus Lutheran Church. Sadly, there are a few members in the congregation that view St. Titus as a rival to St. Timothy, so the thought of sharing a pastor with them is a nightmare scenario to certain members.

Pastor Arbor is asked by the elders to increase his evangelism efforts to the rural community that is quickly growing in population and is becoming more and more of a suburban enclave. However, many of the people in the community that Pastor Arbor reaches out to have trouble following his obtuse and abstract sense of humor. They find it difficult to tell when he is being serious and when he is telling a convoluted story filled with double entendre humor. This also is the case during most of the services he leads, which are unconventional, to say the least.

Several months later as attendance continues to decline, Pastor Arbor is questioned by the elders and the chairman of the congregation about why his efforts have fallen short. With plenty of warning signs, Pastor Arbor explodes on Elder Christopher Yobe and Chairman of the Congregation Bo Wilford, yelling, "Do you think that there are any growing churches on this continent or any other that expect their pastor to single-handedly bring growth to an aging rural congregation that has almost no understanding of what evangelism is? I'm not superman! I'm not St. Paul! I'm not Jesus Christ! What do you guys expect from me? Because every single suggestion that I make you seem to resist or even flat out refuse. If there is ever going to be real change here, then the congregation needs to start buying in a little!"

Please thoughtfully answer the following questions:

1. In your opinion, are the concerns about the decline in attendance by the Chairman of the Congregation, Bo Wilford, and the elders of St. Timothy valid?

2. Do you believe the elders made a reasonable request of Pastor Arbor in asking him to increase his evangelism efforts to the rural community that is quickly growing in population?

3. Do you think Pastor Arbor's explosion on Elder Christopher Yobe and Chairman of the Congregation Bo Wilford was warranted?

4. In your view, are there any words from Jesus in the Gospels that might bring some clarity to this situation?

Derek Is Preaching

Derek Deave was raised with his four siblings in several wealthy communities in three different countries throughout the world. His father served in a variety of middle management positions before working his way up the cooperate ladder to become the vice president of his company. Derek and his siblings grew up with a great many advantages and opportunities at their fingertips. Their father obtained enough wealth for each of his children to attend college without any student loan debts and to receive a sizable trust at the age of thirty years old to supplement their respective earnings in their careers.

Derek earned a bachelors degree in theology from a Lutheran university and upon graduation, was offered a position as a licensed lay deacon in an inner-city neighborhood. Derek accepts and begins assisting his friend, Pastor Kyle, in a variety of mission settings in the community. Although the work barely pays the bills, Derek is not worried because he knows in eight years he will have access to the money from his trust fund to supplement his meager income.

Eight long years later, Derek is working for a different inner-city ministry as a licensed lay deacon and is now making so little that he has four roommates in his eight-hundred-square-foot apartment. He is burnt out, and, once his trust funds are transferred into his checking account, he retires for a period of sixteen years during which he lives almost entirely off of his trust fund. During this time, he occasionally serves as a bartender at a favorite pub or a guest preacher at a local inner-city congregation, but more often than not, Derek saves only a fraction of his earnings.

The problem with Derek's decision is, although his father earned enough to provide a comfortable life for Derek and his siblings, his father did not earn enough for his children to be in a position to retire at a young age. Therefore, after sixteen years of no full-time work, Derek's funds are nearly dried up and he heads back to work as a licensed lay deacon.

One year later his old friend, Pastor Kyle, notices that Derek is once again feeling burnout from his work as a deacon, so, interestingly, he suggests that Derek move halfway across the country to enter a four-year master of divinity program at one of the most academically and professionally demanding seminaries in the world, to work toward becoming a full-time pastor.

Once at the seminary, Derek feels a little out of place. He is reasonably older than most of his classmates and even some of his professors. His love for cigarettes, a stiff drink, and daily grilling of barbecue; his jaunty, borderline cocky, outspoken nature; and his lack of a motor vehicle make him stand out like a sore thumb on the campus. Derek also does not do himself any favors by not arranging ahead of time for rides to his field work church each week, or by saying to professors halfway through the semester at the conclusion of a session that he performed poorly in: "You know, I really don't need to take this course. I took it years ago in undergrad, and I experienced it in real life as a license lay deacon. I'm not learning anything new here."

Derek quickly earns a reputation among faculty, staff, and students as an unteachable person with a lot of odd quirks who is fond of telling embellished tales. Toward the end of his second year on campus, his reputation takes another hit when his field work supervisor, Pastor Holtz, secretly records one of Derek's sermons. When the seminary's director of placement and seasoned homiletics professor hears the sermon for himself, he is so disturbed that he calls the entire faculty together on a Friday evening for an emergency meeting to discuss Derek's future at the seminary.

After almost three hours of deliberation, the faculty concludes that it is wise to postpone Derek's vicarage by one year to further evaluate his performance in the classroom and at his field work church. One year later Derek's academic and professional performance is deemed highly unsatisfactory by the majority of the seminary faculty; therefore he is denied an opportunity to have an internship as a vicar, and there are no other academic degrees for Derek to pursue due to his poor performance in the classroom.

Upon leaving the seminary, Derek is penniless other than the brand-new SUV and small allowance he receives from his sister and brother-in-law. He moves into a dispersed campground inside of a national forest an hour and a half to the south of the seminary. Derek sets up a tent on the top of his SUV. He wraps himself in several quilts and turns on a portable heater full blast to stay warm at night while clutching a revolver for safety. Each morning he builds a massive campfire and cooks baked beans, chicken, carrots, and cornbread in cast iron cookware over the fire. And each night before he goes to bed, he prays to Jesus to give him an opportunity to minister to people in need.

Soon Derek's prayers are answered as he begins to meet large amounts of homeless people camping out in dispersed campgrounds throughout the national forest. Derek travels from site to site by SUV, canoe, and foot, preaching the good news of Jesus Christ to dozens and sometimes hundreds of people each week. Word begins to travel far and wide of Jesus' work through Derek, and eventually his old friend, Pastor Kyle, visits the national forest to encourage Derek and hear him preach once again.

Please thoughtfully answer the following questions:

1. What is your opinion of Pastor Kyle's suggestion to Derek that he move halfway across the country to enter a four-year master of divinity program at one of the most academically and professionally demanding seminaries in the world to work toward becoming a full-time pastor?

2. What is your impression of Derek Deave?

3. If you were Pastor Kyle, how would you encourage Derek while visiting him in the national forest?
4. Is there anyone in the Bible that Derek Deave reminds you of?

Enjoying Nature

Sonya loves nature! When not working at the bank, she can be found outside hiking in the mountains, planting trees, gardening, and swimming. Sunday has become her biggest day of outdoor meditation and rest. Sonya often finds the perfect tree to climb and the steadiest limb to sit on while enjoying a delicious organic coffee alternative.

One brilliantly sunny morning, Pastor Jason and Deaconess Bella meet Sonya for lunch in a famous national park. They sit down under a giant buckeye tree and catch up for the first time in almost six months. After an hour of conversation, Deaconess Bella says, "Sonya, I have missed you in worship. Is everything okay? Where have you been?"

With a completely chill smile, Sonya answers, "Yeah, that is so sweet of you to say, Bella. I'm worshiping God out in nature by myself most Sundays now. I feel closest to the creator out in nature. It's not essential for me to be in the church sanctuary. I still believe in Jesus and everything, but for me there is nothing like being outdoors with the animals, the trees, the sky, and the sunshine. But, don't worry, you'll see me at Christmas. I'm pumped to play Mary in the nativity scene again this year."

Please thoughtfully answer the following questions:

1. What is your opinion of Sonya's choice to worship God out in nature by herself most Sundays instead of attending worship in the sanctuary with her church family?
2. If you were Pastor Jason and Deaconess Bella, what might you say to Sonya to encourage her to start attending worship with her church family in the church sanctuary on Sundays again?
3. Are there any passages from the New Testament that come to your mind while reflecting on this case study?

Dustin's Testimony

Dustin is emerging as a pitmaster star in the world of barbecue. Every food critic that has taken the time to drive down the back county roads to his restaurant has not regretted it. Located in an old barn on the edge of his parents' farm, the barbecue joint emits a rustic charm to all its patrons. One highly regarded food critic famously penned, "This barbecue is close to being the best that I have ever experienced. If Dustin's Old Barn BBQ were located anywhere near a major city, I believe it would gain national notoriety and fame!"

On the weekend of a major holiday nearly one thousand people make their way to Old Barn BBQ for a picnic, a country gospel music festival, and a fireworks show. In the middle of the music festival Dustin goes onto the stage and gives his testimony to family, friends, and patrons. With a nervous smile he says, "Hey, you all having a great time today? We have some fireworks coming up in a couple of hours! And our bands are doing fantastic, too!

"Most of you know that I'm a little bit of an introverted person normally, but I'm becoming more extroverted, I guess. I wanted to tell you a little bit about what God has done in my life. About ten years ago, I was on the verge of dropping out of high school due to horrible anxiety. Thankfully, my parents and guidance counselor were really supportive, and I ended up sticking it out and graduating. Then I wasn't sure what I wanted to do, and I saw a barbecue chef on TV cooking some brisket. And I just fell in love with barbecue at that moment, and I knew that I needed to become a pitmaster.

"By chance that day Pastor Fritzman and his wife, Hailey, from over at the Lutheran church were visiting my parents and me for lunch, and when I told him about what I wanted to do with my life, he put his hands on my shoulders, and I'll never forget what he said. He prayed, 'Jesus, you are Lord of all creation. Pour out your Holy Spirit upon your brother Dustin. If it be your will, we pray that he will accomplish his goal of becoming a great barbecue pitmaster. All to the glory of you, and your Father and the Holy Spirit, three unique persons, one God, now and forever. In your holy and precious name, Jesus, we pray. Amen.'

"I share that story with you all just to highlight what Christ can do when you share your needs with him. He may not answer you exactly as you think he will. But he promises to hear us, and Jesus wants us to pray that his Father's will be done on earth as it is in heaven. So today, I just want to encourage you to pray that your Heavenly Father's will be done on earth as it is in heaven, while you lift up your needs to Jesus Christ. Thanks for listening to a little bit of my story, you all! Lord bless!"

Please thoughtfully answer the following questions:

1. What did you think of Dustin's testimony?

2. What is your opinion of the prayer Pastor Fritzman prayed for Dustin?

3. Are there any characters from the Bible that remind you of Dustin?

Hot Tub Fellowship

Yosemite is a Lutheran pastor who loves Jesus! Every Friday night he invites fellow clergy people from a variety of Christian denominations over to his ranch for "Hot Tub Fellowship." Each pastor soaks in the giant tub and takes turns sharing what they love about Jesus. For about two hours these pastors focus on their common love for Jesus and forget about their differences for a while.

On a crisp autumn day, Yosemite takes several of his colleagues wild boar hunting in his woods. While breaking for water Harold, who serves as the pastor of a Mennonite church, is charged by a giant male razorback. Yosemite quickly fires his crossbow and kills the porker instantly. Yosemite, Harold, and the rest of the pastors say a prayer of thanksgiving to Jesus for his hand of protection on Harold and for Yosemite's quick reaction with the bow.

That evening as the pastors feast on the gamey wild boar, Leslie, who serves as an Anglican priest, begins to belt out an inspired rendition of the "Boars Head Carol"! Soon the entire group joins in. Hours later the singing continues in the hot tub as the group watches the sun rise and listens to the sound of razorbacks squealing in the distance. The next Sunday as each pastor and priest leads worship at his and her respective churches, they all feel refreshed by the fellowship and camaraderie they recently enjoyed together, and look forward to continuing as followers of Jesus Christ.

Please thoughtfully answer the following questions:

1. What can be learned by the fellowship and camaraderie that these Christian pastors and priests share?
2. Are there any passages from the Bible or stories from the early church this case study reminds you of?
3. What are some ways regular fellowship meetings like this could be started in your ministry context?

The Good Old Days

Several times a week Connie tells her pastor, the Reverend Justin Stanford, that the founding pastor of St. Titus Church was the godliest person she has ever known. On the verge of tears, Connie tells of Pastor Brandon's willingness to knock on front doors up and down county line road inviting people to the first ever worship service at St. Titus held in the township hall. Connie makes a point of sharing nearly every one of her fond memories of Pastor Brandon's nine years of service to St. Titus, which made him the longest serving pastor in the congregation's almost fifty-year history.

Overcome with emotion at the memory of the congregation's growth to over sixty members within two years of its founding, and over one hundred members in its fifth year, Connie has trouble keeping her composure as she shows visitors forty-two-year-old pictures of the construction of the fellowship hall and church office. Some visitors are impressed, but more often than not visitors seem to feel uncomfortable with Connie's eagerness to share about the early days of St. Titus church.

One evening at a mission and evangelism brainstorming session with the district mission coordinator, Pastor Devin, Connie interrupts him and says, "We need to get back to the good old days when Pastor Brandon started this church! He went door to door and everyone felt the Holy Spirit, so they were happy to show up and worship! Now we only have twenty people here most Sundays. What's wrong with this godless and wicked generation? Don't they want to worship Jesus and teach their kids the Bible? I made all ten of my children attend church each week! Even if their father wasn't going, we were. Now none of my kids and grandkids even attend church. We have to take this community and take this country back! Pastor Devin, what are you and Pastor Justin going to do to grow this church?"

Please thoughtfully answer the following questions:

1. What is your impression of Connie's speech and her incredibly high opinion of the founding pastor, Pastor Brandon?

2. If you were Mission Coordinator Pastor Devin, how would you respond to Connie's question, "What are you and Pastor Justin going to do to grow this church?"

3. Are there any stories in particular from the Bible that remind you of this case study?

Axl Is Filled with Rage

Axl lives on a four-hundred-acre rice farm that he purchased from his brother last winter. It makes him sad to drive into the crowded city one hour away and see people living in little apartments and houses with limited green space.

Recently Pastor Zellner mentioned during Bible study that a large housing development is set to begin construction next May on a newly purchased farm in between Axl's land and St. Paul's Church. This news is surprising and disgusting to Axl. He believes that some of the best farmland in the state is being destroyed to make way for unimpressive, overpriced homes. If he had been aware a housing development was set to be built near his farm, he never would have purchased the land to begin with.

Axl is filled with rage at his brother as he feels Ted did not disclose the building plans of the farm next door during the sale of the property. One late Saturday evening, Axl pours himself a scotch and calls Pastor Zellner and says, "I am having a really tough time forgiving Ted for this, pastor. I feel like he misled me to buy this property from him. Now he's living up in the mountains hundreds of miles away, living the high life! Does Jesus really expect me to forgive Ted for this betrayal of my trust? I mean, after all, Ted basically robbed me blind! And if Jesus does want me to forgive him, how am I supposed to do that, practically speaking?"

Please thoughtfully answer the following questions:

1. Do you think it was wise for Pastor Zellner to mention the construction of the new housing development during a Bible study?
2. What is your impression of what Axl said to Pastor Zellner over the phone?
3. If you were Pastor Zellner, how would you respond to Axl's question, "Does Jesus really expect me to forgive Ted for this betrayal of my trust?"
4. How do you think Pastor Zellner should respond to Axl's question, "And if Jesus does want me to forgive him, how am I supposed to do that, practically speaking?"

Chapter 11

Separation and Divorce

Johnny and Martha Binx

MR. JOHNNY BINX IS in the honeymoon stage with his wife, Martha. He is thrice divorced and is excited about this new chapter in his life. Martha is twice divorced and is tickled to have found just the right lover for marriage number three. Together, she and Johnny are an absolute power couple! Martha is a seventh-grade mathematics teacher at the local junior high and Johnny is ramping up his real-estate business thanks, in part, to the generosity of his eighty-five-year-old mother. They are ready to take the town by storm! Most importantly, they have the full support of their pastor, their families, and their congregation. Last but not least, they believe that they have the full support of God, who they feel would want them to live their best lives and be filled with all of the happiness and blessings life has to offer.

Over the last two weeks, Pastor Bob has been looking for a couple to lead the second adult Bible study. It has been without a teacher since the associate pastor took a call last month. Eventually, Johnny and Martha come to Pastor Bob's mind. Johnny is a child of the congregation and serves as an elder. Martha has a degree in education and teaches at the local junior high. Pastor Bob feels that they would be perfect to teach this class!

Johnny and Martha are happy to accept the offer to teach the class moving forward. The first few weeks of the Bible class seem to go pretty smoothly under the new teachers. From time to time, Pastor Bob peeks his head into the room and listens to the discussion before he begins his own Bible study. He is pretty happy with what he's seeing and hearing. There doesn't seem to be any type of false teaching taking place, and the class has several young newlywed couples attending. Everything looks great!

However, on week four of the study, Pastor Bob overhears Johnny teaching something rather curious as he peeks his head into the doorway that morning: "When the passion is gone, the marriage is over. It's time to move on and seek out the love and passion that is so vitally needed for your emotional and spiritual well-being. That's what you deserve, and that's what God wants for you. Only the best. When the passion is gone, you must move on. Say that with me. When the passion is gone, you must move on."

Right when Pastor Bob is ready to leave for the Bible class that he is teaching, he hears Martha add something to the conversation: "When God places a desire in your heart, he places it there for a reason. He is placing it there for you to act upon it. There is a season for everything, and I have no doubt that God placed Mr. Johnny Binx into the heart of this cowgirl at just the right season in life for me. At just the right life stage."

Before Pastor Bob can take a sip of his coffee, he hears twenty-four-year-old Brian, recently married to Karen, hesitantly pose a question to both Johnny and Martha. "So, earlier in the class you were talking about how homosexuality is a sin . . . and I agree with that. But how can you say being a homosexual is wrong, but at the same time say we should get divorced and find someone new if the passion is gone? And Martha, when you said God places a desire in your heart, he places it there for a reason . . . it sort of sounds like you think God wanted you to get divorced . . . am I understanding you guys correctly?"

Johnny begins speaking in a raised tone. "Listen to me, young man. Your parents were divorced. And I'm sure if they could do it over again, they would not have gotten married. The pastor that was here before Pastor Bob one hundred and ten percent supported me in all of the difficult decisions I had to make in my previous marriages. And he supported Martha as well. I am completely confident God and Pastor Bob would agree with everything we have done also. So, if you have a problem, then you, me, and Pastor Bob can all sit down and talk about this over in his office sometime!"

Please thoughtfully answer the following questions:

1. If you were in Pastor Bob's place, how would you exercise pastoral leadership in addressing this situation?
2. Did Pastor Bob use sound theological reasoning in his choice of choosing Johnny and Martha to lead the Bible study that was previously under the leadership of the associate pastor?

3. What, if any, theological issues are associated with the statements made by Johnny and Martha during the Bible study they were teaching?

Three Old Friends

Travis and Malachai are both recently divorced from strong, independent women they miss dearly. The only silver lining in their situations is these two college roommates are once again sharing a bachelor pad. In fact, they reminisce about their college days nearly every night over a bottle of wine and dinner, which has led them to the idea of holding a little reunion with old friends at their apartment.

One month later, they are reunited with five of their closest friends from college. Both Travis and Malachai are blown away by the sight of their fraternity's adopted little sister Nicki. It's the first time that they've seen her in almost twenty years.

The slight crush from their younger years is now a full-blown obsession. Yes, as it turns out Travis has a passion for Nicki, and Malachai has a passion for Nicki, and Nicki has a passion for both of them. In fact, Travis and Malachai have even developed feelings for one another. All three believe earnestly that they are meant to be together. Their friendships have turned into a polyamorous relationship.

Six months later a wedding is in the works, and the three begin an intense search for the most beautiful and welcoming wedding venue that they can find within their price range. All that's left is to find a pastor that will preside over this wedding ceremony. They hunt online for churches in their favorite area of the city, and several weeks later it appears they have found just what they're looking for.

Travis, Malachai, and Nicki sit patiently in the narthex of the church, voicing their dreams for the future with giggles and smiles. After a short wait they are greeted by Pastor Saxon, a cheerful second career pastor who spent twenty years serving in the army before attending seminary and taking his first call to his current parish.

After a few minutes of basic introductions and pleasantries Pastor Saxon says to Malachai, who has a head of premature gray hair, "So, are you Travis's father or Nicki's?" Nicki quickly answers for him. "He's neither my father or Travis's father. He is my future husband and Travis's future husband. The three of us are getting married to one another, and we would love for you to perform the wedding ceremony, Pastor Saxon."

With little hesitation Pastor Saxon responds, "I see, well that is an impossibility for me because the teachings of my church hold that marriage is between one man and one woman. And, in fact, that has been the traditional teaching of the catholic church since the first century. So, there is no way that I am able to preside over any type of polyamorous wedding ceremony." At that, Nicki, Malachai, and Travis politely say farewell to Pastor Saxon and leave the church in some haste.

Please thoughtfully answer the following questions:

1. Do you believe Pastor Saxon gave a fair reason for why he could not preside over the wedding of Travis, Malachai, and Nicki?
2. Can you think of any passages from Scripture that Pastor Saxon could have quoted to support his position?

A Curious Voice Message

Pastor Levi is making a forty-five-minute drive back to his house after visiting an elderly home bound parishioner. When he stops for a soda, he checks his voicemail and listens to a message from a fifty-year-old parishioner by the name of Brendon Gibson.

On the message Brendon says, "Hi Pastor, I really need your advice. Last week while I was watching the basketball game with my wife and our friend, Boblet, something sort of weird happened. Um, we were all laughing and having a good time, and then I looked over and saw Boblet massaging my wife's feet, and then she started stroking his hair. I didn't really know what to say at the time. Do you think I should be concerned? Anyway, please give me a call back when you get a chance and maybe we can meet up for coffee to talk about this in person. Thanks. Bye." Pastor Levi then calls Brendon back, but does not get an answer, and cannot leave a message because Brendon's voice mailbox has not been set up yet.

About twenty minutes later, Pastor Levi pulls into his driveway to find a distraught Brendon talking to his wife, Ann, and two of their teenage daughters, Heather and Grace, over a glass of lemonade. Brendon greets him and says, "Hi Pastor, I'm sorry to intrude like this. Your wife and wonderful daughters have been encouraging me. My wife, Barb, is moving away with Boblet. She wants a divorce so she can marry Boblet. They told me this morning about their love for each other, and they don't have a wedding date set up yet, but I'll definitely be invited to the wedding once they know the exact date. Boblet even asked me to be his best man for the wedding. I guess that makes sense since he was my best man when Barb and I got married.

I told him I would think about it. What do you think I should do, Pastor? I mean, what would you do if you were me?"

Please thoughtfully answer the following questions:

1. If you were Pastor Levi, what would be the first piece of advice you would give Brendon after listening to his story?
2. What passages from the Bible might be helpful for Pastor Levi to read prior to speaking with Brendon and Barb in the days and weeks to come?
3. If you were Pastor Levi, would you attempt to reach out to Boblet to speak with him about this situation?

It Happened at the Factory?

Brett Rawson is a thirty-six-year-old, mild-mannered factory worker. He has three sons, and he and his wife, Tessa McCullough Rawson, are nearing their fifteenth wedding anniversary in May. Often the appearance of Brett and his wife Tessa take their fellow churchgoers by surprise . . . in fact, usually when they are out in public together, people in general are a little bit shocked at what they see. Brett stands at five feet four inches tall and weighs approximately one hundred and twenty pounds, in stark contrast to his wife Tessa, who stands at six feet four inches tall and weighs approximately three hundred and fifty pounds.

Their appearances are not the only difference between them. Brett is incredibly introverted and meek. He loves reading science fiction novels and gardening. Tessa, on the other hand, is a former power lifting champion who enjoys riding her motorcycle to heavy metal concerts and underground illegal cock fights. She is loud and is often highly aggressive to most everyone she comes in contact with.

Lately their pastor along with most of their fellow parishioners have noticed a lot of large bruises on Brett's face and arms. Every time that someone inquires about where these bruises came from Brett tells them, "It happened at the factory the other day while I was loading some stuff." Pastor Charleston decides that it is time to make a home visit to see Brett and Tessa to drop off some new small catechisms and say hello.

As Pastor Charleston knocks on the door, Tessa answers the door quickly and shouts "Pastor Charleston! Why didn't you call before dropping by?" Pastor Charleston slowly responds, "Well, I tried several times, but I received no answer. I wanted to drop off these new small catechisms for you and Brett and the kids, and say hello. Is Brett here?" There is a long pause as Tessa tries to find the right words. Finally, she says, "Yeah, but he's really busy.... Why don't you try and get a hold of him later this week?"

Just at this moment Pastor Charleston spots Brett limping out of the restroom toward the living room sofa. He is only wearing underwear and his entire body is covered in bruises. Pastor Charleston shouts out, "Brett! My gosh!" and walks into the house straight toward his feeble parishioner, who is a shell of his former self. He appears to weigh less than one hundred pounds, and is hunched over as he slowly walks with a limp.

Pastor Charleston says, "Brett, you're in need of medical care. I am calling you an ambulance." As Tessa yells out, "No, he doesn't want one!" Brett says, "Thank you, Pastor. I need to see a doctor." Pastor Charleston phones an ambulance, and Tessa hurls insults at him and begins cursing him out. Pastor tries to stay calm; he wants to leave the house, but he doesn't want to leave Brett unattended with Tessa. He starts saying the Lord's Prayer while clutching his cross necklace with his right hand and placing his left hand on Brett's shoulder.

About two minutes later an ambulance comes roaring into the drive and two EMTs come rushing into the house. They seem a little shocked at the sight of Brett and somewhat disturbed by the belligerent, toxic behavior of Tessa. As they take Brett out on a medical stretcher, Pastor Charleston follows them and is soon approached by a police officer who has just arrived on the scene. The officer asks him for a witness statement and he agrees. Toward the end of the statement the officer asks him if he suspects Brett has been abused by his wife Tessa. Pastor says, "Yes, I and many others have suspected that she has been emotionally and physically abusing him for some time. However, I have never seen her hit him, and every time I asked Brett where his bruises came from, he would answer 'It happened at the factory the other day while I was loading some stuff.'"

Later that afternoon, Pastor Charleston is informed by the police that Tessa, under investigation, has admitted to assaulting Brett repeatedly, and that Brett's father and mother have been awarded temporary custody of the children while Brett begins his long recovery in the hospital.

Two days later Pastor Charleston arrives at the hospital to find his battered parishioner in a somber mood. He tells his pastor about the physical and emotional abuse that his wife started inflicting on him not long after they were first married . . . on the second night of their honeymoon, to be exact. And how he didn't want to give up on his marriage especially once his sons were born.

However, Brett is now strongly leaning toward divorcing Tessa and seeking sole custody of his three sons. Eventually he says, "Pastor, I can't take any more. I have put up with the abuse for long enough. If I stay with Tessa, then next time she might kill me. I'm probably going to file for divorce. Will I be sinning if I file for divorce so that I don't have to endure any more physical and verbal assaults?"

Please thoughtfully answer the following questions:

1. What biblical or extrabiblical resources might be helpful to Pastor Charleston as he shepherds Brett during his time of crisis and recovery?

2. Do you believe that it would be wise of Pastor Charleston to advise Brett that he has just cause according to the Scriptures to divorce Tessa for her many years of physical and emotional abuse toward him?

3. In your view, should Pastor Charleston personally reach out to Tessa or should he ask a fellow pastor to since she is possibly not receptive to seeing Pastor Charleston after she cursed him out as he phoned an ambulance for Brett?

Marriage Counseling with Vicar Justin

Pastor Skip is nearing his fortieth year of parish ministry and has served at his current call for eleven years. He serves alongside an associate pastor named Eric Growling who is primarily occupied with off-campus outreach efforts in the community and family time. Therefore, Pastor Skip often delegates extra tasks to the church vicar, Justin Stanford, a thirty-one-year-old second career man who, in his first career, served as a Christian missionary and a parochial school teacher.

One dangerously cold winter morning Vicar Justin arrives at church to conduct a marriage counseling session with Roy and Shannon. Normally Pastor Skip would take the lead on marriage counseling with parishioners, but he is currently enjoying a two-week tropical vacation at an all-inclusive resort outside of the country.

Roy begins the session by saying, "Well, we really want different things at this point in our marriage. I'm a homebody and Shannon is more extroverted and sociable. I want to continue living out in the countryside at the farm house, and have lots of animals and three or four vehicles. And she wants something different. I'll let her tell you."

Shannon quickly adds, "I really want to live closer to work. When we first got married, I thought it might be fun to live out in the middle of nowhere. Now I can see that I want to live in town in a nice new subdivision. I want a ranch-style home, three bedrooms, two and a half baths, central air conditioning and heating. I only need two cars and one cat. Well, we just want different things at this stage in our lives, and that isn't going to change. We have both agreed it's for the best to move on. Haven't we, Roy?"

Slowly Roy says yes and nods his head in agreement. And then adds, "We are actually meeting with our attorneys tomorrow to finalize our annulment. We are going to work together to be the best parents in the world to the kids. It's basically already a done deal. We just thought the leaders of the church should know."

Vicar Justin responds, "Okay . . . do either Pastor Skip or Pastor Eric know about this?" Roy responds, "Yeah, I think so. We've been keeping them up to date as things progressed." Vicar Justin is a little stunned by what he is hearing and almost doesn't know what to say. Finally, he asks, "Well, since this is your first marriage counselling session, would you be willing to attend counseling with me, Pastor Skip, or Pastor Eric for two months before making your final decision on the annulment?"

Roy and Shannon agree to consider Vicar Justin's offer to attend marriage counseling for two months before making a final decision. They then leave his office for other engagements after Vicar Justin leads them in a word of prayer. About two weeks later, Pastor Skip returns from his vacation tanned, refreshed, and ready to cast visions.

Justin walks into his supervisor Pastor Skip's office to say hello and check if he received any of the emails he sent to him and Associate Pastor Eric about the situation with Roy and Shannon. Pastor Skip responds, "Yes, I most certainly did. And after speaking with Roy and Shannon, I was absolutely devastated to hear that you strongly advised them to pursue a divorce without even considering marriage counseling. It is my expert opinion that you will need to stay on as the vicar of this church for an extra month in order for me to observe you performing more pastoral tasks before I can recommend that you pass your vicarage to the seminary."

Vicar Justin does his best to explain to Pastor Skip the truth of the situation, but Pastor Skip refuses to listen and says, "You're already in deep enough water as it is. If you're smart you'll, listen to me and follow my instructions on this one."

Please thoughtfully answer the following questions:

1. In your opinion, do Roy and Shannon have valid, biblically based reasons for seeking an annulment?
2. Do you believe Vicar Justin's offer for either himself, Pastor Skip, or Pastor Eric to meet with Roy and Shannon for marital counseling sessions was reasonable before they make the final decision on an annulment?

3. Do you believe Vicar Justin should contact the seminary's head of vicarage placement to let him know about the conversation with Pastor Skip and the plan to have Vicar Justin's vicarage last another month in order for him to pass vicarage?

Love Sign Proposal

Armani and her husband, Daniel, are enjoying the beautiful zoo lights on their day off. The smell of hot cocoa, roasting chestnuts, and caramel popcorn fills the air. It's a wonderful break from the high-speed pace of their work schedules. As they hold hands, the stresses of work start to melt away like snow under the warm zoo lights.

Upon turning the corner toward a large sign decorated in lights that read LOVE, they see a man proposing marriage to a woman. This sight brings Armani and Daniel joy as it reminds them of their proposal nearly ten years earlier during the same season of year. The woman accepts the marriage proposal and a crowd of onlookers applaud, and a few people shout out words of congratulations.

However, as Armani and Daniel move a little closer to the couple, they realize the man who proposed marriage is Logan Kingston, a married parishioner of Daniel's. They are stunned because Logan and his wife, Emma, were in Bible study yesterday, and spoke of the desire to start hosting dinner at their home more often.

Logan spots his pastor and Armani and says in a sheepish voice, "Hi Pastor Daniel, I didn't know that you were going to be here." Pastor Daniel responds, "Yeah, I didn't know that you were going to be here either." Logan says in a hurried, nervous voice, "Listen . . . I bet you are wondering what in the world is going on. Um, it's basically over between Emma and me. We are probably going to get divorced soon. I read this great book from Johnny Binx. And he says in it, 'When the passion is gone you must move on.' Well Emma and I just don't have the passion anymore. So, I'm moving on. This is my fiancée Kewpie." And with that, Logan and Kewpie quickly walk away, and Logan says, "See you later, Pastor; maybe we can get coffee soon!"

Pastor Daniel then walks after Logan and Kewpie and says, "Listen Logan, I don't know everything about your marriage to Emma, but if you are planning on divorcing her and marrying Kewpie you need to let her know. You definitely don't want her finding out through gossip." Logan responds, "Yeah, at some point I will. Probably after Christmas or something."

Pastor Daniel raises his voice and says, "No! You are going home right now like a man, by yourself, without Kewpie, and telling her what you did here tonight. And if you have any common sense left, you will beg her for forgiveness and get into marriage counseling." Logan raises his voice and answers, "Yeah, you can't run my life, man! You aren't Jesus!" Pastor Daniel responds, "No, I'm your pastor and I'm telling you that if you are not man enough to speak to your wife, then I will." Logan quickly responds, "Yeah! Whatever! I'm going to a new church. You're judgmental and not loving like Jesus!" And with that Logan and Kewpie take off to the other side of the zoo.

Please thoughtfully answer the following questions:

1. Do you believe Pastor Daniel responded in a pastorally responsible way to Logan telling him that he is now engaged to Kewpie and is soon divorcing his wife, Emma?

2. In your opinion, should Pastor Daniel inform Emma of what he and Armani saw and heard from Logan right away?

3. Do you think it would be wise for Pastor Daniel to take Armani with him to meet with Emma since she also witnessed the proposal and heard a good portion of what Logan said in a public setting?

Herbert and Jelly418

Herbert is a traveling businessman who is on the road approximately two hundred and eighty days a year. He and his wife, Marilyn, have slept in separate bedrooms for eighteen of their twenty-five years of marriage. Their relationship is cordial and, at times, warm as they reflect on the accomplishments of their two teenage daughters.

One evening Herbert returns home from a five-week cross country trip to a freshly cooked pizza and a pitcher of ice-cold lemonade. He and Marilyn quietly sit down on the sofa and watch a new sitcom. Following the show Marilyn turns to Herbert and calmly says, "So we need to discuss how we start to unwind our marriage. It's time to end this marriage. You are never home. It has been a loveless mess for a long time, and we need to do what is best for ourselves and for the girls." Herbert tells Marilyn, and all of his family, friends, and coworkers, that he is completely shocked by Marilyn's request for a divorce. He says, "I never saw this coming in a million years! I mean, I knew that things were messed up, but I had no idea that she was thinking this way!"

Within a month of Marilyn requesting a divorce, Herbert signs up for a Christian dating site. Each evening from the privacy of his bedroom, he searches the dating site for eligible, single, Christian women. His search includes an area within fifty miles of his home; eventually he expands it to a radius of one hundred miles within his home. And after a week of finding very few profiles that he is attracted to, Herbert expands the search to include women on the site within two hundred and fifty miles of his home.

One lonely night as Herbert hears Marilyn cleaning her bedroom across the hall, he receives a notification that a woman with the username Jelly418 has smiled at him. Herbert messages Jelly418 right away. After several messages back and forth, Herbert finds out that Jelly418 is Jessica Sanders Schmidt, a divorced mother of three who works as a dental hygienist over two hundred miles away. About ten minutes into the conversation Herbert writes "Well, I think that you should know that I'm still married, and I'm not officially divorced yet." Jessica responds, "Oh, well I guess we have nothing to talk about then." To which Herbert responds, "Good, because if you hadn't said that then that would have disqualified you."

Over the next several months as divorce proceedings continue between Herbert and Marilyn, Jessica and Herbert begin to fall in love. They dream of possibly getting married one day, while at the same time they spend hours in prayer asking Christ to salvage Herbert and Marilyn's marriage, if at all possible, for the sake of the couple's daughters and one another. However, the divorce is eventually finalized, and one month later, Herbert and Jessica begin planning an international destination wedding that will be held in a place of great religious significance. They ask a pastor who is leading a tour group to that place to lead them through premarital counseling sessions and perform the wedding ceremony.

However, Pastor Denny is hesitant to agree to this request, because Herbert and Jessica are planning on tying the knot only two months after Herbert signed his divorce papers. Pastor Denny is concerned that maybe his friends are rushing into marriage, and he does not want to enable them in rushing into such a serious decision. After a great deal of conversation and prayer with Herbert and Jessica, Pastor Denny agrees to walk them through premarital counseling sessions and perform their wedding ceremony in a country thousands of miles away, in a specific spot of great religious significance.

Please thoughtfully answer the following questions:

1. What is your opinion of Pastor Denny expressing concern that his friends are rushing into marriage?

2. If you had been in Pastor Denny's shoes, would have you agreed to walk Herbert and Jessica through premarital counseling sessions and perform their wedding ceremony?
3. Are there any passages from the Bible that come to your mind when reflecting on this case study?

Long Term Plans

Brock puts no money away for retirement each month, but he loves his wife's new high heels. Money is not an object to this pastor and husband who prides himself in his attention to detail. Yet Brock pays no attention to the worries of the years to come. When the forty-nine-year-old is asked what his plan for retirement is, he responds with a smirk and says, "I have faith that God will provide just like he always has."

On a rainy night of relaxation with his beloved wife, Allison, Brock is reminded of the importance of his duty to provide for his wife and children financially long after he has gone to be with the Lord. The next morning, he schedules an appointment with his attorney to discuss the possibility of selling two of his three duplexes that he rents out. Brock would love to put the proceeds of the sale of the properties into various retirement accounts and college advantage funds from which his wife and children can benefit.

With deep concern, Brock's attorney, James, informs him that his wife Allison sold all three of their duplexes last week and had the entirety of the proceeds from the sale transferred to an account exclusively in her name. James says somberly, "Allison didn't come right out and say it, but I believe she is planning on divorcing you. I tried to convince her to call you before finalizing the sale of the properties and she refused."

Brock goes out into the lobby and phones his wife to confront her. Allison insists that the sale of the properties was done out of desperation to put money away for needed expenses and retirement. Brock asks her directly if she is planning on divorcing him and she answers, "Yes, honey, I am. I need financial stability in my life, and although I appreciate all of the clothes and shoes you buy me, I would rather see that money tucked away in a retirement account."

Brock does his best to explain that he went to the attorney's office that morning to arrange the sale of two of their three duplexes for the purpose of putting the money into retirement accounts and college advantage funds for Allison and the children. However, Allison has decided there has been too much damage done to their marriage due to their financial disagreements to reconcile at this point.

Brock is beside himself searching for a compassionate ear to confide in. He then decides to phone his ecclesiastical supervisor, the Reverend Bishop Tomlinson, and immediately he hears words of rebuke and is essentially guaranteed that he will be removed from ministry for being divorced. As the Bishop bluntly puts it: "You have not loved your wife as Christ loved the church! Can you honestly say that you have done everything in your power to save this marriage?" Brock responds, "Bishop Tomlinson, you're a legalistic pharisee!" Brock then hangs up the phone and checks into a hotel for the evening.

Please thoughtfully answer the following questions:

1. If you were giving Brock pastoral advice, how would you advise him to try to save his marriage to Allison?
2. What words of Christ-centered comfort would you speak to Pastor Brock during this devastating time?
3. Are there any biblical or extrabiblical resources you would recommend to Brock and Allison?
4. If you were sitting down for coffee or tea with the Reverend Bishop Tomlinson, what would you say to him?

Dealing with the Trauma

Pepper is an eighteen-year-old high school senior with a massive crush on a famous TV actress. He loves his family, friends, and favorite football team. His family is relatively close despite the fact his parents both work long hours, and his father is often away for several days at a time at conventions.

One evening while Pepper is reading the latest news on his favorite actress, he receives a message through social media from a girl that he is not friends with. The message reads, "Hi, I'm Taylor, I think that we have the same dad. He lives with my mom and sisters and I part of the week, and then he always says he has to go to a convention and leaves. I'm guessing he goes to your house."

Pepper studies every detail of the message multiple times as well as Taylor's social media page thoroughly. She is also eighteen years old and lives with her sisters and mother in a town only twenty miles away. Taylor and her siblings bear a striking resemblance to Pepper's father, Stan. That night, with a sick feeling in his stomach, Pepper shares the social media message and his research with his mother, Betty.

A day later when Stan returns home from his travels, Betty confronts him with the message. Stan answers, "Yes, I admit it. I'm sick of living this way! I have two families that I love to death! Does that make me a horrible person, Betty?"

Within a year, Stan and Betty are divorced and Pepper is working seventy hours a week at a major retail store. He soon earns a position as a manager and often celebrates his new position and higher earnings by hosting movie nights at his apartment, where there is usually a great deal of drinking.

By the age of twenty-two, Pepper's life is filled with nights of drunkenness and reckless behavior. He often has fits of rage and lashes out at the people who love him the most. Pepper's life hits a crisis point when he attends a professional soccer match with friends and becomes so inebriated that he drops his phone and wallet into a bathroom urinal. By the time he fishes these items out they are ruined, and he loses contact with his friends at the game. Pepper then proceeds to hitchhike home, and somehow ends up stranded four hundred miles away in one of the most dangerous communities in his country.

Pepper eventually returns home, and he has lost his job for failing to report to work, and as a result, he soon loses his apartment for failure to pay the rent. Pepper moves in with friends and begins attending weekly counseling with Dr. Seth Dublin, an experienced licensed professional counselor and pastor. After months of counseling sessions, Pepper comes to the conclusion that he is responsible for his reckless behavior and that a great deal of his behavior is a coping mechanism to deal with the trauma of his father's infidelity and double life as well as his parents' difficult divorce.

One afternoon at the end of a counseling session, Pepper says to Dr. Dublin, "I've never asked anyone to do this before, but since you're a pastor, I'll ask you to. Will you please pray to Jesus for me that I continue to stay focused on attending counseling, and that I can continue to heal?" Dr. Dublin answers, "Of course I will, Pepper. The Lord be with you."

Please thoughtfully answer the following questions:

1. How do you think you would feel if you were in Pepper's position and learned your father had two families who knew nothing of each other for years?
2. If you had been in Betty's position, would have you filed for divorce with Stan upon learning that he had a second family that he was living with also and keeping secret from you?

3. If you were Dr. Seth Dublin's pastor, what words of encouragement might you speak to him as he counsels people during some of their darkest times?

4. Does this case study remind you of any stories from the Bible?

A Bad Match?

Al Schmidt is a twenty-one-year-old pre-seminary student. He has dreamed of being a pastor since the age of five. Al has a B grade point average, as he struggles tremendously with ancient Hebrew, classical Greek and Koine Greek courses. Al is thrilled to be finishing his junior year as he begins to prepare to move out of state for seminary studies in one year. More importantly, he is preparing for his wedding in less than a year to his stunningly beautiful fiancée, Bridgette.

Both Al and Bridgette are from devout Christian families. There are some differences between them, though. Al's family barely had enough money to send him to college, and Bridgette's family is one of the wealthiest in the state. Actually, many students, professors, and even family members of the couple have quietly been wondering how this relationship came together in the first place. Bridgette is a charming tall beauty with thick blonde hair, in great shape, with a perfect olive complexion. She is an excellent student with a ton of career options after college, and has been asked out by nearly every eligible, intelligent, good-looking male student on campus.

In contrast, Al is noticeably shorter than Bridgette, he is introverted, and looks ordinary. He is bald and is an average student, preacher, and conversationalist. The differences have been so glaring that Al's mother sat down with him in the kitchen one month before the wedding and said, "Al, honey, I love you. What I'm about to say is coming from a place of love as your mother. Al, this engagement between you and Bridgette doesn't make any sense. You are a sweet, normal, average guy from a family with lower middle class means and connections. You are getting ready for four more years of schooling to become a pastor. Once you're ordained you won't be making a ton of money. Bridgette looks like a super model. She is almost six feet tall, she is in amazing shape, she is incredibly charming and wealthy, and is a great scholar. Bridgette is a year ahead of you in school and is one year older biologically, but maturity wise she is a decade ahead of you.

"I think as you two get older and you are further and further away from college life, you will grow apart. I'm trying to save you both heartache, honey. Al, I can tell you are not really listening to me so I'm going to say it bluntly. Al, honey, Bridgette is out of your league! End this before she rips out your heart! It's much easier to end things before you are married. Once you're married things get a lot more complicated. Trust me!"

The wedding goes ahead as planned and the two honeymoon on an island famous for its gorgeous sunsets. They return home and move into a modest apartment off campus and four years of seminary fly by. Al receives a call to a loving and generous congregation on the coast that provides him and Bridgette with a spectacular parsonage that was donated by a wealthy member.

Less than three years into his first call, Al meets with his elders and then schedules a meeting with his bishop. With a broken heart Al says, "Bishop Melbourne, I have some bad news. My wife, Bridgette, and I are getting a divorce. She is filing for divorce actually. In a way, the marriage was never really legitimate in the first place. In the six and a half years that we have been married we have only had sex five times, and she claimed each time not to enjoy it and to not really feel anything. Of course, as you know we have no children.

"So, with basically no romantic component to a marriage from the start, was this marriage really ever legitimate to begin with? I don't think so. That's what I see in Scripture. This is essentially an annulment of a marriage that existed in name only. I entered this marriage ready to fulfill my husbandly duties, and she entered this marriage not ready to fulfill her wifely duties. I acted in good faith and she did not. Bridgette and I are ready to move on and live our lives as if this marriage never happened. Sadly, two years of marriage counseling helped us very little."

Please thoughtfully answer the following questions:

1. What is your opinion of what Al's mother said to him concerning his engagement to Bridgette?
2. What is your reaction to what Al said to Bishop Melbourne?
3. If you were Bishop Melbourne and served as Al's ecclesiastical supervisor, how would you respond to what he shared with you?
4. Are there any passages from the Bible or extrabiblical resources you think would be helpful for Al and Bridgette to read together during this difficult time?

Chapter 12

Sexual Misconduct

An Accusation against Tonya

Ms. Tonya Wellington is celebrating her fiftieth birthday by throwing herself the finest party of the decade. She is inviting a wide range of friends and acquaintances to celebrate with her. Of course, her pastor is on the guest list as well, and Tonya is delighted to introduce him to colleagues from her firm along with friends from the expatriate community. Pastor Dennis has brought with him two guests: his wife, Amy, and the congregation's new vicar, a young man by the name of Brian Wu. The party is an exciting celebration filled with dancing, laughter, and a wide variety of food and drink. All of the guests mingle and, after several hours, Pastor Dennis, Amy, and Vicar Brian all grab a taxi back to the church.

During the taxi ride Amy notices Brian is uncharacteristically quiet. She asks him if everything is okay. He does not respond and instead looks away. Pastor Dennis is now showing a good deal of concern and says, "Brian, what is it? Why are you crying?" Brian answers, "Tonight while I was using the restroom . . . I felt someone come up behind me and grab my privates. It was Tonya. She said, 'Not only am I a senior member at my firm, but I'm also the head of the hospitality committee at church. I think it's my job to welcome you to our congregation.'"

Brian starts to tremble and says, "I didn't know what to do. I'm sorry I didn't stop her. I thought if I said no or ran away that I'd be in trouble with the church. Please don't end my vicarage! I'm sorry! Are you going to end my vicarage?"

Please thoughtfully answer the following questions:

1. If you were in Vicar Brian's place, would have you told your supervisor, Pastor Dennis, and his wife, Amy, what happened at the party?
2. If you were Pastor Dennis, how would you respond to the story Brian had just shared with you?
3. If you were Amy, how would you respond to the story Brian had just shared with you?

How Should J.T. Handle This?

J.T. Thompson serves as a director of Christian education at a medium sized congregation. He is one of three full-time staff members at this church. J.T. enjoys serving alongside his sister-in-law, Ellen, the church secretary, and Pastor Rick. Most of the congregation feels comfortable with J.T. and are thrilled that Pastor Rick has been asking him to preach on a regular basis at the third Sunday service. In fact, J.T. just finished up a full month of preaching at every service over the last four Sundays while Pastor Rick was on vacation.

Several days later as J.T. is loading up his van in preparation for a much-needed mini-vacation with his family, he hears someone call out, "Hey man! Your sermon the other day was amazing!" It's Frank Alex, a free-spirited beach bum who owns a series of successful bed and breakfast rental properties down the road from the church. Frank has recently joined the congregation through the new member class.

Before J.T. even has a chance to say hello, Frank says, "Pastor J.T., I have a massive praise report for you, man! The other day my lady was out of town visiting her college friends, and God worked it out that my neighbor Angie's boyfriend was out of the country on business. Angie and I have had a thing for each other for months. And God just worked things out that we could finally hook up! I thought you would want to hear the good news. You're a great friend and Pastor!" J.T. is completely speechless as Frank drives away on his scooter yelling out, "See you at church on Sunday, bro!" while waving goodbye.

Please thoughtfully answer the following questions:

1. What do you think J.T.'s first responsibility is in this situation?
2. Should J.T. cancel the much-needed mini vacation with his family in order to try to address this situation involving Frank Alex?
3. Are there any passages in the Bible you think J.T. should meditate upon when reflecting on this situation?

Dylan Seeks Refuge

Dylan is twenty-three years old and is fresh out of university. The young graduate has just been hired on at one of the world's largest real estate investment firms. It's Dylan's first real, proper job, and the youthful entrepreneur is elated for the opportunity. Dylan decides to move directly from the school flat to the city. The twenty-three-year-old has little money and is in the process of searching for a place to live.

Luckily Dylan's new boss, a Mr. Frank York, is an old family friend and has volunteered to let young Dylan stay with him while getting settled in the city and saving up a little money to buy a proper flat in a suitable area. This is a massive relief to Dylan, as the recent graduate has very little savings left after attending an expensive university and also incurring great debt in pursuing two degrees. If Frank York had not volunteered to let Dylan stay at his home, there would have been no other choice but to commute from his dad and mom's house an hour and a half one way by rail to work each day.

Three weeks into Dylan's stay with Frank York, the young entrepreneur is having a fantastic time. Dylan is working long hours six days a week, but after work nearly every evening Frank York takes his new employee out to a high-end restaurant or whiskey bar with other colleagues. Dylan is rubbing shoulders with some major players at the firm and with rival firm members as well. Most of Dylan's family and friends are incredibly impressed by the opportunities that their young friend has been blessed with, and they say at least once a week, "Make the most of this, Dylan! You may never get an opportunity like this again! You get to live with and learn from Frank York. There are people all over this country who would kill for that opportunity."

One evening while out at a whiskey bar, Dylan inquires of Frank about the arrival time of work colleagues to the bar, and says, "What time is the rest of the gang going to arrive, boss? I bet they'll love this place. It has loads of character and history." Frank York then looks at Dylan in a way that Frank has never looked at his young employee before. In a way that is reminiscent of how Dylan's father would look at his only child when Dylan was home from university. A look that conveyed concern or even disappointment.

After a pause that only lasted about ten seconds but felt like ages, Frank responds with, "Our colleagues won't be joining us tonight, Dylan. They have other engagements. It will be the two of us. I think this is a great opportunity for us to take our professional relationship as well as our personal relationship to the next level. We can build the foundation of a life partnership, and also an incredibly lucrative financial partnership. As you know, I have no children of my own. I now fancy you to be my heir one day. But

I would like to cut you into my business plans now. And share everything with you fifty-fifty."

Frank York then places his hands on Dylan's shoulders and says, "I see you not only as my child, but also now realize that you are the great romantic love I've been waiting for all my life. I can't wait for us to be lovers! This will move you forward in business and in love." Upon hearing this Dylan begins coughing violently and rushes to the WC.

Once in the WC, Dylan tries to find a way out of this situation at once. All of a sudden the young entrepreneur cares little for this job, title, and financial future it may provide. Dylan just wants to be away from Frank and to feel secure. However, this young business-minded scholar is on the edge of panic because there are so few close friends in the city that would be willing to come to the door around the midnight hour.

Suddenly Dylan remembers that a childhood priest, Father Noah, and his wife Ashley started serving at a church in the city a few years ago. They live in the church rectory next door. Dylan locates the address on an old mobile contact list, and then proceeds to exit the WC and make a mad dash out the door. Thirty minutes or so later, Dylan's on the steps of the rectory. Only the front door light is on, and for a moment Dylan hesitates to knock. "What will Father Noah say? Will he understand? He's probably fast asleep in bed with Ashley . . ."

But after a moment or two, Dylan feels that it is imperative to knock. The young entrepreneur has almost no other options for lodging or to borrow cash for a train ride back to his dad and mom's home. Dylan knocks the old stone knocker and within a minute or so Father Noah comes to the door. He looks almost exactly as he did a few years earlier except he has some gray hairs now. "Yes, may I help you," Father Noah says in a cautious voice, while squinting through the dim front light. "Hi, Father Noah. You probably don't remember me. I'm Dylan Brown. You were my priest at your last church for a number of years in the town of—" At that moment Father Noah lets out a great jubilant laugh and says, "Young Dylan Brown! It's so good to see you! My, you have grown up! Ash! Honey, come downstairs! One of my former parishioners is here! I baptized this sophisticated young adult as a little baby, and then Dylan was a part of one of the last catechism classes that I taught at St. Matthews. Come into the house, Dylan, and let's have some refreshments by the fire!"

Over the next thirty minutes Dylan tells Father Noah and Ashley about the situation regarding work and living arrangements. Dylan then hesitantly shares with them about what took place approximately an hour earlier with Frank York. They insist Dylan stay the night in the guest room, and share with their young friend that the church has a small cash fund reserved for young people in situations like his. Dylan says to them both, "I feel so conflicted. There is a part of me that wants to return to Frank's house and just pretend the entire incident never took place. Or maybe I should return home and just try to commute every day to work from my parents' place? But that's about three hours on the train each day. That makes for long days. There is another part of me that thinks . . . well, maybe I should file a report with the police about Frank's advancements towards me? I think since he's my boss that what he did was essentially sexual harassment. What do you think that I should do Father Noah?"

Please answer the following questions:

1. Does Father Noah have an ethical duty in this situation to advise Dylan to file a police report on Frank York for sexual harassment?

2. Should Father Noah caution Dylan about returning to work at the real estate investment firm due to the fact it might be a step into a hostile work environment?

3. Since Dylan shared this story openly in front of both Father Noah and his wife Ashley, do you believe Ashley has an obligation to make a report to the police concerning Frank York's behavior based on what was said by Dylan?

Abby's Story

Ray McCrae is a forty-one-year-old guidance counselor at one of the largest private high schools in the city. He also serves as an associate pastor at a non-denominational church near the school. Ray has an eye for identifying each student's unique ability and promise. Nearly every morning as he arrives at work, he pops into Principal Lisa Coldwater's office and steals a kiss before he meets students. Ray is thankful he has the opportunity to work at the same school as his new girlfriend. Never in a million years did he think that the woman who hired him would end up being both his boss and his girlfriend. What a joyful surprise this has been for Ray!

One Friday evening, Ray is finishing up a few tasks at work before heading to a local Italian restaurant to meet Lisa for dinner, when an eighteen year-old high school senior named Abby enters his office crying. Ray asks Abby, "What's wrong?" and requests that she sit down while he makes her a cup of tea. Abby then begins telling Ray a story that almost puts him into a state of shock.

In a voice that is not much more than a whisper Abby says, "For the last year Principal Coldwater and I have been having lunch together in her office about once a month. At first it was a lot of fun... then she started telling me stories about some of her favorite yoga gurus, and how to test each other's willpower they would both get naked and try to resist sexual temptation. And that we should do that together, so we did. We sit together naked in her office and just talk for an hour or two. This happens about once a month... but lately things have become more intense. The last couple of times Mrs. Coldwater's secretary, Rita Smith, has come in and sat down across from us, and made sketches of the two of us while we talk. I'm really uncomfortable with the whole situation. There hasn't been any physical contact or anything like that, but the whole situation is feeling really weird. You're the only one that I've talked to about this so far. I haven't even told my parents yet. I just want this to stop. What do you think that I should do?"

Ray responds, "Abby, thank you so much for having the courage to share this with me. You have done absolutely nothing wrong. First off, I'm going to phone the police so that a police report can be filed, and then I'm going to phone your parents and inform them of the situation." Abby is thankful to Mr. McCrae for his support, and understands that calling the police and her parents is the best course of action.

The police arrive about five minutes later, and Abby requests to have her parents present before she makes a statement. Her parents walk in only moments later and are incredibly supportive of Abby as she gives her statement to the police. About an hour later two detectives meet Ray at his apartment and inform him that they have spoken to both Lisa Coldwater and Rita Smith, and they each told similar stories that Lisa broke up with Ray last week and that he threatened to find a way to get back at her.

One of the detectives has informed Ray that they believe Principal Coldwater and her secretary, and they think he has manipulated Abby into going along with this preposterous story that he has created for the purpose of gaining revenge on his ex-girlfriend. And he would be wise to say nothing more on the matter or else he runs the risk of being sued by Lisa or Rita, and may also face criminal charges for convincing someone to file a false police report. Ray McCrae is nearly speechless and simply says, "Oh, I understand. Thank you, officers." The two detectives leave, and Ray begins praying for direction from God on what to do next.

Please thoughtfully answer the following questions:

1. Do you think Ray McCrae acted in an ethical manner by phoning the police and Abby's parents upon hearing the allegations Abby made against Principal Coldwater and Rita Smith?

2. Given that the police believe Abby's entire story was created by Ray out of spite toward Lisa, who might Ray look to for professional or legal guidance in this situation?

3. What biblical or extrabiblical resources do you think might be helpful to Ray in this situation?

4. What biblical or extrabiblical resources do you think might be helpful to Abby and her family in this situation?

5. In your view, what might be a wise next step for Ray?

6. In your opinion, do you think it is likely the police are correct in their assumption that Ray manipulated Abby into telling this false story to the police and her parents in order to gain vengeance on Principal Lisa Coldwater?

Johnny's First Act as a Sole Pastor

Mr. Johnny Binx has recently become the sole pastor of a medium sized church that is no longer affiliated with any denomination. He has always believed in celebrating victories and feels that his new position as sole pastor of a church is well worth celebrating. He also believes fervently in the value of building a strong team. He decides that he will both celebrate and build up a strong sense of teamwork with two of his elders by taking them out to a fine dinner, followed by a night at his favorite gentleman's club.

As the three men enter the club Johnny says, "Gentlemen, this may not be what God meant when he said be fruitful and multiply . . . but when the heart has a burning desire you must oblige, and you must comply. It is pointless to try and defy the heart." Johnny then greets two of his favorite dancers, and then shows his elders around the club. The three men leave the club ten hours later and, as they are leaving, Johnny says, "Now, remember gentlemen, not a word of this to the wives or anyone else in the congregation. Their hearts and minds aren't ready for this type of information yet. This was a fantastic evening of team building. Keep up the great work!"

About four weeks later at a Friday night worship service, Johnny is preaching a sermon on the need to celebrate victories when Chris, one of his parishioners, interrupts him. "You're up here preaching on the need to celebrate victories! Taking elders out to a strip club all night! Is that how you celebrate victories, Pastor?" Without hesitation Johnny sharply responds, "I admit to no wrongdoing. I am only guilty of building a dynamic team with two of my most trusted elders, who were in desperate need of a little R and

R. I am so sorry that your tender little heart and mind is not ready to hear of the ways that mature men need to bond after a long week at work. I forgive you for your ignorance, Chris."

In reaction to Johnny's response, a handful of members storm out of the worship service, and Johnny continues preaching his sermon. After the service, during the announcements, Johnny's beloved wife, Martha Binx, addresses the congregation and says, "This man of God is casting a vision. We all celebrate victories differently. Pastor Johnny leads with flare and panache! That's just one of the reasons that I fell in love with him, and we as a congregation chose him. Pastor Johnny is the closest thing to a modern-day King David or King Solomon that you will ever see. He is a biblical man of God straight out of the Old Testament. We should be thankful for that type of biblical leadership and example!"

Please thoughtfully answer the following questions:

1. In your opinion what would be an appropriate way for a parishioner to speak to Pastor Johnny Binx about his trip to a local gentleman's club with two of his elders?
2. Do you agree with Martha Binx's assessment, "Pastor Johnny is the closest thing to a modern-day King David or King Solomon that you will ever see. He is a biblical man of God straight out of the Old Testament. We should be thankful for that type of biblical leadership and example!"?
3. What biblical passages come to mind when you reflect on Pastor Johnny Binx's pastoral leadership style?

The Landlords Upstairs

Norm is a thirty-year-old hospital chaplain who typically works the night shift five days a week. He is grateful to have a cozy four-hundred-square-foot basement apartment that he rents from Jay and Isabella, a middle-aged married couple who reside above the basement in the three floors of their brownstone. Occasionally, the couple invite Norm upstairs for dinner and drinks. To say the least, Norm feels blessed to have such friendly landlords that rent him a good apartment for an affordable price.

One morning as the sun rises and Norm begins to settle into bed after a long night at the hospital, he suddenly hears aggressive pounding on the first-floor door. He looks out his window and sees people standing above in suits and ties along with men and women in casual dress. Norm hears a woman say to Isabella, "Ma'am, we are the federal police and we have a warrant to search the entire premises. You need to comply." And a man yells, "Let's back the processing truck up to the door quickly!"

A few moments later Norm, hears banging on his apartment door. He rushes to answer in his old shirt and gym shorts, still wired from the three cups of hospital cafeteria coffee. Quickly about ten agents rush into his dwelling with a warrant giving them permission to conduct a search. A man and a woman each take Norm by an arm and lead him out to a large van where they ask him if he would like a lawyer present. Norm declines the offer and then is interrogated for several hours about his knowledge of Jay and Isabella. Toward the end of the interrogation, the federal officers inform him that Jay is being arrested for sex tourism that he engaged in while visiting foreign countries along with five counts of human trafficking. The agents then calmly tell Norm that he will have to find another place to stay for at least two months while the top three stories and the basement of the brownstone are processed for evidence.

That afternoon, Norm checks into an inexpensive hotel. As he enters his room he begins to pray for Jay and Isabella. He then reflects on the times that he had dinner with his landlords and their various guests. Norm ponders if the charges that have been brought against Jay are possibly valid. To his alarm, he unexpectedly feels a sense of panic as he starts to imagine having to testify in a criminal trial and being cross examined by attorneys. This sense of panic stays with Norm as he finally falls asleep on his hotel bed.

Please thoughtfully answer the following questions:

1. If you were in Norm's position, how would you specifically pray for Jay and Isabella?
2. If you were Norm's pastor, what words of comfort would you offer to him?
3. If you were a pastor visiting Jay and Isabella, what might you say to them after hearing what they have to say?

Knocking on the Front Door

Sophia Herz is a twenty-five-year-old single woman who serves as an elementary public school teacher in an affluent suburban enclave. She is excited about how her third year of teaching is going and is thrilled to have recently upgraded from renting a small studio apartment to owning a two-thousand-square-foot condominium within walking distance of her school.

One gorgeous late October evening, Sophia's town celebrates Halloween with a trick or treat night. Her neighborhood is packed, and Sophia passes out candy from her porch while dressed as a nurse. A great number of her students stop by with their siblings and parents. Each child is thankful to receive one large full-sized candy bar from her. At about 8 p.m. that evening as trick or treat ends, Sophia goes inside to her living room to watch a scary movie and enjoy some popcorn and a strawberry daiquiri.

Three hours later, Sophia showers, puts on her pajamas, and snuggles into bed with her cat Scampi. As she begins to fall asleep, she hears loud, playful knocking on her front door. Sophia unlocks her bedside safe and grabs her handgun. She then proceeds to walk to the front door to see who could possibly be knocking at such a late hour. Staring at her through the living room window while standing on her porch is a man dressed as a character from a famous 1800s novel. As Sophia looks closer, she realizes that it is none other than the uncle of one of her students. His name is Steve Vanlue, and he is a mathematics teacher at the local high school. In fact, he is only a year or two older than Sophia, and he went on several dates with Sophia's friend and colleague Kay a few years ago.

Before Sophia can say a word, Steve says, "Hi Sophia! I loved the sexy nurse's outfit you were wearing tonight! After I stopped by for candy with my niece and brother and his wife, I couldn't get how you looked out of my mind. I just want you to know that I am in the mood. So do what you want with that information. You look vivacious! Smoking hot tonight!"

Sophia says in the sternest teacher voice that she can muster, "Steve, it is inappropriate of you to show up at my house at this hour and talk to me this way! I would like you to leave right now!" Steve answers, "Yeah, I think you are right. I hope I didn't scare you or anything. See you later, Sophia." After Steve walks away Sophia double checks to make sure that all of her doors and windows are locked and that all of her outdoor lights are on.

As she curls up in bed with her handgun close, she begins to shake and contemplates calling the police. She then considers calling her parents for advice, but hesitates to do so because she does not want to worry them. Suddenly she sees the shadow of a figure at her bedroom window. Sophia picks up her handgun and peeks out the blinds. Sophia is disgusted to see Steve Vanlue masturbating outside of her bedroom window. She grabs her cell phone and quickly snaps a photo of him before yelling, "I'm calling the police, Steve! You need to get out of here!"

The police arrive within five minutes of her call, and Steve is nowhere to be found. Sophia gives a statement to the police and shows them the photo she took. It is dark and blurry and of low quality. It is not clear who is in the photo. Rapidly the police begin checking with neighbors to see if they have any security camera footage of the incident, and a few people do hand over their footage happily. Unfortunately, all of the footage is not of good quality. The scene is processed but no fingerprints or DNA evidence of any kind is found. This makes proving it was Steve a little tough with only Sophia's testimony, the blurry photo, and the unclear security camera footage as evidence. To make matters more difficult, Steve was dressed up in makeup and a popular outfit for Halloween, which creates some doubt of the identity of the person who was harassing Sophia.

Upon questioning Steve, he has an alibi that at the time he was sleeping at his brother and sister-in-law's home on the other side of town in their guest bedroom. This makes it almost impossible for Sophia to press charges on Steve Vanlue, but she does take out a restraining order on him and alerts her family and friends, school principal, and school superintendent of what took place. Everyone is incredibly supportive, and the school district places Steve on paid administrative leave while a thorough investigation is launched into the incident. Sophia's church family is highly supportive as well, and Father Johnathon Dublin and Sister Maria Sanchez let her know that they are available if she ever needs to talk.

Sophia's family, friends, colleagues, and church family all encourage her to go to counseling for a mental health checkup as she processes the traumatic, violating experience that she suffered because of Steve Vanlue's appalling behavior.

Please answer thoughtfully answer the following questions:

1. If you were Father Johnathon Dublin or Sister Maria Sanchez, what would you do to try to continue to show Sophia love and support?
2. Are there any words from Jesus in one of the Gospels that you think would be good to share with Sophia as she deals with her trauma?
3. If you were Father Dublin or Sister Maria, how would you pray for Sophia during this difficult time?
4. Have you ever encouraged someone to go to counseling for a mental health checkup as they process a traumatic, violating experience?

A Wicked Idea

Mr. Frank York has struck up a friendship with a young man who is making a name for himself in the expatriate community. This extroverted, theatrical party animal is none other than Steve Vanlue. He and Frank are kindred spirits that have a big bro-little bro, fraternity-style friendship. After only a month of hanging out they are starting to think of one another as family. To say the least, Steve is happy with his decision to relocate and escape what he describes as "the hassles and drama of back home."

One evening while watching a classic movie and enjoying a stiff drink in Frank's penthouse, a wicked idea comes to Frank's mind. He tells Steve about a situation that took place several months earlier. A member of the church that Frank occasionally attends accused a woman by the name of Tonya Wellington of sexually assaulting the church's vicar, a seminary student by the name of Brian Wu.

"In my opinion Vicar Brian was embarrassed that he was caught messing around with an older woman, and probably felt like he needed to say it was a sexual assault to save face. That would be my guess!" Frank makes this proclamation before pouring himself another stiff drink. He then suggests that they invite Tonya and Brian over for what he says will be "a smashing sequel to their first encounter." Several minutes later Frank is texting Tonya and inviting her to his penthouse while Steve is texting Brian and inviting him over. Tonya is unaware that Brian has been invited, and Brian has no idea that Tonya is on her way.

Brian is buzzed up to the penthouse moments after Tonya arrives. As soon as Vicar Brian spots Tonya at the bar he runs out the door and heads for the elevator. Frank, Tonya, and Steve erupt in hysterical laughter as Brian flees. Moments later there is a sharp pounding on Frank's penthouse door. Frank answers in his smoking jacket and says in a calm, motherly voice, "Brian, you've returned. We were concerned about you. Why on earth did you leave in such a hurry?" With beads of sweat dripping down his face, Brian answers, "Um, I didn't feel well. Sorry! Listen, I need the code to the elevator so I can get back down. Can I have it please?" Frank answers, "Well of course you can, Brian. I'll have to look through my files for it, though, and see if I have it still. While I look for it why don't you come back in and have a drink?"

Brian hesitantly accepts Frank's offer. The next day Brian awakes in a strange bed that overlooks the beach. He is wearing only his underwear and has a horrible headache. The last thing he remembers is drinking a glass of bourbon that Steve Vanlue poured for him at the bar. Brian quickly gets dressed and rushes down the hall past the dining room where Frank, Tonya, and Steve are enjoying a continental breakfast. "Will you be joining us for breakfast Brian?" asks Frank in a concerned, motherly voice. Brian does not answer but instead rushes out the door where a doorman puts in the code for him to enter the elevator. Once outside of the main entrance there is a taxi waiting to take Brian back to his humble apartment. The driver pulls up next to the guard hut. The armed guard takes a photo of Brian and then opens the gate. The taxi driver then rushes Brian home. Vicar Brian opens up his wallet to pay and, unbelievably, sees a large amount of cash stuffed inside. The driver tells him the ride has already been paid for and speeds off down the coast.

Please thoughtfully answer the following questions:

1. If you were Vicar Brian's pastoral supervisor, what advice would you give him if he were to confide in you about this situation?
2. Did this story remind you of any stories from the Bible or perhaps of a story you have first- or second-hand knowledge of?

The Misconduct of Piston

Piston enters the classroom twenty minutes late with a confident swagger, proudly sporting a T-shirt that says "DESTROY THE PATRIARCHY!" She addresses the all-girls high school freshman class with a commanding voice. "Okay! Listen up! You're either a penis or you're a vagina! All penises go to the left side of the room! All vaginas go to the right side of the room!" Over the course of the next two minutes twenty girls go to the right side of the room and three girls jokingly go to the left side of the room, while two girls choose neither side of the room. Piston demands that the girls who did not choose a side answer for their lack of choice. The two girls respond with a united statement, "We are young women, and we do not appreciate being objectified in this way, and being identified as either a penis or a vagina."

Piston then proceeds to project images onto the classroom's projector screen of naked adult people with both female and male sexual organs. She then demands that each girl who identified as a vagina is to show her their vaginas in order to prove that they are in fact vaginas. Only one girl agrees to Piston's demand. Moments later, the girls who identified as penises are given the order to show their penises to Piston. Thankfully it is at this time that the school's principal, Ms. Molt, enters the room and informs Piston that there is a phone call for her in the school's office.

Later that afternoon, outraged parents and their attorneys flood Principal Molt, Superintendent Stansberry, and School Chaplain Reverend Grover's email inboxes and voicemails with complaints. Piston is placed on paid administrative leave while a thorough investigation is conducted by the school district as well as by the sheriff's department.

As parents demand answers, Superintendent Stansberry, Principal Molt, Reverend Grover, and the school board all issue a joint apology to the students and parents for the inexcusable behavior of Piston. All claim that they were led to believe Piston was going to follow her submitted lesson plan for the health class that period. They are unified in their claim that they had no idea that twenty-three-old Piston was going to behave the way that she did and sexually harass the underage high school freshman girls, as that behavior is inexcusable at any institution and is not in accordance with the standards of a Christian day school that seeks to instill ethical, Christlike morals in each young woman in their care.

Please thoughtfully answer the following questions:

1. In your opinion should criminal charges be brought against Piston, and should she also lose her job as a high school health teacher as a result of her misconduct?
2. Do you believe School Chaplain Reverend Grover has an ethical responsibility to reach out to Piston and speak to her about the incident?
3. If you were Reverend Grover, would you share any passages from the Bible with Piston if you had the opportunity to speak with her?

Ray Knocks on Glenn's Door

Ray Burlington is a twenty-five-year-old, self-proclaimed, world-class musician, painter, linguist, actor, director, fashion icon, poet, and social media influencer. His appearance changes drastically depending on the time of the day and or the setting. Ray is well known by people throughout the nation, yet nearly every person who knows him has a completely different impression of him.

For instance, Ray might walk to his favorite local bakery for fresh bagels and coffee dressed in a tailor-made, three-piece suit with penguin tails and a top hat while acting as pleasant as can be, conversing with nearly everyone he comes in contact with and thanking the person who checked him out with a gold coin for a tip and a farewell bow. Yet that evening he might attend a formal dinner party acting stoic while dressed as a grunge rocker. In fact, his own identical twin sister, Glenn, has said on multiple occasions, "I hardly know the man. He's a riddle wrapped in an enigma. He's a complete mystery to me."

One late evening in the middle of the worst snowstorms the area has experienced in five decades, Glenn hears Ray's signature playful knock on her apartment door. She looks through the peephole and sees a visibly shaken Ray. She quickly unlocks the door and embraces her disheveled brother with a hug and is told an alarming story. Ray says, "Glenn, I was sexually assaulted tonight. My girlfriend, Blair, invited me over to her place for drinks and a movie. When I arrived, eight of her friends from the modeling agency were there too. We were all chilling out on the sectional couch enjoying some red wine, when all nine of the women tackled me and began ripping off my clothes and touching me. I was violated! I was violated, Glenn! Some people might laugh at me because these are really beautiful women, but I kept saying no! I didn't ask them to do that. I know that I'm theatrical and I'm always method acting in preparation for auditions and different plays and stuff, but this is real! Please believe me, Glenn! I'm going to call the police to file a police report on Blair and her friends. Do you believe me Glenn?"

Ray phones the police and the detectives arrive ten minutes later to take his statement. After they speak with Ray, they ask him if he would like to speak with Father Alberto, a chaplain for the police department. To Glenn's amazement Ray says yes. About twenty minutes later, Father Alberto sits at the dining room table with Ray and listens for several hours while Glenn sits by her twin brother holding his hand and rubbing his back. She leaves his side only to refill his water glass and bring fresh tissues.

Father Alberto primarily listens to Ray and provides a ministry of presence. He speaks a few Christ-centered words of compassion and love to Ray and to Glenn. At the end of the visit, Father Alberto leaves Ray a card with both his personal cell phone and email information as well as his professional contact information. He encourages Ray and Glenn to call him day or night if they ever need to talk, and Father Alberto promises to contact them both in the next two days.

Please thoughtfully answer the following questions:

1. If you had been in Father Alberto's position, what Christ-centered words of compassion might have you offered to Ray and his sister Glenn?
2. Do you think it would be wise for Father Alberto to encourage Ray to seek out professional counseling to deal with his traumatic sexual assault?
3. If you were Father Alberto, how would you specifically pray for Ray and Glenn each day?
4. If you were Father Alberto, how would you specifically pray for the models who sexually assaulted Ray?

Chapter 13

Shut-Ins and Homebound Ministry

Visiting the Viddletons

LAFYETTE AND TANNER VIDDLETON cuddle up together nightly on their sofa and binge watch their favorite political news channel while enjoying multiple bowls of buttery popcorn washed down with ice cold soda. They both work remotely from home and have bonded so closely they almost cannot stand to be apart from one another for a single second.

Lately Pastor Kris has been curious as to why Lafyette and Tanner no longer attend church in person. One morning as Pastor Kris makes a pot of coffee, a well-meaning parishioner by the name of Santa Valeria approaches Pastor Kris and says, "Wow! Can you believe that Lafyette and Tanner are shutting out their family, friends, and church family? I mean, I understand that they are on this journey together, but come on, you can't pick up your phone anymore, and every time someone comes to the door you are only allowed to speak to them through the living room window? What's up with that? I don't think they have any serious physical problems, and I live across the street from them, and they never leave their apartment anymore. It's scary! Don't they need sunshine, fresh air, love, and encouragement? Don't we all need that? What's wrong with these two? What's wrong with the world, Pastor?"

Pastor Kris pauses for a moment and responds to Santa Valeria with, "Well, I truly had no idea that Lafyette and Tanner's situation had become so serious. They have always been a little bit of homebodies, but they would still attend church in person often, and I know they enjoyed going out to eat and the occasional political rally. I'll make a point to visit them sometime before Christmas. Thanks for giving me the heads up on their situation, Santa Valeria."

Over the course of the next three weeks, Pastor Kris tries several times to reach Lafyette and Tanner with phone calls, text messages, and even a handwritten letter. Finally contact is made through a private message on social media, and Pastor Kris is invited over for a visit and to bring holy communion. A week later while approaching the door of their apartment Pastor Kris hears, "Come on in, Pastor Kris! The door is open and the popcorn is hot! We saved you a seat!"

Once in the apartment Pastor Kris is hit with the glow of the television and several blacklight lamps. The walls are decorated with posters of Lafyette and Tanner's favorite political figure. Lafyette gives an inviting tap for Pastor Kris to sit in between the two on the sofa as their eyes are glued to their favorite political program of the night. Two hours later the three are filled with laughter to the point of tears as they share stories and enjoy television together. After about four hours of visiting and catching up, Pastor Kris gives communion to Lafyette and Tanner and says good night.

On the train ride home, it comes to Kris's mind that there was no mention or thought to discuss why these two fun-loving, political junkie parishioners had not been in church in person for the last six months or so. The entire evening was so pleasant, the thought to ask about their church attendance completely left Kris's consciousness during the visit. For the time being, Pastor Kris is okay with that, but has every intention of checking in on Lafyette and Tanner in the near future and inquiring at that point about their in-person absence from church.

Please thoughtfully answer the following questions:

1. What are your initial impressions of Pastor Kris's home visit with Lafyette and Tanner?
2. If you were Pastor Kris, would you try to contact Lafyette and Tanner to set up another visit in the near future?
3. On your next home visit, how would you broach the topic of Lafyette and Tanner's absence from in-person worship with them?
4. What Scripture passages about the importance of gathering together in worship might be helpful for Pastor Kris to share with Lafyette and Tanner?

Shut in with a Shut-In

Trace is elated to be starting his second career. His first career was serving in the Army. Trace served two tours of duty, and after twenty-five years of service he received an honorable discharge and retired with full benefits. Upon retirement he entered a seminary that is typically designed to work with older, second career students. Its curriculum was practical in nature and gave students the meat and potato teachings and tools to become solid pastors.

Two years later Trace is placed at a church for his vicarage internship with the understanding, if things go well, he will receive a call to that congregation in one year and serve as its full-time pastor. Trace is excited about this opportunity, as this congregation has a good mix of younger families and older members. He also likes the fact that the church is located near his wife Sandy's parents.

A week after arriving Trace, Sandy, and the kids are getting settled into the parsonage and the swing of everyday life. Late on Monday afternoon, Vicar Trace is exhausted from the moving and nearly reschedules his shut-in visit for the day, but he decides to drink one more can of soda and press on. Trace follows his map down an old stone lane near the outskirts of town not far from a posh, brand-new housing development.

He pulls into a yard that serves as a parking lot. A large mutt barks furiously at Vicar Trace as he steps out of his station wagon and approaches the front door. Slowly an old screen door opens and an elderly gentleman says, "You must be our new pastor! It's a pleasure to meet you." Trace responds with a smile and a booming, "Yes, I am! It's a pleasure to meet you as well. You must be Hennessy!"

Vicar Trace walks into the home that has seen utter neglect. It appears as a time capsule of a home from thirty-five years earlier, except little to no cleaning has taken place in those years. Spider webs, mouse droppings, and what sound like the clamoring of raccoons in the attic immediately stand out to Vicar Trace. The two men enter the parlor and begin to converse next to a roaring fire. The glow of the embers bounces off of the marble hearth and onto the stained glass window over Hennessy's head.

The experienced veteran-now-vicar listens to Hennessy's confession and reassures him of God's forgiveness. He then spends the next hour listening to the radio with his elderly parishioner, and suddenly hears a news flash that the area is under a level three extreme winter storm advisory that will be in effect until 8 a.m. the following morning. Hennessy insists Vicar Trace spend the night and not risk driving on the road. Trace reluctantly decides to accept Hennessy's offer, and he uses the home's land line phone to call his wife Sandy and tell her of his plans for the evening.

That evening around midnight, Hennessy makes up the sofa in the parlor for Trace and brings him a cup of boiling hot tea with a shot of whiskey. The two men pray before saying good night, and as Hennessy walks to his room on the second floor he says, "Just let me know if you need anything. Make yourself at home!"

The next morning around seven thirty Trace awakens to the smell of freshly ground coffee brewing, and eggs, bacon, pancakes, sausage, and French toast cooking in the kitchen. As it turns out, Hennessy is one of the finest cooks in the county. He always serves as the cook on church fishing trips to the north. As Trace sits down to a splendid breakfast, he begins to see Hennessy's home differently. As snowflakes fall down outside the window his eyes are opened to the home's rustic, maverick charm, and he sees the unsanitary qualities as mostly cosmetic problems.

Right before Vicar Trace leaves that morning Hennessy says to him, "Your visit has breathed new life into this house. I'm inspired to clean it up a bit and give it a few updates so I can entertain people more often. I'm also inspired to get out of the house more often. I'll see you at church on Sunday!" Trace is honored and humbled by Hennessy's generous words. He thanks him for his kind hospitality and leads him in a prayer before leaving.

Please thoughtfully answer the following questions:

1. Had you been in Vicar Trace's position, would have you accepted Hennessy's offer to spend the night?
2. What is your impression of what Hennessy said to Vicar Trace right before he left that morning?
3. If you were Vicar Trace, how would you specifically pray for Hennessy?
4. If you were Hennessy, how would you specifically pray for Vicar Trace?
5. Does this story remind you any stories from the Bible or from your own life?

Osmond Is Concerned

Osmond Jones is a twenty-six-year-old man who has recently accepted his first call to serve as a pastor. The congregation is located in an economically struggling area with a crumbling infrastructure. Upon arrival Osmond learns that a number of the younger families in the congregation left during the church's seven-year pastoral vacancy, which means there are currently only about forty people in attendance in worship each week, and there are twenty-five people who are either permanently shut-in or are homebound for the time being.

Pastor Osmond is cautious when it comes to visiting shut-ins or those in the hospital or assisted living facilities. He always wears a mask when visiting any type of hospital or care facility or someone in their home. What he and only his doctor, and a few close family members and friends, know is that he is HIV positive, which means his immune system is more susceptible to various illnesses and infections. Pastor Osmond also typically wears a mask at church or while in public, which has caused some of his new parishioners to tease him about how cautious he is being.

Two weeks after being installed as the pastor of his first congregation, Pastor Osmond arrives at the home of a parishioner named Ellie Hopkins. He rings the bell multiple times over the span of five minutes. Finally, Ellie's eighteen-year-old daughter, Lindy, answers the door and nonchalantly invites him in. The home looks like a giant rat's nest. Boxes are stacked to the ceiling, and old containers of food, clumps of pet hair, and newspapers liter the floor. As Pastor Osmond climbs over an old couch that blocks Ellie's bedroom door, he is hit with the stench of rat urine. His eyes are watering, dust covers his suit, and the stench of the house burns his skin.

Inside Ellie's bedroom is a woman that at first looks like a skeleton to Pastor Osmond. Her bed is a basic queen-sized mattress without a frame or box spring. Her window is blocked by cardboard boxes stacked almost ten feet high, and her only source of pleasure is a thirty-two-inch television, sitting atop a mini fridge in the corner of the room, playing reruns of old black and white television shows.

Pastor Osmond sits down on a three-foot-tall stack of plastic totes and visits with Ellie for almost an hour. Pastor Osmond offers her communion, but she declines, saying, "I want communion at some point, but I just don't feel up to it today." Before he leaves for an appointment with another shut-in ten minutes away in a neighboring town, Ellie says, "It was so good to meet you, Pastor. Next time please bring your wife along. I would love to meet her." Pastor Osmond politely informs Ellie that he is single and says, "Take care and Lord bless, I'll see you later."

After leaving, Osmond is convinced that Ellie is going to die soon, and he fears that if he had spent another hour in that filthy house he might die soon as well. Seven months later Ellie is still alive, but Pastor Osmond has not returned to see her in that time. This is brought up at a monthly elders meeting. The elders are insistent that their new pastor start visiting Ellie every two or three weeks. "She deserves to be visited just as often as the rest of the shut-ins and hospital bound people of our congregation!" exclaims Elder Riley Brunswick.

Pastor Osmond agrees to start visiting Ellie more often, but quietly he has no intention of doing so. The normally private Osmond has considered confiding in his elders and telling them that he is HIV positive and is concerned that his immune system may be vulnerable to the filthy conditions of Ellie's home, and that is precisely why he has not been to visit her in the last seven months. However, Osmond decides it is best not to make them aware of his condition, as he is afraid they will not understand and will pass judgment on him for his illness. To say the least, the young pastor feels isolated and depressed and not sure who to turn to for help and advice.

Please thoughtfully answer the following questions:

1. If Pastor Osmond reached out to you for advice on this situation, how would you advise him?
2. What pastoral words of comfort would you speak to Osmond as he struggles with feelings of isolation and depression?
3. Are there any words from Jesus in one of the Gospels you think would be good for Osmond to hear from a friend?

Myrtle the Matriarch

Myrtle is ninety-one years young and is nearing her ninety-second birthday celebration. She has been blessed with remarkably good health throughout her life. Family and friends have a tough time keeping up with this soon-to-be ninety-two-year-old. In fact, they are stunned whenever she leaves a visit early to deliver meals to shut-ins or pick people up for church each week in her minivan. Without reservation, Myrtle gives all the glory to God.

As Myrtle's friends decorate the church fellowship hall in preparation for her ninety-second birthday celebration, Pastor Alexiou receives a phone call from Myrtle's eldest daughter, Clara. Apparently Myrtle has gone into a coma and may have suffered a stroke. She was rushed to the ER by ambulance earlier in the day. Twelve hours later Myrtle comes out of the coma, and by this time the doctors have concluded that she did in fact suffer a light stroke.

Clara and the rest of Myrtle's children, as well as nephews, nieces, and friends, are devastated to hear that their dear Myrtle is facing a long recovery and will likely have to give up driving and all of her volunteer activities, and may never return to her beautiful home on Sycamore Street. Three months later, Myrtle defies the odds and the advice of her doctors and moves back into her two-story home on Sycamore Street. She takes the liberty to hire a private nurse named Kellogg to carry her up and down the stairs. She continues to sleep in her master bedroom on the second floor and reads the paper from her balcony with a cup of coffee each morning.

Unfortunately, this beloved matriarch and leader is not well enough to return to volunteering. It's also a struggle for her to socialize for a long period of time, and she has not attended church in person since her stroke. However, she enjoys visits from Pastor Alexiou and watching services online. At the same time she misses in person worship and receiving communion on a weekly basis and does not feel satisfied with communion only once every two weeks when Pastor Alexiou visits.

One Easter morning Myrtle arrives at a packed church accompanied by her nurse Kellogg. Most everyone is joyfully shocked to see Myrtle back at church in person. Some thought that this day would never come. Some even thought that Myrtle was on the verge of death and are speechless to see her again. What is more shocking than anything to the congregation is the fact that this normally mild-mannered matriarch is dancing and singing loudly with a tambourine during the traditional service. And not just during the hymns, but for several one- or two-minute periods during Pastor Alexiou's sermon as well. A great number of people watching the service online share the service on their own social media pages and comment how much they enjoy Myrtle's singing and dancing. Several people worshiping in person cheer on Myrtle as she sings and dances and applaud her each time she finishes.

Less than one week later, Myrtle passes away peacefully in her sleep at the age of ninety-two. Friends, family, admirers, and her church family all attend the service to pay their respects. To the surprise of some at the service, approximately half of the five hundred people in attendance sing and dance during the traditional hymns with tambourines in hand. This touching tribute brings tears to the eyes of Myrtle's eldest daughter, Clara and several of Myrtle's other children.

Please thoughtfully answer the following questions:

1. In your opinion was Myrtle's recovery a miracle?
2. If you had been in Pastor Alexiou's position, how would have you reacted to Myrtle singing and dancing with a tambourine for several one or two minute periods during your sermon on Easter Sunday?

3. If you were Pastor Alexiou, what Christ-centered words of comfort would you share in your sermon with those in attendance at Myrtle's funeral?

4. Does Myrtle's story remind you of any stories from the Bible?

In a Dense Forest

Brently, Ron, and AP live in a trailer located deep within a dense forest that has a number of trees over one thousand years old. They hunt for a majority of their food and entertain one another by discussing a wide array of conspiracy theories while playing video games or sitting around the campfire. About once every two months, the three drive their ATV to town and attend Saturday night worship at a Presbyterian church.

From time to time Pastor Matt says cheerfully, "Brently, Ron, AP! One of these days I'm going to hike into the forest and visit you three at your place!" One bright, warm Thursday morning, Pastor Matt is feeling ambitious and decides to hike five miles one way through the forest to visit three of his members. His map leads him to their isolated trailer, but he first passes dozens of signs with skulls that read "No Trespassing" and "Intruders will be shot!"

He knocks on the trailer door and Brently welcomes Pastor Matt inside. Over the course of the next hour and a half Pastor Matt watches the three play a first-person shooter game and listens as his parishioners share conspiracy theories with him that range from corruption in the global banking system to the possibility of a zombie apocalypse. Eventually Matt starts to feel overwhelmed and a little frightened by what he is experiencing. He wants to leave, but he also feels a responsibility to stay for lunch because he realizes that Brently, Ron, and AP rarely get to have visitors, and they are enjoying hanging out with their pastor.

After lunch as Pastor Matt prepares to hike home, Brently says to him, "Pastor, before you go we want you to see one more thing." The three lead him to an old barn about half a mile away. Once inside they show Pastor Matt hundreds of semi-automatic weapons, swords, and knives. Matt keeps his composure and pretends to be impressed by what he is seeing, but deep down he feels utterly sick and thinks to himself, "Why on earth would these three have all of these weapons? Are they planning some sort of attack? Do they honestly believe all of the conspiracy theories that they have been sharing? Is that why they are hiding out in the forest?"

After about thirty minutes of viewing his parishioners' extensive weapons collection, Pastor Matt finally starts to hike home. As he walks into his kitchen, he gives his wife, Veronica, a quick synopsis of his visit and says, "They never prepared me for that at the seminary."

1. If you had been in Pastor Matt's position, would have you visited with Brently, Ron, and AP as long as he did?
2. Do you believe that Pastor Matt has good reasons to be concerned about his three parishioners who are living in an isolated area of the forest?
3. If you were Pastor Matt's pastor, what Christ-centered words of comfort and advice would you share with him as he reflects on his visit with Brently, Ron, and AP?

Passionate about Visiting Shut-Ins

Toby and Ryan are elders at a medium sized church. They are passionate about visiting shut-ins! Before every elders' meeting they request a pre-meeting with the senior pastor, Chase, and the associate pastor, Justin, to discuss essentially every aspect of each person's life who is currently a shut-in. These pre-elders' meetings often last two hours or more. And usually just as a meeting is about to end, Toby says, "And just one more thing. I just have to mention this one last thing."

Pastor Chase and Pastor Justin decide to sit down for a beer and discuss ways that they can address the length and repetitive nature of these pre-elders' meetings with Toby and Ryan. Pastor Justin suggests that they say to Toby, "If you or anyone else has a reasonable request, then we as the pastors of this congregation have a duty to fulfill that request. However, a two plus hour-long pre-elders' meeting to discuss virtually every aspect of each shut-in's life on a monthly basis is not a reasonable request. It's not the best use of our time as the pastors of this church. Any updates or questions concerning the shut-ins can be discussed during a regular elder meeting as was the practice up until a year ago."

Pastor Chase agrees with Pastor Justin's suggestion, and they inform Toby and Ryan of their decision in person and through email. The two elders seem disappointed by the decision but overall seem to accept the change fairly well. Unfortunately, a few weeks later, Pastor Chase and Pastor Justin begin to hear reports from several trusted parishioners that Toby and Ryan have been telling almost anyone who will listen that neither Pastor

Chase nor Pastor Justin care about the shut-ins of the congregation. And they are referencing a list of four persons who are shut-ins who have not had a pastoral visit in almost three months as proof.

Both pastors agree that it's best to invite Toby and Ryan out for coffee to discuss this matter. The meeting begins with everyone acting courteous to one another, and a few minutes into the conversation Pastor Chase asks Toby and Ryan directly, "Have you been telling people that I and Pastor Justin don't care about the shut-ins because there are four people who have not been visited in a month?"

Ryan remains calm and sheepishly looks to the ground, while Toby reacts by turning beet red and crying. He yells with a high-pitched voice, "You two don't care! The shut-ins have no one. You have help from the elders in visiting them, and there are still people that you hardly ever visit. You can't even make time for a pre-elders' meeting to discuss them each month anymore! It just makes me so upset! So upset I want to scream!"

At this point nearly everyone in the café is staring at the two pastors and two elders. Toby storms outside with Ryan sheepishly following behind him. Shocked and disgusted, Pastor Chase and Pastor Justin apologize to the staff and fellow patrons for Toby's outburst, before paying for the four drinks and leaving. The two young pastors spend the entire drive back to the church discussing how they should handle the difficult situation concerning Toby and Ryan.

Please thoughtfully answer the following questions:

1. In your opinion, did Pastor Chase and Pastor Justin do a good job in following Jesus' words from Matt 18:15–20?
2. What is your opinion of how Toby and Ryan each behaved at the café?
3. If you were to give pastoral advice to Pastor Chase and Pastor Justin in this situation, what would you offer?

Online Worship to In-Person Visit

Amber works most nights and has started the habit of worshiping online. She loves singing the contemporary worship songs and the time of confession and absolution that are included in every service at U-Turn Church. Amber is always intrigued and often captivated by the sermons of Pastor Jed, a worker priest who loves sharing the good news of Jesus with people all over the south side.

Shut-Ins and Homebound Ministry

Lately Amber feels like she has been engulfed in a hurricane while listening to one of Pastor Jed's forty-five-minute sermons from his sermon series "Jesus—The Selfless Servant." Pastor Jed apologized at the end of the service for preaching so long, but explained that he had extra notes from Bible study that he wanted to include in the sermon. However, Amber did not mind and is looking forward to hearing more about Jesus' perfect servant love toward everyone in the world.

Three weeks later Amber is feeling depressed because her hopes of attending in-person worship are sidetracked when she has a bad fall at work. So, Amber worships online again, but the next day she receives a knock on the door. She calls out, "Who is it?" A booming voice rings out, "It's Pastor Jed from U-Turn Church. We received your message through our website that you have been worshiping online and would like more information on our church. I'm here with my wife Sarah." Amber looks through the peephole and sees that it really is Pastor Jed and his wife Sarah.

After answering the door Sarah and Pastor Jed gift Amber with a box of assorted flavors of donuts and a brand-new leather-bound journaling Bible. They seem genuinely kind and interested in Amber as a person and invite her to continue watching their clips online and attend in person-worship when she has an opportunity. Lastly, they provide her with information about the church's bus transportation system, which is free.

After the visit Amber is struck with a strong sense that Jesus is real and that he cares tremendously for her. In fact, she is curious if Jesus sent Pastor Jed and Sarah to visit her that day. For one of the first times in her life, Amber prays aloud to Jesus and asks him to help her become one of his followers. Amazingly, one month later to the day Amber is baptized in the name of the Father, and the Son, and the Holy Spirit at U-Turn Church. Her mother, Lucy, is in attendance to support her along with two friends from work.

Amber begins a new member class and is soon receiving holy communion each week. She is eternally grateful for Pastor Jed, Sarah, her entire church family, and most of all for Jesus, who loves her unconditionally and used Pastor Jed and Sarah to visit her and welcome her to U-Turn Church.

Please thoughtfully answer the following questions:

1. What might have happened if Pastor Jed and his wife Sarah had not visited Amber at her home with gifts of donuts and a leather-bound journaling Bible to introduce themselves and welcome her to U-Turn Church?

2. Are you able to specifically think of any churches whose members visit and bring gifts to people who have requested information on their church?

3. How did Pastor Jed and Sarah's actions and words show Jesus' love to Amber?

Visiting Every Shut-In

Pastor Nate is determined to visit each shut-in within his first two months at his first call. The new pastor has tried repeatedly to reach forty-five-year-old Runyan, a member who is said to be in excellent health, yet was placed on the shut-in list by the previous pastor one year earlier.

On the eleventh try, Pastor Nate finally reaches Runyan. The two men have a good conversation about hunting, fishing, and boating. Eventually Runyan says, "So I'm guessing that the old pastor told you about what happened. He came out to the house to visit me once uninvited, and when he stepped onto my ten acres, he saw that I'm a full-time nudist now. He was awfully embarrassed and took off. When we talked on the phone, I told him what I'm going to tell you . . . I'm young, wild, naked, and I'm free! That's how I was born and that is exactly how I want to live my life from now on! I just don't feel comfortable with clothes on anymore. That's why I moved out of the city in the first place. I needed privacy out in the country to live the way I wanted to."

After a ten second pause Runyan continues speaking to young Pastor Nate. "I would like communion sometime, though. Pastor, would you mind bringing me communion and leading me in a short devotion sometime soon?"

Please thoughtfully answer the following questions:

1. What is your opinion of Runyan's decision to live as a nudist?

2. If you were Pastor Nate, how would you respond to Runyan's request to bring him communion and to lead him in a short devotion sometime soon?

3. If you were to give Pastor Nate pastoral advice, what words of wisdom would you share with him?

4. Are there any biblical or extrabiblical resources you would recommend to Pastor Nate to help him navigate this strange situation?

A House Guest

Hud is attempting to see every corner of his country for as inexpensively as possible. While his friends are working summer jobs, he is enjoying a wide variety of terrains, cultures, and cuisines. The only downside to Hud's explorations is the worry they cause his mother, Rosie.

Early Tuesday morning Rosie's older half-sister, Kerry, is captivated by a social media post from her nephew Hud, which reads, "Hello friends and family! I'm throwing out a Hail Mary pass to all of my social media family! I'm not ready to go home yet. I have three weeks until summer break is over, and there is a lot more beautiful weather left. If anyone has a couch, air mattress, cot, guest bedroom, or even space for me to set up a sleeping bag or tent, I would be eternally grateful!"

After an extensive conversation with her husband, J.P., Kerry responds to Hud's post through a private message and happily invites her twenty-one-year-old nephew to stay at her new dream home. Upon Hud's arrival, J.P. sips his coffee at the kitchen table and watches Kerry greet the young traveler with a hug and the words, "Hello Hud! It's so great to finally meet you! Wow, you look just like Rosie! Let me get your bags and show you to your room."

In the course of Hud's three-week stay, he earns several small acting roles for regional television commercials. The parts pay modestly well and lead to a significant supporting role in a nationally broadcast miniseries. Hud celebrates his blossoming career by treating Kerry and J.P. to dinner at their favorite restaurant. Over cocktails Hud says, "Kerry, J.P., my career is really starting to take off. Would you be willing to let me live with you for a while if I pay rent and keep helping out in the garden? I love you guys. Not just because you're my aunt and uncle but also because you have great vibes. I can really feel Jesus' love in you both."

Kerry agrees almost instantly and J.P. firmly informs Hud that at the very least he will need to discuss the idea with Kerry in private before any commitment can be made. That evening Hud listens in the hallway as J.P. and Kerry fight for five hours about the possibility of Hud moving into their home long term. At one point, Uncle J.P. even accuses Kerry of being infatuated with Hud and having an affair with him. Kerry flatly denies the accusations. Sadly, six hours later J.P. begins the process of moving out and starts searching for a stellar divorce attorney.

One year later, Hud has not worked since his miniseries debuted and is no longer leaving the house. Kerry tries her best to convince her nephew to go out for auditions and interviews but he refuses. Hud has effectively become a shut-in. Eventually Kerry calls her favorite author and guest speaker,

Pastor TNT. Kerry requests that TNT visit Hud and listen to what is on his young heart. TNT agrees with joy as he was once a struggling young actor himself before he became a pastor. He has a heart for young people that are in need of encouragement and direction.

Please thoughtfully answer the following questions:

1. If you were Pastor TNT, what would you say to Hud to encourage him with Jesus' love?
2. Do you believe that Kerry was wise in allowing her nephew Hud to stay past his summer vacation?
3. If you were Pastor TNT, what specifically would you be most concerned about in this situation?
4. Is there any passage from the Bible that comes to your heart or mind as you reflect on this situation?
5. Do you think TNT should recommend to Hud he speak with a licensed professional counselor?

Pepper Prays Out Loud

Pepper proudly uses his medical marijuana card as he picks up his favorite gummies from a local dispensary. The thirty-seven-year-old pops one into his mouth as he strolls through a bustling casino. Minutes later he sends a flurry of text messages to an old acquaintance inviting her out. Pepper writes his eighth text and says, "Hey Tina! Are you around? I've been texting you all night. I'm enjoying one of the best gummies of my life and I'm digging the energy of this casino. You should come over and play some slots with me!"

Tina never responds to a single text from Pepper. The silence concerns Pepper, so he decides to reach out to Tina's father, Pastor Philmont, via social media. He quickly receives a response from the old pastor that reads, "Hi Pepper, thank you for being such a great friend to Tina and checking on her. I'll be honest with you. Tina isn't doing well. She hasn't been out of the house in nearly six months. Her anxiety has become severe, and she is struggling to do her job while working remotely from home. Her mother and I are worried about her. If you have any ideas on what might encourage Tina, feel free to share them. In fact, why don't you come over for dinner tonight around five thirty? Seeing you might cheer her up! Blessings, your old catechism teacher."

That evening, Pepper chomps down three gummies as he walks to Tina's place. He prays aloud to Jesus for the first time since he was in catechism class twenty-three years earlier. Pepper prays, "Jesus, I love Tina like a sister. You know there have been times when I have even wanted to date her. I know that she has no idea! Please help me to encourage her tonight. Please help Tina to feel comfortable about leaving the house again. I want her to know that you love her. And I want her to know that I love her like a sister and a little bit in a romantic way too. In your name Jesus! Amen!"

After Pepper finishes praying, he notices that two college women heard him while walking to their car. Normally that would embarrass Pepper, but not tonight. Pepper was praying for his friend Tina and she needs Jesus' help.

Please thoughtfully answer the following questions:

1. Do you think it was wise for Pastor Philmont to invite Pepper over for dinner to cheer Tina up? Why or why not?
2. What is your reaction to Pepper's prayer to Jesus on behalf of Tina?
3. If you were a friend or family member of Tina, are there any passages from the Bible you would consider sharing with Tina if a good opportunity arose?
4. Do you believe Pastor Philmont and Tina's mother should recommend Tina attend counseling with a licensed clinical therapist and maybe speak with a psychiatrist about the possibility of being prescribed medication for anxiety?

Chapter 14

Urban and Inner-City Ministry

Kevin Loves His New Apartment

KEVIN HAS RECENTLY GRADUATED from a rural college that is almost entirely surrounded by corn fields. One day after graduating, Kevin lands a job in the tech industry, and he quickly packs up his small electric car and makes the sixteen-hundred-mile drive to meet his new bosses and colleagues. Upon his arrival he is given a tour of the two main facilities that he will be working in.

About halfway through the tour he realizes that his tour guide is actually his new boss, Kyle. With an ironic half smile and silly laugh Kyle says, "Yeah, people are always surprised when a massively successful boss and innovator is giving the new kids a tour. But I say, why not! I want you kids to feel comfortable as you start out here. That's why we bought the apartments in the city, and match up each new employee with roommates that will fit their personalities based on the personality tests that you completed. Unless, that is, you already have an apartment?" Without hesitation Kevin answers, "No! I don't. Thanks, Kyle!" Letting out another silly laugh, Kyle answers, "That's what I thought. You'll be rooming with Laci and Ren. Our corporate buses will pick you up for work Monday to Friday 7:30 a.m. sharp. Let me know if you need anything."

Kevin really likes his two new roommates and he loves his brick warehouse-style apartment. It's located in an ethnically diverse area of the city that is walkable and has numerous restaurants, entertainment venues, and waterfront views within minutes of his front door. However, after about a month of getting used to the area, Kevin starts to feel a sense of loneliness, and he realizes he misses attending church. While at college, he would attend daily chapel every chance that he got.

Thankfully, he finds a church which seems to have a relaxed, welcoming spirit while staying focused on Christ. He has even decided to start volunteering to help serve meals at the church's basement food kitchen once a month. For his first time volunteering, Pastor Fernando serves alongside of him and introduces him to some of the other volunteers and regular visitors.

Toward the end of the evening a regular named Miguel approaches and says, "So, did you move into the neighborhood to work for one of the big tech companies?" Kevin answers sarcastically, "Yeah, I did. But one of these days I'll move back to my home town to live with my parents and work as a telemarketer." Miguel gives no reaction to Kevin's answer and responds with, "Do you live in one of the apartments down the block?" Kevin has a short nervous laugh and says, "Yeah, I do. It will do for now, I guess."

Suddenly he notices that Pastor Fernando seems uncomfortable, and Miguel starts to shake as he says, "I was priced out of those apartments when you rich tech kids came in and gentrified the area. Now I live in a tent in a park ten minutes in the other direction, and my bus trip to work at the dock takes twice as long. I hope your good deeds of working at the food kitchen help you sleep well at night, bro."

After Miguel leaves, Pastor Fernando puts her hand on Kevin's shoulder and says, "Try not to take it personally. Miguel is still hurt about losing his apartment. It was your company that bought the building and raised the rent, not you. You came in way after it happened. Pray that the church can help Miguel find permanent housing for him and his wife soon."

Please thoughtfully answer the following questions:

1. Do you feel that Kevin's sarcastic remarks provoked a blunt response from Miguel?
2. What is your opinion of Miguel's response?
3. Do you believe that Pastor Fernando gave Christlike pastoral words of encouragement to Kevin?

Shaw Shaw Is on Guard

Shaw Shaw is a sixty-one-year-old convenience store owner who immigrated to this country when he was eighteen years old. He and his wife, Strawberry, and their three children live in an apartment above their shop that is open six days a week and closed only on Sundays so they can attend

Mass and enjoy family time. Shaw Shaw set up roots forty-three years ago in what would be considered an urbanized old city area within a ten-minute walk of the central city hub.

Lately there has been a rise in break-ins and violent crimes in Shaw Shaw's neighborhood. In fact, a fellow shop owner and dear family friend by the name of Ali was violently gunned down in the back by two cowardly robbers a mere eight months ago. Sadly, they are still at large. This rise in crime and, more specifically, Ali's tragic murder has inspired Shaw Shaw and other business owners in the area to create a neighborhood watch program.

One early Friday morning, Shaw Shaw is patrolling the neighborhood with a large samurai-style sword that he recently purchased from a pawn shop, and his patrol partner, James, is armed with a forty-five-caliber handgun as well as a pair of nunchucks and brass knuckles. After about thirty minutes on patrol, they spot a man in a ski mask attempting to break into a side window of their friend Connie's restaurant. Shaw Shaw and James encircle him and James yells, "Don't you move an inch, you twit, or I'll blast you!" The two men hold him captive for a moment and debate whether to phone the police or to take justice into their own hands and hang him on the spot. Thankfully they make the wise decision to phone the police. James stuffs his gun in his back pocket so the police won't charge him with illegally possessing a firearm.

After the police take witness statements from Shaw Shaw and James, they seriously warn the two men not to take justice into their own hands or apprehend anyone in the future. They are warned to always immediately phone the police. As it turns out, the man they apprehended is a highly dangerous person who was wanted on three counts of attempted murder.

As the sun rises Shaw Shaw walks home, and he decides to stop into his church and see if his priest is in the building. As it turns out, Father Morton has recently arrived and is happy to see one of his favorite parishioners. The two men sit down for tea, and Shaw Shaw relates the night's events in detail to his priest.

Father Morton responds to the story with, "Well Shaw Shaw, I am grateful that you and James made the wise decision not to take justice into your own hands. God has placed the governing authorities in a position to administer justice on his behalf. As long as the authorities are not doing something blatantly amoral, we should obey them.

"Also, I would like you to consider that perhaps some of the people committing these heinous crimes in our neighborhood also need love. What if you split your time working on the neighborhood watch with volunteering in some charitable capacity? I have seen several studies that show people who are exposed to trees and green spaces typically feel more relaxed and have better overall mental health. Now, this neighborhood is a little bit of a tree desert. There is a need for trees to provide shade on hot days, a block from harsh winds, a habitat for wildlife, and something for children to climb. I would like you to consider joining me in partnering with the city in planting trees along sidewalks, parks, and in vacant lots. This is an opportunity to care for God's good creation together and make a real difference in our community."

With little hesitation, Shaw Shaw accepts Father Morton's invitation and soon convinces his family and even James to participate as well. Ten years later their group, with the help of the city, has planted nearly a thousand trees and beautified their neighborhood. As they have planted trees, there have been countless conversations with many people in the neighborhood who found out that Father Morton and Shaw Shaw's group were composed primarily of Christians, and a number of conversations about Jesus have organically come about as a result. This work has been far more fulfilling for Shaw Shaw than any work he has ever done on the neighborhood watch.

Please thoughtfully answer the following questions:

1. What is your opinion of Father Morton's advice to Shaw Shaw when he said, "Well Shaw Shaw, I am grateful that you and James made the wise decision not to take justice into your own hands. God has placed the governing authorities in a position to administer justice on his behalf. As long as the authorities are not doing something blatantly amoral, we should obey them"?

2. Had you been in Shaw Shaw's position would have you joined Father Morton in partnering with the city in planting trees along sidewalks, parks, and in vacant lots in an effort to care for God's good creation?

3. Do you find it surprising when many people in the neighborhood found out Father Morton and Shaw Shaw's group were composed primarily of Christians, a number of conversations about Jesus organically arose as a result?

Unity in a Time of Disunity

Artem is an Orthodox priest serving in a thriving old city that is filled with character and tradition yet simultaneously embraces modern technology. His congregation was founded over six hundred years ago, and the church building they worship in is over four hundred years old. However, his congregation and its building are relatively young for the neighborhood, as there are three congregations that are almost eight hundred years old with buildings that each date back nearly seven hundred years.

Six months ago, his nation was invaded by military forces from a large neighboring country. A substantial portion of Artem's beloved city has been decimated by air raids and artillery bombardments. Sadly, fourteen of the fifteen church buildings in his area of the city have been destroyed.

Artem and his parishioners have responded by opening the doors of their church to welcome in Christian neighbors from a variety of denominational backgrounds for prayer, conversation, and rest. Their church building has also become a place to shelter during attacks for people of different religions as well as for atheists and agnostics. Artem and his parishioners strive to welcome all of their guests with love and open arms.

One Saturday evening during a particularly violent bombing raid, approximately three hundred Christians from eleven different denominations, and around fifty people who either identify with another religion or none at all, take shelter in Artem's church basement. Suddenly an elderly Lutheran pastor begins to pray the Lord's Prayer. In an awesome moment nearly everyone in the basement joins him in prayer.

During this time of desperation, the group who is uncertain if they will live another hour or even another minute, finds themselves focusing on their common humanity as opposed to their differences. It seems almost every man, woman, and child in the basement is overwhelmed with love toward one another, as they pray the prayer Jesus taught his first disciples to pray a little over two thousand years earlier.

Please thoughtfully answer the following questions:

1. What is your opinion of how Artem and his congregation responded to the crisis they and their local neighbors were dealing with?

2. Do you believe Christian congregations and communities in general should focus more on their common humanity as opposed to their differences with those around them?

3. If you had been in the church basement during the bombing raid, would have you joined the Lutheran pastor and the majority of the people in praying the Lord's Prayer?

Pastor Chris

Two years ago, Chris resigned as pastor of his first call out of seminary. The ten-month experience was so traumatic that Chris told his bishop privately he feels like his life has been ruined. After deleting his social media accounts, creating a new email address, and getting a new phone number that he gives exclusively to close family and friends, Chris moves to a large coastal city in a different region of the country.

After a year of settling into his new career as a human resources agent, Chris begins to heal from the trauma that he experienced in his first call. Soon he starts to pray about whether or not he should try to reenter parish ministry or if he should pursue some type of specialized ministry. It is at this time that he invites friends and colleagues to a Thursday night weekly Bible study at his favorite pub. For the first three years, the study has an average of five or six people each week. It then grows to about twenty people a week, and after six years the Bible study becomes too large for the pub.

The Bible study participants soon begin to rent out a school gymnasium for two worship services each Sunday morning. Chris is once again serving as a pastor. Except this time, he is in a large urban setting that is primarily composed of younger adults, and he is now a non-denominational pastor, but in his heart and in his teaching and preaching he is still very much a Lutheran.

As Chris continues to work as a full-time human resources agent, he serves part time as a pastor and watches with amazement at what God does in his neighborhood and city as a whole. Chris's church, Living Savior, partners with other Christian churches in the area to set up a food pantry and job training center in a beautiful Art Deco–style building that was formerly a bank. The ecumenical Christian partnership also begins to buy up loft apartments that are in disrepair and rehabs them into beautiful, livable spaces, which they then rent out at a low, affordable rate to single mothers in need.

"Jesus Christ is doing everything here. He deserves all of the credit. We simply allowed him to use us for his glory. We saw needs in our community and prayed that God would give us an opportunity to make a difference in Jesus' name," Chris tells a local news reporter who interviews him about Living Savior and the ecumenical Christian partnership's positive impact in the neighborhood and city as a whole.

Please thoughtfully answer the following questions:

1. Does Chris's story remind you of any stories in the Bible?

2. Are you surprised by how much the Bible study grew over the course of a six-year period to the point it was too big for the pub and eventually had to start worshiping in a school gymnasium as Living Savior Church?

3. What is your opinion of the work Living Savior and the ecumenical Christian partnership is doing in the neighborhood and city as a whole?

4. What do you think of what Chris said to the news reporter who was interviewing him?

Riley Calls for Action

Riley Dalton was born sixty-nine years ago in what he calls "the most beautiful city on earth!" He purchased his dream home forty years ago on the north end of Rocky Side Park. Riley and his wife, Lana, chose their dream home in part because of the location. The iconic neighborhood is densely populated, welcoming, eclectic, and electric! It has traditionally been full of life, fantastic resources, imagination, community engagement and collaboration, and endless possibilities.

Riley and his wife have watched in horror as their neighborhood and a majority of their city has been transformed into a humanitarian crisis of homeless encampments. This sharp decline started when the mayor of their city, Rod Loria, decided three years ago that Rocky Side Park would be the perfect place for several massive homeless encampments. According to Riley and Lana, these homeless encampments have brought several nightmares to their neighborhood, which include enormous amounts of trash, a total lack of sanitation, endless health issues, unregulated propane tanks, and a variety of other safety and security issues, as well as so many other tragedies that are now connected to their dying neighborhood.

For the first thirty-seven years that Riley and Lana lived on the north end of Rocky Side Park, they freely rode their bikes to the zoo with friends and family members. Now, in the last three years their beloved bike paths have become impeded with trash, encampments, and human feces and puddles of urine. They are attacked verbally or physically nearly every time they go for a walk or bike ride in their once beautiful and safe community.

Riley has spoken with the amazing men and women of his police department about these issues, and they tell him that they act at the direction of their mayor, Rod Loria. And that Mayor Loria has instructed them to "Deescalate any situation involving the homeless no matter what. Treat their tents and propane tanks on public space as a permanent residence just as if you were approaching the mayor's mansion. Lastly, handle all homeless people with kid gloves, and be very hesitant to charge a homeless person with a crime if they are breaking the law for assault, menacing, trespassing, littering, exposure, public urination or public defecation. We want to be humane and have a live and let live approach to the homeless crisis in our city."

After almost three years of trying to work with Mayor Rod Loria to solve the humanitarian crisis in his neighborhood and throughout the city, Riley eventually becomes fed up, as he feels that his efforts have been ignored and that he is being condescended to by Mayor Loria and his office. He decides to hold a public press conference on the steps of his church expressing his great concern about the massive homeless encampments in Rocky Side Park and throughout the city. Riley also does not shy away from calling Mayor Rod Loria out by name to the media. He even goes as far as to demand the mayor resign from his office as result of failing to govern effectively and solve the homeless crisis as he promised on inauguration day.

Riley's speech angers the mayor's office to the point that they issue a response accusing Riley of using his church, his faith, and his celebrity as weapons to attack those struggling with homelessness as well as the mayor for being openly gay and a person of color.

Riley responds two days later in a second press conference at his home. "I want clean, stable housing and medical services for our homeless brothers and sisters in our city. I have a compassionate view of those who are homeless. Unlike Rod Loria, I don't want them to be stuck living on the sidewalk or in a park without any services or permanent housing. Lastly, I have never said one word about the mayor's sexual orientation or his race or ethnicity. To accuse me of being upset with him for any other reason other than the horrible way he has governed and handled this humanitarian crisis is absurd! As a Christian I love everyone, people of all races, ethnicities, and sexual orientations. How dare Rod Loria and his office and anyone else who has attacked me in this baseless way! My record speaks for itself and is beyond reproach. Ask any of my colleagues, family members, friends, or my pastor, Pastor Phil Jones. They will all happily tell you that I don't have a homophobic or racist bone in my body."

Please thoughtfully answer the following questions:

1. In your opinion was it wise of Riley to hold his first public press conference on the steps of his church?
2. If you were Pastor Phil Jones, what words of advice would you give to Riley and Lana if they sought your counsel?

3. From what you have read, what is your opinion of Rod Loria's performance as a civil leader?

4. Are there any words from Jesus in the Gospels that come to your mind when reading and reflecting on this story?

5. If you were Pastor Phil Jones, how would you specifically pray for Riley and Lana?

6. If you were Pastor Phil Jones, how would you specifically pray for Mayor Rod Loria and for those serving in his office?

A Disappointing Voters' Assembly Meeting

City Hope Church is a growing congregation located in the heart of a thriving, densely populated downtown city center. Its leadership team is a vibrant and energetic group of people composed of both men and women from a wide variety of diverse backgrounds. Together this team is preparing to renovate their sanctuary with the latest technology and fresh décor.

Strangely, the emeritus chairman of the congregation, Earl, is displeased with the recent growth and proposed renovations. In fact, most everything about Earl is a little strange. For example, at the last voters' assembly meeting Earl was overheard saying to Hannah, the wife of Pastor Donny, "I don't know why Pastor has been praying for the people displaced because of the war. I think that countries should end every war by dropping nuclear bombs. That would save a lot of fighting and a lot of money."

In that same voters' assembly meeting Earl stands up and opposes the sanctuary renovations, saying, "We only have five years' worth of operating funds in our emergency account. Is it really justified to dip into our emergency account for this renovation? I mean, this is going to eat up a quarter of the funds in that account! What if there is another financial crisis? We will need all of those funds. Things could get really tight around here! Call me a worrier if you want, but I say we play it safe and make do with what we have. Now isn't the time to take any risks."

Earl's speech convinces twenty-three of the forty-two voters to vote no on the sanctuary renovation. After the meeting, several of his acquaintances congratulate him with handshakes and hugs. And one person can be heard saying, "Earl, you saved this congregation a great deal of financial hardship. Good job and thank you for your leadership!"

Moments later Earl overhears Pastor Donny saying, "It's amazing how one or two people can hinder the work of the Lord. Our leadership group worked tirelessly for half a year planning these proposed renovations, and Earl wrecked it in a few minutes. The people of this area of the city should have a modern, beautiful, and functional space to worship Jesus in. Not a space that is barely adequate."

Please thoughtfully answer the following questions:

1. Do you think Pastor Donny and the rest of the leadership team should reintroduce their proposal for renovations to the sanctuary in a few months at the next voters' assembly meeting?
2. What is your opinion of Earl's speech at the voters' assembly meeting?
3. Do you think Pastor Donny's comments after the voters' assembly meeting were warranted?
4. Are there any passages from the Bible you would recommend to Pastor Donny and the rest of the leadership team to reflect on at this time?

Urban Prairie

First English Church is surrounded by urban prairie. The older members of the congregation can remember a time when their street was lined with handsome storefronts, an Art Deco–style movie theater, and dozens of well-built brick bungalow homes. Today all that remains on Oak Street is their church building, the parsonage, and three bungalow homes that are in poor condition yet are still inhabited. The area has become so rural that deer have started to roam around the block, and recently a poacher drove into the area and took a six-point buck.

Late one evening at a church council meeting, Vivian shares her thoughts on the state of the neighborhood and the congregation saying, "My grandparents helped found this congregation, and my parents paid for half of the cost of the construction of our current church building as well as the parsonage. Today if they were alive, they would be shocked to see the state of this once beautiful neighborhood. It's obvious that the city is unable or unwilling to help this neighborhood. We have tried to get their help multiple times, and where has it gotten us? Where?

"We need to ask our sister churches and social service agencies in other areas of the county to help us. We need to let them know that this is a real mission opportunity. With their help, God can use us to revitalize this area with the construction of affordable decent housing and new parks. As people move in and they see how much we care, then we can share the good news of Jesus with them as well. What do you folks say? Are you willing to swallow your pride and ask for help and give this a shot? What on earth do we have to lose? There's only forty people left in this congregation! Pastor Fenster, I know you're close to seventy-five years old, but will you put off retirement a few more years to lead us in this effort? You've been here thirty-seven years already. What will another three years hurt?"

Please thoughtfully answer the following questions:

1. What is your opinion of Vivian's speech to the church council?
2. If you were in Pastor Fenster's position, would you prayerfully consider putting off retirement a few more years to lead an effort to revitalize the neighborhood?
3. What biblical or extrabiblical resources would you recommend to a person or team that would lead the effort to revitalize First English's neighborhood?

Relating Jesus to the Needs of the Time

Pastor Joseph Lee is elated by his new call to Sunset Lutheran Church in the affluent old city neighborhood of Bellersville. It is far away from his previous congregation on the outskirts of a declining small city. Bellersville has the best of premium urban amenities yet has easy access to gorgeous wooded parks and the ocean.

Each Saturday night Pastor Lee enjoys his favorite jazz clubs until early on Sunday morning. He then heads directly to church to lead worship. His congregation loves their new pastor's style! A mere five months after his arrival Pastor Lee spearheads a church plant by Sunset Lutheran Church inside of his favorite spot, The Old House of Bourbon Jazz Club. The name Pastor Joseph Lee gives this satellite is Bourbon Jazz Lutheran Church.

People from far and wide journey to the famous jazz club for great music and dynamic, Christ-centered sermons! Within three years of Bourbon Jazz Lutheran Church's founding, it swells to over four hundred members, and Lutheran churches throughout the country have copied their ministry model by founding churches in jazz clubs, bars, and coffeehouses.

Amazingly, one Lutheran pastor by the name of Craiger Cunningham writes on a famous blog, "The Reverend Joseph Lee has led our church down a dangerous path. We should not strive to conform to the ways of the world, but instead should be set apart as holy. From what I know, Pastor Joseph Lee is not even wearing a clerical collar in most of his services. Shameful! The church is not to be a whore to the world, but instead it should be a shining example of doctrinal purity in the midst of the pagans."

One blogger responds to this pastor's comments by writing, "First of all, it is always good to speak with a brother in Christ directly whenever you have a concern and put the best construction on things. I know Pastor Joseph Lee, and he is a faithful pastor and theologian who loves Jesus. Secondly, if Bourbon Jazz Lutheran Church is sharing the good news of Jesus Christ, why on earth would any Christian be upset with them or churches with a similar ministry style?" This blogger receives no response from Pastor Craiger Cunningham.

Please thoughtfully answer the following questions:

1. What is your opinion of Pastor Joseph Lee planting a church in The Old House of Bourbon Jazz Club and naming it Bourbon Jazz Lutheran Church?
2. What is your opinion of what Pastor Craiger Cunningham wrote on the famous blog about Pastor Joseph Lee and the congregation of Bourbon Jazz Lutheran Church?
3. How do you feel about the response of the blogger to Pastor Craiger Cunningham's comments?
4. Are there any passages from the Scriptures that come to your mind while reflecting on this case study?

A New Year's Eve Toast

Pastor Cray and fifty other city pastors and their families have been invited to a local New Year's Eve party hosted by philanthropic businessman Frank York. He is hosting the celebration at his newly acquired apartment that was formerly a firehouse on the edge of an industrial park. As guests enter the mid-century modern complex that has been turned into a massive four-story loft-style apartment, they discuss Frank York's acquisition of the industrial park that he will soon develop into luxury apartments and penthouse suites, complete with lush green space, high end dining, and entertainment options.

At about ten minutes till midnight, Frank takes the microphone and addresses his guests, while enjoying champagne. "Ladies and gentlemen! Thank you all for allowing me to celebrate with you and your families this evening. I thank God that I get to ring in the new year with you! What an honor it is to host you in my new apartment on the edge of the York Town

Innovation Village. Yes, ground was broken and construction began yesterday. Next year at this time phase one of the project should be complete.

"If I may share a personal note, I have had one or two bad experiences in the church over the years, yet spending time with godly pastors and their lovely families has strengthened my faith in God. The love that you are showing the people of this city is fantastic! You are helping people get much-needed resources like health care, housing, job opportunities, and, most of all, you are pointing them to the cross of Jesus Christ. I applaud you all!

"Now, I know this isn't possible, and maybe it's my glass of champagne talking a little, but wouldn't it be amazing if everyone in this room planted a church and everyone here became members? Can you imagine a church that is primarily composed of pastors? Wouldn't that be marvelous? In fact, I could turn one of my apartments into our church building! Hahaha! Oh well, we can dream. A toast to all of you! May God bless you in the year to come! Amen!"

Please thoughtfully answer the following questions:

1. What, if any, issues might arise if a church was planted primarily by fifty pastors and only they, their families, and close friends attended?
2. What is your overall impression of Frank York's New Year's Eve toast?
3. If you were advising the pastors who attended this party, would you encourage them to read and reflect upon any passages from the Bible specifically?

A Car-Free City

Gabriel's city is on course to be a car-free city within ten years. This move will cut down on every type of pollution substantially and will provide a better quality of life for not only people but also animals and plant life. Most of the people in Gabriel's martial arts class are excited for these changes.

One early morning after class, Gabriel is discussing with Mike and Cray the city's transition to car independence and the expansion of bike and walking paths as well as solar powered underground and above-ground trains. The typically stoic Mike becomes agitated and proclaims, "I'm not going to swear because I know you two are pastors, but this stuff makes me sick! This city has always been famous for muscle cars! If the government believes they are going to outlaw my car that I restored or the cars of other men throughout this city, they are gravely mistaken. They'll have to pry my dead hands off of the steering wheel. That's a promise."

Pastor Cray responds, "Well, I wish that you would just come out and tell us what you really think, Mike." For a few moments Mike lets out a fake pretentious laugh and then says, "Yeah, Cray, I know that you are a tree hugging liberal, and you are totally into this program. I've heard you carry on about how important it is to care for God's good creation, but what about me? Aren't I God's good creation too? Shouldn't my needs matter too? Have fun riding your bike around town when it's thirty-nine degrees out next January!"

Please thoughtfully answer the following questions:

1. What is your opinion of what Mike had to say?

2. If you were Pastor Cray, how would you respond to what Mike said to you?

3. What words of wisdom do you think Pastor Gabriel should offer to his two friends?

4. Are there any passages from the book of Genesis that come to your mind as you reflect on this case study?

Chapter 15

Youth and Young Adult Ministry

The Recommendations of Debbie Hancock

REVEREND HEROLD IS FINISHING his first week as intentional interim pastor at one of the most conflicted congregations he has served to this point in his long career. Thankfully there is only one more meeting for the day, and he arrives ten minutes early. As Reverend Herold approaches the church conference room, he hears a parishioner by the name of Debbie Hancock making an impassioned speech, saying, "Well, I have been volunteering to clean the youth room for nearly a decade, and the sight that I saw this morning was heartbreaking! I was appalled. Simply appalled! Dirty dishes in the sink, davenport pillows on the floor. Disgusting! It is my recommendation as the church's sanitation supervisor and board of properties vice president that the youth room be closed until the space can be respected and cherished as it deserves. Secondly, we must obviously suspend this rogue youth director without pay, and begin a thorough investigation into her life prior to her becoming our youth director!"

There is a brief pause and then Howard Schmidtler announces, "Debbie, you are an invaluable member of this congregation. Your dedication to this family is beyond compare. I believe that I speak for the whole board of elders when I say that your recommendations will be followed. Reverend Herold will fall in line with these recommendations as well, I guarantee it. And, may I say also, your speech at the festival of bratwursts last August was tremendous and it brought tears to my eyes, but today I think that you may have topped that speech. Thank you so much!"

Please thoughtfully answer the following questions:

1. Does it appear Debbie's recommendations to the board of elders are reasonable?
2. In your opinion are Debbie and Howard following Matt 18:15–20 in this situation with the youth director and the youth room?
3. What Bible passages might Reverend Herold read to Debbie and the board of elders to help them reflect on this situation in a Christlike way that is focused on love and forgiveness?

Visiting Justin at College

Pastor Albert has been at the same call his entire twenty years of ministry. During this time, he has grown close to his congregation and has baptized nearly a quarter of his flock. One of the members he baptized nineteen years earlier is finishing up his first semester of college at a prestigious liberal arts university about an hour away. Pastor Albert and his wife Sarah decide to take a Saturday morning to drive down and encourage Justin as he finishes up his first semester of college, while also enjoying the last of the autumn colors.

When they arrive at Justin's address, they pull up to a fraternity house that seems eerily out of place on such an idyllic and well-maintained university campus. The large Victorian-style home has missing shutters, chipped paint, and a large, collapsed porch. As they enter the side door they see beer cans scattered throughout the downstairs and several plastic soda pop bottles filled with urine placed on coffee tables and bookshelves. The smell of vomit, mildew, and rotting food permeates the entire building.

As they try to locate Justin's room, a young man walks out of the bathroom wearing a towel and says, "Are you the people from the church who are visiting Justin?" Pastor Albert responds, "Yes, I'm Pastor Albert and this is my wife Sarah." The young man responds, "Good to meet you guys. Justin has been really looking forward to your visit. He's been sort of depressed ever since he was banished to the basement for not being available to help decorate for the Golf Pros and Tennis Hoes party a couple weeks ago. I can show you where he's staying, if you want?" Pastor Albert speaks up, "Wait ... what do you mean, Justin was banished to the basement? Who banished him to the basement?" The young man in the towel responds, "Uh, I think it's best if he tells you. Come on, I'll show you where he's staying."

They walk down a shaky wooden staircase to a filthy basement with a six-foot ceiling that has a mural of a giant rat painted on the wall. For a moment they don't see any sign of Justin until they spot him in the far corner sleeping on a mattress that is placed next to several boxes of clothing, textbooks, and toiletry items. "Oh my gosh, Albert! There is Justin. He's sleeping in the corner of the room," says Sarah in a voice of alarm.

Albert and Sarah take Justin out for brunch, and over the next several hours they hear dozens of stories of hazing directed at him and other freshmen by upperclassmen living in the house that began at pledge week and has lasted ever since. Eventually he talks about having had to miss the decorating event for the Golf Pros and Tennis Hoes party due to a group study date at the library, and being called in front of the whole house by the fraternity president, who declared, "Normally we would spank someone for their disobedience. But Justin isn't even worthy of that! He's banished to the basement until I see a renewed sense of commitment in him. His lack of dedication is unacceptable. Take your stuff and get down in the basement, Justin!"

Please thoughtfully answer the following questions:

1. If you were Pastor Albert and Sarah, and had heard and seen what they had that day, what words of advice would you give Justin concerning his living arrangements and involvement in this fraternity?
2. In your view do Pastor Albert and Sarah have an ethical responsibility to report the condition of the fraternity or the stories of hazing to the authorities and to the university?
3. Clearly Pastor Albert and Sarah should encourage Justin to inform his parents about the situation at the fraternity house. However, if he does not, do you feel it is appropriate for Pastor Albert and Sarah to inform them?
4. What biblical passages might help Pastor Albert, Sarah, and Justin think through this situation with the fraternity?

Waking Up to an Awkward Sight

Hank is a forty-four-year-old retired construction worker who has lived on disability for approximately one year. Over the last five months he has found joy in serving as the volunteer youth director at his church. To his surprise the parents have asked him to lead the high schoolers on the yearly summer youth service trip to a city nearly five hundred miles away. Hank drives the majority of the students in the church bus, and his wife, Ariana, drives the remaining six students in the family minivan.

After almost nine hours on the road, the group finally arrives at the church that will serve as their home over the next six days. As they register their group in the narthex, Hank and Ariana are expecting one classroom space for the girls to camp in and one classroom for the boys to camp in. Instead, they are informed that the girls will have their own classroom but the boys will have to sleep in the corner of the gymnasium so that a group of girls from another youth group that registered late can have their own private classroom. When Ariana asks the woman running the check-in desk why the boys are being dislocated, and not the late registering female students, the woman answers, "It would be inappropriate to expect young ladies to sleep in an open area like a gymnasium. Boys are more suited to handle situations like that. Girls need privacy more than boys do."

Hank and the twenty boys in his group camp out in a three hundred square foot corner of the gym that is no bigger than a small living room. The rest of the gym is crammed with boys from other church groups along with their youth leaders. On the fourth night of their stay just before wake-up call, Hank awakes to a boy and three girls just inside of his group's camping space watching an exceptionally graphic movie on a cell phone that depicts extreme scenes of violence, nudity, and sexual acts. For a moment Hank is not totally sure if he is awake or dreaming, but as he smells the strong aroma of coffee brewing from the cafeteria, he realizes he is awake. Hank feels a responsibility to ask the students to turn off the movie they are watching and return to their camps. When he does, one of the boys, who appears to be about sixteen years old, responds, "It's okay, this is Miranda, she's an adult camp counselor. This is a movie that she ordered for us to watch. Just let us finish and then we will leave."

Upon further conversation with the boy, Hank realizes the two girls and boy are all only fifteen years old and the camp counselor, Miranda, is twenty-one years old. After they leave Hank's camp area, he considers how he should handle this awkward situation. For about an hour he thinks about reporting this incident to the church leaders that organized the camp or possibly even to the local sheriff's department. After talking it over with his wife Ariana, they come to the conclusion together that the best course of action is to forget the situation took place. The rest of the service trip goes relatively smoothly, and two days later they drive their students home.

Please thoughtfully answer the following questions:

1. Do you believe that Hank and Ariana were wise in not reporting what Hank witnessed to the church leaders that organized the camp?
2. If you had been in Hank's place would have you considered reporting what you had witnessed to the local sheriff's department?

3. Hank's church has had a pastoral vacancy for almost two years, but a new pastor just accepted a call to his church. Would you advise Hank to tell his new pastor about what he witnessed on the trip once they arrive?

Kim and Adam

Aaron and Sharon are parents to a rambunctious, free-spirited fourteen-year-old son named Adam. There are many mornings they are awoken to the sound of video game tournaments or electric guitar solos blasting from Adam's bedroom. Recently Adam started his freshman year of high school and has made a new friend, Kim Prescot, an incredibly beautiful seventeen-year-old senior who serves as class president and is a state champion in the four-hundred-meter dash and long jump as well as leading the varsity volleyball team as captain. Although there is a noticeable age difference between Adam and Kim, Aaron and Sharon are thrilled their son has a new friend who enjoys playing video games with their son and listening to him play the guitar.

Early on a Monday morning, Pastor Jacob notices an email that is marked urgent and is entitled "One of your youth group members is having an inappropriate relationship!" The email was sent by an ex-member named Holly Marshall. The five-paragraph message makes the accusation that seventeen-year-old Kim Prescot is manipulating Holly's next door neighbor Adam into kissing her under his backyard magnolia tree in exchange for her attention while he plays the guitar and her participation in video game tournaments with him.

Holly Marshall ends the message to Pastor Jacob with the lines "Adam is a starry-eyed fourteen-year-old youth who is being seduced and manipulated by a vivacious, voluptuous seventeen-year-old who is only a month away from adulthood! Kim Prescot is a parishioner of yours. It is your duty to correct this situation, Pastor Jacob! So far you are the only one I have spoken to about the situation so that I could save Adam and his family from any further heartache. How do you plan on correcting Kim Prescot?"

Please thoughtfully answer the following questions:

1. If you were Pastor Jacob, would you respond to Holly Marshall's email?
2. Do you believe Pastor Jacob should take extra time to ask Kim Prescot how her senior year is going at the end of the next youth group meeting over soda and snacks?

3. What, if any, Bible passages are you reminded of when reflecting on this situation?

Celebrating a State Championship

Trey, LJ, Deon, Christopher, Paul, Mario, Baxter, and Gerry are celebrating winning the boy's state championship game in basketball earlier in the day. They have been waiting nearly an hour for Paul's Uncle Riley to meet them in Paul's hotel room with beer. Eventually, they become impatient with how long it's taking Riley to arrive with beer, so they decide to walk across the street and try to find someone who is old enough to buy it for them.

As the boys cross the street to the convenience store, they spot a guy who used to be married to Trey's first cousin, Lisa. His name is Harrison, and they are pretty sure that he is in his mid-twenties and will likely buy them beer for a little bit of cash. Trey approaches Harrison and says, "Hey Harrison! The guys and I want to celebrate our win with some drinks. If we give you enough money to buy yourself something to drink, and we give you money to get us five twelve packs of beer and two bottles of whiskey, will you buy it for us?" Harrison responds, "You guys played your hearts out today, and gave the area something to be really proud of. I would be honored to help you guys celebrate tonight. Your money is no good here. Drinks are on me."

Ten minutes later Harrison emerges from the store with the alcohol for the guys and, as they say thank you, Harrison looks right at the boys without expression and says, "You know, you might think that your bodies are made mostly out of water . . . well, they're not. They are chiseled out of pure granite rock. Each one of you looks like a Roman god, but you played like superheroes in today's state championship victory. You are heroes to an entire generation of young people in our area. And quite frankly you're my heroes as well. Nicely done today, gentlemen. Nicely done."

The boys say thank you and then walk toward Paul's hotel room with their alcohol. As soon as they are out of Harrison's sight, they have a good laugh at how weird Harrison was acting. Once back in the room, they start talking about how much they will miss playing on the same team again next year, and about how they will have reunions after graduation and come back next season to see Baxter and Gerry play as seniors with new teammates.

At around this time, they hear playful knocking on the door to the room. It's Paul's Uncle Riley with his best friend from high school, Harrison. They enter the room with a lot of alcohol to add to the celebration. Harrison is elated to be sharing this moment with his heroes. The boys are stunned to see Harrison because they had no idea that Riley even knew him.

The celebration continues on for several more hours, and eventually everyone starts to pass out on the beds and the couches except for Trey and Harrison. Trey tries to make conversation and says, "Hey, let's see what's on TV." Harrison responds, "I wish that I could reenact today's game with you. Instead, I'm going to grab more ice from the hall. When I come back, I'll have something stronger than alcohol for you to try. It will make you feel amazing. Get ready, because it is going to change your life, young man."

After Harrison leaves the room Trey locks the door behind him and quickly calls his older brother Stephen, who is staying in a hotel room down the hall. He asks him to come to room 809 as fast as he can. Upon arrival Stephen says to Trey, "Hey buddy, what's up?" Trey gives him a quick synopsis of the night and tells him that he thinks Harrison is a creepy guy who is making him feel uncomfortable. About two minutes later Stephen answers the door and sees Harrison with a bucket of ice and a little brown paper bag. Stephen says, "Hey sorry, the party is wrapped up and these kids need some rest before the drive home tomorrow." Harrison responds, "I know you. You're the pastor at the church that my mom goes to sometimes. I heard you preach last Christmas Eve." Stephen responds, "That's fantastic that you joined us for worship. You're welcome at St. Michaels anytime. Talk to you later. Have a good night," and then slowly closes the door.

Please thoughtfully answer the following questions:

1. In the morning after everyone wakes up, do you think it would be wise for Trey's brother to speak to the boys about the fact they were drinking under age?

2. Are there any passages from the Bible that might be helpful for Stephen to meditate on while reflecting on his responsibilities as a brother, a pastor, and a citizen?

3. In your opinion do you believe Stephen has a moral or legal obligation to alert the boys' parents about the underage drinking that took place and the situation that occurred which brought him to the room?

4. Should Stephen make a special phone call to the school or possibly to law enforcement concerning the underage drinking Trey, LJ, Deon, Christopher, Paul, Mario, Baxter, and Gerry took part in? Or should he allow each of their parents to deal with their child as they see fit?

5. Should Stephen make a special phone call to the school or possibly to law enforcement concerning the actions of Riley or Harrison?

An Odd Encounter

Stewart, Mel, Andy, and Neil are sixteen-year-olds heading into their junior year of high school. All four of the boys are above average students and are active in athletics and other extracurriculars such as drama team, tech club, and marching band. All four of the boys get along well, but they are prone to one-upmanship toward each other.

One beautiful late June night, they decide to drive far into the countryside to smash mailboxes. Stewart says, "Hey, let's go over to that one abandoned farmhouse on Creek Road and smash its mailbox! No one will care about that place!" The boys turn down several sparsely populated roads and eventually turn onto Creek Road. It is terribly dark outside; the road is bumpy and filled with loose stone. The four boys approach the mailbox at the end of a half-mile lane that leads to the farm house that either is abandoned or in total disrepair. Andy hops out of the back passenger side door of the car with a large metal baseball bat.

In mid swing someone rapidly emerges, seemingly out of nowhere ... perhaps from the ditch near the lane. The person who appears seems either to be severely burned throughout his face or else is wearing some type of latex mask. He stands only about five feet six to eight inches tall and has a slight build. This ambiguously aged person grabs Andy's arms and shakes him, while staring fiercely straight into his eyes, and yells in a high-pitched, tortured voice, "Get out of here!!"

Andy, who is normally tough and unshakable, flings the bat into the air and yells in terror as he moves his six-foot tall, two-hundred-pound frame into the backseat of the car with a head-first jump. As the vehicle pulls away the mysterious person tries to grab Andy's legs and pull him out, while scratching up the frightened sixteen-year-old's lower legs with his fingernails. The boys look back two or three seconds later, and they see no sign of the person who had just confronted them.

Not surprisingly this incident has frightened, confused, and shocked the boys to the point that not a single one of them intends on ever smashing another mailbox or vandalizing property of any kind again. In fact, this incident was so traumatic that the once close friends no longer feel comfortable hanging out together and go to great lengths to avoid one another.

A few months after the disturbing evening, Andy relates the story in detail to his parish pastor, Pastor Ronny. Andy is visibly shaken as he tells the story to him and reveals that he fears God is angry with him and feels the man he encountered might have been someone or something angelic. Pastor Ronny reassures Andy with these words: "Andy, God has forgiven you for the sake of his beloved Son Jesus Christ. You are a baptized child of

God. All of your sins are forgiven. I do not know if the person you encountered was someone angelic or not, but what I do know is Jesus loves you and your friends dearly. Depart in peace and serve the Lord."

Please thoughtfully answer the following questions:

1. Do you have any opinion on the person who confronted the boys or where he may have come from?
2. In your opinion did Pastor Ronny give a Christlike response to Andy after he related the story of the encounter and his fear of God being angry with him?
3. If you were in Pastor Ronny's shoes, would you try to think of a way to reconnect the once close friends Andy, Stewart, Mel, and Neil?

Dobie in the Wilderness

Dobie is a fifty-nine-year-old volunteer youth director at a congregation in the exurbs. The values of the area exalt rigidly frugal living; therefore, the congregation has seen fit not to have a youth budget or to reimburse their volunteers for gasoline or art and crafts supplies. This has caused Dobie to sell her pickup truck and buy a miniature two-seat electric car in order to save money. She works as many hours as she can as a dental hygienist to send her son, Ian, to college and also pay for her church's youth group. Yet even with cutting out all luxuries and a few items of need, she is still struggling to make ends meet.

Recently in a moment of complete desperation, Dobie decided to start working as a drug mule for a statewide dealer. Each Saturday she transports three large bricks of cocaine two hours north to an affluent suburban neighborhood home. Once the drop is made and she is paid, a wave of relief washes over her. This work is terrifying for Dobie, but it is more terrifying to imagine her beloved youth program dying and her baby Ian not being able to afford college.

One particularly beautiful Saturday morning as Dobie parks her miniature electric car that she has nicknamed Zippy in the circle drive of the drop-off home, Mr. C invites her into the living room for a drink. This gesture seems a little unusual, but Dobie feels she has no other choice but to accept. Once inside she is angrily confronted by Mr. C and four intense women she has never met before. They are accusing her of stealing cocaine from them. She does her best to deescalate the situation while denying the accusations.

Moments later Dobie is knocked unconscious, and when she awakes, she is in a wooded area with Mr. C and the women. Dobie is tied to a rotten tree stump, which is followed by Mr. C and the women threatening to set her on fire with gasoline and matches unless she confesses. Dobie begs the gang for her life while also crying out to Jesus. She promises to pay each person whatever they want. Eventually the gang decide to leave her for dead in the woods. They take off and about thirty minutes later Dobie manages to pry herself loose from the ropes as she continues to pray to Jesus for help.

Once free, Dobie makes her way through the pitch black, mosquito-infested, swamp-like woods. She follows the sound of traffic to the nearby highway and climbs over an old barbed wire fence and hitchhikes her way home. Once home she immediately phones Pastor Milliard and tells him the entire story from the very start. Pastor Milliard responds, "Oh, Dobie, I am grateful that you are still alive! If only you had made your need for youth funding and college support for your son clearer, the church certainly could have helped." Dobie painfully blurts out, "I've begged for funding for the last ten years! And every time people at this church passive aggressively imply that I am being greedy and go on their way as if nothing was said in the first place. I felt desperate and without options, Pastor!"

Please thoughtfully answer the following questions:

1. After hearing Dobie's confession, what advice would you give her if you were Pastor Milliard?
2. Do you feel any compassion for Dobie after the ordeal she has been through?
3. Does Dobie's story bring to mind any passages from the Bible?
4. Do you believe that Jesus saved Dobie's life in the woods?

What Should Be Said to A.T.?

A.T. is a twenty-nine-year-old man who works as a substitute teacher at rural schools three or four days a week. He has a bachelors degree in art education from a local college and is hoping to land a full-time teaching position soon. Most of A.T.'s friends have either relocated to major metropolitan areas or have large families with demanding jobs and little time to socialize. As a result, A.T. is scarcely invited to events or parties and has taken up the habit of inviting himself places.

Recently A.T. has gotten back in touch with Justin, an acquaintance that he worked a summer job with years earlier. Oddly enough, it had been so long since Justin had seen A.T. or heard from his old acquaintance that he almost completely forgot about him. The two start to reconnect and talk about their faith, which leads Justin to casually invite A.T. to speak to his church's youth group. A.T. happily accepts and does a good presentation on apologetics for the students.

Almost two years later, A.T. is substituting at a local high school and strikes up a conversation with Justin's dad, Karl, who serves as a teacher. Karl mentions in passing that Justin is getting married to a beautiful woman named Josie in June. The next day A.T. contacts Justin through social media and strongly hints he would like to attend the wedding. Justin speaks with Josie and they determine there is enough room on the guest list for A.T.

After the wedding ceremony the reception is held in the party barn at the family farm. Mid-way through the celebration A.T. asks Justin's older brother Neil for a tour of the historic family home on the property, which is also where Neil resides. Graciously Neil takes A.T. on an extensive tour of the home.

Later that evening, guests make their way to the pond for a fireworks show about half a mile away from the party barn and home. At about one in the morning most of the guests have made their way home, and Justin and Neil's younger sister Sarah is invited by Neil to head up to the house to crash on the couch in the parlor instead of driving back to her apartment. A few minutes later, Neil gets a phone call from Sarah, who is noticeably concerned and frightened. She tells him there is someone in his home and is calling his name.

Neil rushes to his home, where he sees his younger sister standing outside of the front door. Neil slowly enters the home, where he sees A.T. dressed only in underwear wandering around the parlor. A.T. is crying out for him, saying, "Neil! Neil! Neil, is that you?" Hesitantly Neil responds, "Yeah man, it's me. This is my home. What are you doing in here?" A.T. sheepishly responds, "I was tired and had a few drinks so I didn't want to drive home. I thought it would be okay if I crashed on the couch. Is that okay?" Neil answers, "Yeah, I guess that's okay . . . just make sure you lock the door behind you when you leave in the morning."

The next morning Neil hears the clanging of pots and pans as well as rummaging through the refrigerator. The noise is so intense he checks to see who is causing the disturbance. It is his overnight guest, A.T. Neil says, "A.T., what are you looking for, man?" A.T. responds in a monotone voice without expression and says, "I need meat." A few moments later Neil spots A.T. exploring near the guest bedroom where Sarah is sleeping. It is at this point that Neil firmly asks A.T. to leave his home.

About three weeks later, Justin and Josie return home from their honeymoon. Neil tells his brother about A.T.'s strange behavior, and steadily Justin starts to hear other reports from various people as well about strange behavior that A.T. was exhibiting at the wedding ceremony and at the reception.

Several months later, as Justin begins his first semester of seminary, he is contacted through social media by A.T. with the following message that reads, "So I saw through social media that your church's youth group is looking for a full-time youth director. I had a great time presenting on apologetics to them that one time. I used to help out at my old church with the youth, and I have a bachelors degree in art education. Would you be willing to put in a good word for me at your church if I applied for the position?"

Please thoughtfully answer the following questions:

1. If you were Justin, how would you respond to A.T.'s social media message regarding the youth director position?
2. Do you think Justin should bring up to A.T. the story he heard from Neil and others about his odd behavior at the wedding and reception?
3. Are there any passages from the Bible that might be helpful to remember in this situation?
4. Do you believe there is a clear, Christlike way for Justin, as a pastor in training, to handle this situation?

Ned Survived

Ned is a junior in college who is striving to become a full-time teacher at a Christian high school. His father passed away when he was sixteen, and his older brother, Ron, became a second father to him. In order to pay tuition, Ned works as a campus maintenance employee and sells his blood every few months. Lately he has been on the verge of dropping out of school as tuition has increased dramatically at the Christian liberal arts university he attends.

Ned's RA, Damien, has noticed how much he is struggling. For instance, last Christmas break while the campus was almost completely shut down, Ned stayed in his dorm room and took all of his meals at fast food restaurants he walked to in the snow, due to the fact that the campus dining hall was closed and he did not have access to a vehicle.

Eventually, to save money, Ned moves out of his dorm room and in with friends off campus. Soon rumors begin to circulate that Ned is living in a small apartment with fourteen other adults and is forced to find space in a walk-in closet to sleep each night. Damien finds these rumors to have credibility, so he sends Ned a text message to check on how he is doing, but he gets no response.

Four days later, Damien walks through the dorm to double check that all of the entrance doors are locked when he spots Ned sleeping on a couch in the common area with an old ragged blanket wrapped around him and his head resting on a scrunched-up sweatshirt acting as a pillow.

Damien understands immediately what is taking place. Ned is essentially homeless and is taking shelter in his old dorm hall common area. This is a difficult situation for Damien because the university has strict rules prohibiting non-dorm residents from spending more than two nights in a row in any single dorm hall. For a night or two Ned's presence in the common area shouldn't be a problem, but eventually he will have to leave or else Damien might lose his job for allowing it to take place.

Ultimately Ned starts to camp out for a night or two in different dorm common areas before moving onto a different location. He stores his clothing and books in his maintenance locker and sneaks into the men's locker room a couple nights a week to shower. When asked by caring friends why his mother or older brother Ron can't help him out a little financially, Ned responds, "My mom doesn't believe in college. She thinks it's pointless, and my brother works a really low paying job. He works over eighty hours a week every single week just to survive. So, I'm pretty much on my own, and the university is giving me basically all the aid that they can, I guess. At least that's what they keep telling me."

Amazingly, in the span of five and a half years, Ned, by the grace of God, is able to overcome a variety of challenges and obtains his degree in education and is hired as a high school math teacher at a Christian school. Damien is amazed at how much his friend has overcome, and he is simultaneously disgusted by how little help he believes the university offered his friend. Damien hears from Ned years later that the university president and campus chaplain wrote him a joint letter of apology for the lack of support that was offered to him during his time of need as a student five years after he graduated. Ned accepted the apology but Damien felt that it was too little, too late.

Please thoughtfully answer the following questions:

1. Do you believe it was fair for the university president and campus chaplain to write a joint letter of apology to Ned for the lack of support that was offered to him by the university?

2. Do you agree with Damien the apology letter was too little, too late?

3. If you were Damien's pastor, what biblical or extrabiblical resources might you share with him that would emphasize the need for forgiveness toward the university?

The Youth House

Christopher Yobe has recently joined the elders and started serving as the youth director at St. Timothy Lutheran Church as a way to say thank you to the senior pastor, the Reverend Timothy Hersh, for donating a kidney to Christopher and saving his life. Christopher and his wife Sheri have grown accustomed to hosting weekly youth group meetings in their home, but would like to see a permanent space designated specifically for the youth to use and take ownership of.

An opportunity for a permanent youth space arises when the old teachery's future is brought up at a voters' assembly meeting. Some suggest that the antique home and its one-acre lot be sold, while others believe the home must be torn down because the building is almost beyond repair.

Christopher stands up and makes a compelling plea for the house to be transformed into a beautiful youth house that would be primarily used by the youth and could also serve as a meeting place for other church groups to sew in and use for euchre tournaments. Christopher guarantees that if the church designates a small amount from the mission budget, then he and other retired people in the congregation will provide the labor to transform the house into a functional space. A vote is cast and Christopher's proposal is approved by a mere two votes.

Over the course of three years, retired people throughout the congregation as well as youth volunteers transform the downstairs of the house into a functional space under the leadership of Christopher. The garage is still a wreck and the upstairs bathroom is the only completed space on the second floor. The volunteers essentially decide to pause work on the youth house and return to the project in a year or two.

However, work on the upstairs and garage are never resumed, and for the next five years essentially only the downstairs is used for events. It is at this time Justin Stanford, a twenty-four-year-old recent college graduate and former missionary, is commissioned to work with the youth and start a young adult group at St. Timothy while simultaneously serving as a school teacher and coach at the church's day school. Justin is a child of the congregation and is generally well liked by people at St. Timothy.

Initially Justin sees the youth house as a fantastic blessing for his work with the youth and young adults. He views it as a great location for Bible studies, lock-ins, and picnics, a wonderful spot for the youth, young adults, and their families to be rejuvenated after completing a human care project or outreach event or a place to chill out while home from college on break.

Unfortunately though, it soon becomes evident to Justin that the majority of people at St. Timothy view the youth house as a space the youth should primarily stay in and be so satisfied with that they rarely ask for any type of further support. Secondly, there are so many other groups using the space that it is difficult for Justin to book the youth house for youth and young adult events.

Justin goes from initially scheduling approximately 45 percent of the youth events in the youth house, and about 55 percent off campus in public to scheduling 20 percent in the youth house and 80 percent off campus in public. Once Justin makes this change, he begins to hear complaints from a number of congregation members and parents about how few youth events are taking place in the youth house. Ironically, many of these same people also complained weeks earlier about how much time the youth were spending in the youth house.

By the grace of God, a number of unique and positive improvements are made to the youth program and a young adult program is created at St. Timothy, under Justin's leadership. However, after about a year into his service, he begins to feel a little isolated and attacked personally by some in the congregation. These feelings surface when there is occasionally an event that is delayed or has a low turnout due to the busy schedules of the students during a hectic time of year.

What is more frustrating for Justin and others who are invested in the youth and young adults is, whenever there is an event that has great conversations about Jesus, whether it have a large or small turnout, a member or two goes out of their way to bring up the fact that forty or fifty years earlier the church often had thirty students confirmed per year and another fifty at youth group each week. Therefore, these members are not impressed with any event that has five to fifteen people in attendance, and sadly they feel the need to disparage current youth events to Justin and others.

Eventually, after almost three years of serving at St. Timothy, Justin begins seminary only two months after marrying his beautiful wife, Josie. He primarily looks back at his time working with the youth and young adults at St. Timothy positively. After all, that's where he met Josie, who was also a recent college graduate working as a teacher at the day school. And, of course, Jesus was at the center of Justin's time there. However, he occasionally wonders how much impact his service had at St. Timothy and in the community in general.

Please thoughtfully answer the following questions:

1. What is your impression of how well St. Timothy Lutheran Church supported their youth and young adults to grow in their faith overall?
2. If you were Justin's pastor, what words of encouragement and guidance might you have offered to him as he worked with the youth and young adults and their families?
3. In your opinion was the youth house a blessing to the youth to be refreshed at? Or a place some in the congregation wanted the youth to go to stay out of the way?
4. Are there any passages from Scripture that come to your mind as you reflect on this case study?

Bibliography

Luther, Martin. "The Estate of Marriage." In *Luther's Works*, translated by Walther I. Brandt, 45:14–15. Minneapolis: Augsburg Fortress, 1522.

www.ingramcontent.com/pod-product-compliance
Lightning Source LLC
Chambersburg PA
CBHW071433150426
43191CB00008B/1114